MORE JUNIORPLOTS

MORE JUNIORPLOTS
A Guide for Teachers and Librarians

By JOHN T. GILLESPIE

R. R. Bowker Company
New York & London, 1977

Published by R. R. Bowker Company
1180 Avenue of the Americas, New York, N.Y. 10036
Copyright © 1977 by John Gillespie
Printed and bound in the United States of America

Library of Congress Cataloging in Publication Data

Gillespie, John Thomas, 1928–
   More juniorplots.

   Includes index.
   1. Books—Reviews. 2. Books and reading for
youth. I. Title.
Z1037.A1G52   028.1   77-8786
ISBN 0-8352-1002-2

To
David James Maguire,
whose gentleness and love
will always be remembered

Contents

Preface

IN WRITING a Preface to the current volume, it is difficult not to echo exactly the words used to introduce the previous volume, *Juniorplots,* although the need for active reading guidance by teachers and librarians appears even more acute today. The inroads of television and other nonparticipatory activities, and the dismaying reading scores of today's youngsters, have heightened the need for a more aggressive and positive campaign to introduce young people to reading. Statistics show that the greatest drop in quantity of reading occurs during the sixth through eighth grades. At that time, in particular, librarians and teachers must make a concerted effort to retain and, if possible, expand reading habits. It is hoped that this volume will stimulate these professionals to introduce deserving books to young people. The titles included are generally suitable for children between the ages of 11 and 16, although some titles also will be useful with a younger group, and others with older, more mature readers.

The book consists primarily of plots and related material on 72 books. The titles have been organized under nine developmental goals associated with adolescence. In a supplementary index, the books are also listed under conventional subject headings (e.g., Adventure Stories, Animal Stories). The nine developmental goals are: (1) getting along in the family; (2) developing lasting values; (3) understanding social problems; (4) developing an understanding of the past and other cultures; (5) understanding physical and emotional problems; (6) becoming self-reliant; (7) developing relationships with both sexes; (8) developing a wholesome self-image; and (9) developing a respect for nature and living things.

Various methods were used to choose the books to be highlighted. A questionnaire was administered to young adult librarians from school and public libraries. Many teachers and librarians were consulted directly, as were library school students from the author's young adult literature classes. Standard bibliographies and selection aids also were checked carefully. In addition to criteria involving quality, an important consideration was the desire to provide materials covering a variety of interests and needs at a variety of reading levels. In spite of these concerns, some of the selections still remain personal and, therefore, arbitrary. For example, it was believed necessary to give some representation to that highly endangered species in young adult literature—the quality novel with limited appeal and popularity. On the other hand, a few choices had to be made from the hundreds of slick, superficial junior novels that appeal to popular tastes and are particularly useful with reluctant readers. In both of these categories, only a small representative selection could be chosen, even though several other titles were identified as equally suitable and could as easily have been selected.

The individual titles are covered under five headings:

1. *Plot Summary*. Each plot briefly retells the entire story. The summary includes all important incidents and characters, while trying to retain the mood and point of view of the author.

2. *Thematic Material*. An enumeration of primary and secondary themes found in the book will, it is hoped, facilitate the use of the book in a variety of situations.

3. *Book Talk Material*. Techniques are given on how to introduce the book interestingly to youngsters. Passages suitable for retelling or reading aloud are indicated, and pagination is shown for these passages for the hard-cover and, when available, the paperback editions.

4. *Additional Suggestions*. Related books that explore similar or associated themes are annotated or listed with identifying bibliographic information. Approximately six to eight titles are given per book.

5. *About the Author*. Standard biographical dictionaries (e.g., *Something about the Author, Who's Who in America*) were consulted to locate sources of biographical information about the author. When this section does not appear, no material was found. However, the user also may wish to consult other sources, such as periodical indexes (*Reader's Guide, Education Index, Library Literature*), jacket blurbs, and material available through the publisher.

The detailed treatment of the main titles is not intended as a substitute for reading the books. Instead, it is meant to be used by teachers and librarians to refresh their memories about books they have read and to suggest new uses for these titles.

This volume is not intended as a work of literary criticism or a listing of the best books for young adults. It is a representative selection of books that have value in a variety of situations.

The author has had more helpers than can be identified by name, but special thanks should be given to Mary K. Chelton for permission to reprint her useful material on booktalking; Bette Vander Werf and my graduate assistant, Ilene Baker, for assistance in manuscript preparation; and to my friends, particularly those in Hartsville, Massachusetts, who bore up so well during my periods of "plotting."

JOHN T. GILLESPIE, Professor,
Palmer Graduate Library School
C. W. Post Center, Long Island University
Greenvale, New York

Booktalking

By Mary K. Chelton

SKILL in booktalking remains one of the most valuable promotional devices YA librarians can have at hand to interest teenagers in the library. Once acquired, this skill can be adapted to floor work with individual readers, radio spots, booklist annotations, and class visits in the library or in the classroom. It can be combined with slide-tape, film, or musical presentations, and with outreach skills. Its limitations are set by YA librarians who either refuse to learn the technique, have never learned it (and judge it valueless even after learning it), or who remain inflexible in chosen methods of doing it. The best young adult librarians I have known, whether they see their book selection role as one of expanding horizons and literary tastes or of just giving kids what they want (and most of us usually fall somewhere in between), have a "hidden agenda" for promoting the love of reading for pleasure, and have found booktalks a superb way of doing that.

It should be said here that booktalking skills do not preempt professional abilities in programming, information and referral, traditional reference work, audiovisual collection building, or community outreach, as is often unjustly assumed of the YA specialty. It is my contention, however, that the public still assumes that libraries deal in books and our nonbook related skills and materials will win us no friends or financial support for other information or enrichment media unless librarians do traditional reader's advisory work very well.

In my opinion, the two simplest definitions of booktalks are Amelia Munson's, "The booktalk falls into place between storytelling and book reviewing, partakes of both and is unlike either," taken from *An Ample Field* (American Library Assn., 1950); the other is my own "A booktalk is a

Reprinted from *School Library Journal*, April 1976 with permission of the author.

formal or informal presentation about a book or group of books designed to entice the listener into reading them."

Elaine Simpson, in her YA course at Rutgers, describes a booktalk as "That part of a librarian's visit to a classroom or during a class visit to the library devoted to presenting two or more books to the group. It is an art and a device by which the librarian tries to interest young people in all books in general and in some books in particular through a talk so carefully prepared as to seem spontaneous, in which he or she gives the subject, the flavor, and the appeal of each book presented." Simpson adds, "Indirectly through book talks we are able to show the teenager that he or she is welcome in the school or public library, and that he or she has a place there. We are also able to identify ourselves as friends...."

One of the axiomatic things about booktalking is that the talk is not to reveal everything about the book. This is a common beginner's mistake. Doris M. Cole's suggestion in "The Book Talk" in *Juniorplots* (Bowker, 1967) is that booktalks should give only an "enticing sample of the book's contents." In the same article, Margaret Edwards calls the sample "a little piece of pie so good that it tempts one to consume the whole concoction." Learning how to find and then how to present just the right sample is the essence of learning to booktalk. In her book, *The Fair Garden and the Swarm of Beasts* (Hawthorn, 1974), Edwards states that the objectives of booktalks are "to sell the idea of reading for pleasure; to introduce new ideas and new fields of reading; to develop an appreciation of style and character portrayal; lift the level of reading by introducing the best books the audience can read with pleasure; to humanize books, the library and the librarian."

To all of these objectives, I would add that booktalks keep librarians from becoming hypocrites who despair of their patrons' reading tastes while never reading for themselves or for their patrons.

There are probably as many types of booktalks as there are librarians doing them, but roughly they fall into long or short talks with interesting combinations of the two. A short talk, and the one which should be mastered first, usually presents only one title and lasts from 30 seconds to one minute. In it, the librarian tells listeners about something happening to someone in the book, without either divulging the entire plot or stringing along a variety of superlatives. Examples:

When Bo Jo was 17 and July was 16 and they'd been going steady all through high school, July got pregnant and they ran away and got married, even though both sets of parents were disgusted; July had to drop out of school; and Bo Jo gave up his college football scholarship. *Mr. and Mrs. Bo Jo Jones* will tell you how they made a go of a teenage marriage with three strikes against them.

Even though Harold Krentz went totally blind as a child, his parents refused to send him to special schools, and in *To Race the Wind*, he tells his true life story about how he played football, became a lawyer, got drafted into the army, and inspired the writing of *Butterflies Are Free*.

As a baby, she had been fried alive by alcoholic parents. By the time Laura was twelve and Dr. D'Ambrosio discovered her in an institution, she had been diagnosed as schizophrenic (the severest form of mental illness), had a long list of physical problems, and had never spoken a word. *No Language but a Cry* is about how he helped her.

It is obvious in these examples how easily short talks can be adapted to floor work, when a teen asks what the book's about, to annotated booklists, and to prerecorded radio spots. Depending on the use or situation, the booktalks can be shortened further or lengthened. "Booktalk" is probably too formal a word, but these short talks do demand that YA librarians discipline themselves to think constantly about the books they've read in terms of plot and the teen audience rather than literary quality or a strictly personal reaction. Kids want to know what happens in a book, what is so exciting about it that they should want to read it. Keeping out your own adjectives lets them feel that they make the decision to read the book, despite your predilection, rather than that the librarian is just pushing either personal favorites or some sort of "literary spinach" down their throats. In other words, let the book sell itself.

A long booktalk lasts ten to 15 minutes and usually emphasizes one particular section of one particular title, whether memorized or told in your own words but not read aloud. Some examples of good sections of books to use are the dead horse scene in *Red Sky at Morning*, the first day on the tubercular ward in *I'm Done Crying*, Albert Scully meeting Mrs. Woodfin for the first time and getting drunk in *The Dreamwatcher*, being fitted for braces and shoes in *Easy Walking*, the race at Riverside with no clutch in *Parnelli*, discovering that Madec has left him naked to die in the desert in *Deathwatch*, or Capt. Lebrun's escape in *Escape from Colditz*. Long talks are more formal than short talks and are best used to follow up several short ones on the same theme or as a break in the middle of a variety of unrelated shorts.

Typing out a long talk, double-spaced, helps both with editing it and learning it, because no matter how closely you follow the author's words, there's usually a sentence or two which can be eliminated for an oral presentation. It also helps you incorporate an introduction, ending, and transitions from short talks into one coherent, packaged talk, rather than relying on your own memory. Typed talks can also be kept on file and used repeatedly by the same person or for training new talkers. It is possible to get stale or become dependent on out-of-date talks or, worse still, to forget all other sections of the book except the typed talk, but I have found that because a much-used talk is new to the audience it also remains fresh for the librarian, unless the subject matter is no longer relevant.

The major disagreement among the YA service experts is whether to memorize the long talk or not. Some feel the preparation is too hard, that it is too easy to forget a memorized talk in public, or that such talks are not adaptable enough for all types of audience situations. Some feel the kids will not be interested in so formal an approach or that the librarian will get stale and sound wooden if the same talk is given repeatedly. Others feel that memorization, at least once during a training session, is the only way new booktalkers can learn delivery and talk-cutting techniques against which to evolve their own individual styles later. Having been trained and having trained people by the memorization method, I find the latter to be true, for myself and for most beginners. I do believe, however, that there is no *one* way to do booktalks and that you should do what is comfortable for you— within the guidelines of experience outlined here—and what gets kids to read the books you talk about. It does seem illogical to reject a method just because it is difficult without trying it to see the results or how you might improve upon it.

The combination booktalk presentation can mean a combination of types of talks, librarians, books, genres, or media, and should generally not run more than 25 to 30 minutes. It is the most common type of presentation done for a teenage audience and is usually prearranged with the teacher or group leader to allow time for browsing, card registration, a film, discussion, questions, or just relaxing afterward. Examples would be interspersing poetry, cassette folk-rock lyrics, and short talks on a loneliness theme, or using themes like overcoming handicaps, teenagers in trouble, the future, love, etc.

Short talks could alternate with related slides of the books or the situations described, or of the library itself. Talks can be woven into a creative dramatic presentation or improvisation. If the theme is related to a particular curriculum unit, the combination of readable fun books with magazines, pamphlets, and reference works is valuable. With a little imagination, short talks can even be combined with a lesson on using the catalog. The combinations are limited only by your time, talent, ingenuity, and the audience response. It is always important to remember that your ultimate object in booktalking is to get the kids interested in reading the books you talk about. So if you get so AV-oriented that you are no longer connected with books or so entertaining that only your dramatic ability dazzles your audience, you may be missing the point.

Elaine Simpson further differentiates booktalks into the resource talk done by school librarians, which "is a supplement to a particular unit of work being done in a class, and its purpose is to show the useful, interesting, unusual materials available in the library on the subject"— done at the request of the teacher concerned—and the public library booktalk, which "is to show the great variety of materials and services available for all library users" and is not directed toward a specific subject. This distinction seems arbitrary to me with some of the popular curriculum topics now taught. It does seem unfair to ask public YA librarians to do only curriculum-related resource talks (which are extremely popular with teachers when they discover them) when a school librarian is available, but priorities must be decided by school and public YA librarians based on local circumstances, time, and talent, and should always be a fully cooperative, courteous, joint effort. The teenagers are the ultimate losers in territorial feuds between school and public librarians.

To prepare for booktalks and the accompanying reader's advisory floor work, YA librarians should read widely all types of books and subjects of interest to their teen patrons and keep track of what they have read. Writing a short talk on every title read on a 3″ x 5″ card is a good way to discipline yourself to think of books in terms of how you would present a particular title to a particular teenager. This also helps you keep the names of the characters straight—an eternal problem with teen novels—and the cards can be filed according to themes, which then helps train you in associating similar titles for talks, lists, and reader's advisory service.

The next step is to master talk delivery techniques in private, preferably in a formal training session where the rest of the group is as nervous as you are, and where videotape playback and group criticism are encouraged. The horrible shock of seeing your unconscious mannerisms on a television monitor corrects them faster than any other method I know, and addressing any audience will give you practice in pitching your voice properly.

If you are in a small, isolated library, have no one more experienced to work with you, and have not learned the technique in library school—an all too common problem among YA librarians—practice on your family or clerical staff and use a full-length mirror and a tape recorder if you have no access to videotaping. A tape recorder can help you memorize a talk in addition to correcting mistakes, but there is a danger that learning your booktalk this way will make you bored with it before you ever give it for the first time. Since a formal group training workshop is so valuable in learning to booktalk, I feel isolated YA librarians should pressure local library schools to provide this as continuing education in extension programs and pressure library associations to give regional workshops and create videotapes of different booktalks which can be borrowed.

Once you feel you have mastered the cutting and delivery of a talk in the abstract and have read widely enough so that you won't be undone because a kid has already read one of the books you're prepared to talk about and you can't suggest another one, announce your availability to do this (with a prior agreement with your supervisors as to how often you'll be available) by letters and/or visits to teachers, curriculum supervisors and department heads, school librarians, principals, reading specialists, and youth workers. Be sure to state in the letter what you *will* and *will not* do, and I suggest that you always insist that the teacher or leader remain with the class or group. You are a guest, not a substitute, and it is extremely hard to be an entertaining booktalker as well as an authority figure at the same time. Classes are notorious for going berserk when they think an inexperienced substitute is on the scene, and teachers who have never had booktalkers before are equally notorious for disappearing the whole period.

Be sure to state how long you will talk, usually 25 to 30 minutes, and what you will do in any leftover time. If you will not do curriculum related talks, this is the place to say so, or to list which subjects or books you are prepared to talk about so they can be chosen in advance. English teachers will sometimes want you to discuss the literary merits of the books you talk about to reinforce their classroom objectives, and since it usually is disastrous to do this with booktalks, you can state this in your letter or in person as arrangements are finalized.

Another way to advertise yourself is to demonstrate the technique at faculty and department meetings and to invite teachers of other classes to observe you while you talk to a particular class.

Some schools assume that once you talk there you will never return and they will hit you with double classes and assemblies. So it is wise to state whether you will stay all day and talk to single classes successively or return at another convenient time. While I feel that assemblies are an awkward way to booktalk because of projection problems and the lack of personal eye contact, the Free Library of Philadelphia has perfected "On Your Own," a thirty minute multimedia assembly program featuring short films, slides, a tape of music and narration, and three librarians who present five short one-minute bookspots in person.

Ideally, the school librarian is the contact for the public YA librarian in neighboring schools and booktalk efforts should be coordinated through the school librarian.

A day or two before you are to appear, call to remind the person who invited you and check to see if circumstances have remained the same, and, if you're depending on school AV equipment, to make sure that the equipment is working and will be there when you need it. One piece of equipment you may need is some sort of podium if you're tall, and you can improvise with a dictionary stand or a pile of encyclopedias if necessary, on the spot, or carry a portable one with you. It's a useful crutch, and I suspect short people or those with photographic memories may scorn the use of such props.

You will find, as you booktalk more often, that the sheer public relations value of being so visible in the adolescent community makes rapport with them much easier because they remember you. "Hey, Miss, didn't I see you in my school the other day?" "Hey, what're you doing here?" Other youth service professionals will remember you also as a friendly helpful ally and often reciprocate with help at programs and recommend you as a resource person to others. Your own self-confidence grows immeasurably and you soon find that you're really not scared to talk to anybody anymore.

Best of all, though, is the immediate and immensely gratifying feedback from the kids who truly appreciate your presentation and will charge back to the library to get "the book about the guy who drank the blood" or say, in wonder, "Have you *really* read *all these books*?" or as one teen recently said, "that was a nice thing you did for us the other day."

There is almost no better way to let them know you're on their side than good booktalking, and I can only agree with Doris Cole who said, "Young people are the best, the most responsive audience in the world."

Titles Mentioned

Bradford, Richard. *Red Sky at Morning*. Lippincott, 1968.
White, Robb. *Deathwatch*. Doubleday, 1972.
D'Ambrosio, Richard. *No Language but a Cry*. Doubleday, 1970.
Ferris, Louanne. Edited by Beth Day. *I'm Done Crying*. M. Evans, 1969.
Gershe, Leonard. *Butterflies Are Free*. Random, 1970.
Head, Ann. *Mr. and Mrs. Bo Jo Jones*. Putnam, 1967.
Krents, Harold. *To Race the Wind: An Autobiography*. Putnam, 1972.
Libby, Bill. *Parnelli: A Story of Auto-Racing*. Dutton, 1969.
Lord, Walter. *Night to Remember*. Holt, 1955.
Nasaw, Jonathan. *Easy Walking*. Lippincott, 1975.
Reid, P. R. *Escape from Colditz*. Lippincott, 1973.
Tolstoy, Leo. *War and Peace*. Modern Lib.
Tyler, Anne. *Slipping Down Life*. Knopf, 1970.

A Guide for Booktalkers

Don't wait until the eleventh hour to prepare, nor be unduly concerned by preliminary nervousness.

Make sure you know how to get where you're going to speak, unless the audience is coming to you. If the latter is true, make sure the room is reserved and set up in advance. If you are a librarian going to a school, always check in at the main office first to introduce yourself and announce the purpose of your visit.

Organize your books and equipment. Set them up in the order in which you'll talk about them and have chosen passages marked with a clip at the bottom of the page. Hold your notes up if you have to, use a podium, or clip them to the inside or back of the book.

Do not begin to speak until the audience is ready to listen, and wait for attention with good humor, unobtrusively. Introduce yourself or allow your host to introduce you and any other team members at the beginning of the period and be sure everyone in the room can hear all that is said and understands why you are there.

State clearly the author and title of each book you talk about. Sometimes it is wise to have a list of your talk titles prepared in advance, which you can distribute and let the audience keep and check off as you speak. This is especially good if your charging system or the circumstances don't allow you to circulate the books on the spot at the end of the period or visit.

Speak slowly and clearly, trying not to think too far ahead so you don't forget what you're saying. Talk to the back of the room and don't be afraid to smile occasionally or to laugh with the kids at a funny spot. Avoid any gestures or tones which do not enhance the story and call attention to yourself, and don't try to be hip or you'll be very embarrassing to the audience. On the other hand, don't talk down to them using phrases like "boys and girls" or "you young people," or you'll alienate them.

Try not to be monotonal, a quality which can be discovered and corrected if you have practiced with a tape recorder prior to your appearance and change the pace of your speaking as well as your loudness occasionally. Don't be dramatic unless it comes naturally or you've been coached by more experienced people.

Stand firmly without rocking and try not to lean, or play with rubber bands or paper clips. It looks terrible and distracts the audience. If you hold a book up so they can see it or show illustrations, hold it firmly and consciously and pan slowly so everyone can see it. A book held at an unconsciously lopsided, impossible viewing angle is an all too common fault among beginning booktalkers trying to remember everything at once, and it is very annoying to an audience.

Don't illustrate a book with an example or incident applicable to a class member. I once introduced *Slipping Down Life* to a class saying, "Evie Decker was the second fattest kid in her whole high school," only to see the entire class, to my horror, turn in unison to stare at an overweight member. It was awful, and I never used it again. Try to learn from your own mistakes.

Try to know the characters' names, especially in teen novels, or they all sound alike out loud, and don't frustrate the audience by making every talk a cliff-hanger or they'll tune you out as the tease you are in such a case. Don't get nervous and tell the whole story or no one will read the books. This is avoided by careful preparation and discipline on the spot if the kids beg you to tell them the ending.

Be flexible enough to wind up quickly and go on to another title or activity if the group seems restless or bored, and whatever you do, don't scold the audience for not being fascinated with you. It backfires every time.

Try not to use difficult words they may not understand. Don't be nonplussed if they say, "Hey, what's that mean?" Beware of rhetorical questions. Someone may answer them. Don't use dialect unless it's natural to you or you'll be ridiculed or will unwittingly insult the kids by making them feel you're making fun of them. And avoid profanity and *double entendres* because the kids usually either think it's hilarious from you and go into phony gales of shocked laughter or are actually shocked and forget what else you're saying. There are some exceptions to the *double entendres* like *Night to Remember*, which always got asked about without fail by an unwitting teen who thought it was a torrid love story. One of those is usually enough because tricking the unknowing audience is hardly the point.

Don't oversell average books. There's no bigger bore than a librarian who gushes over every teen or sports story as if each is equal to *War and Peace.* The kids will peg you as a phony each time and you are guaranteed to bore them to death. Be sure of your terms and facts in technical and sports books and do not use explicit factual books on physical or sexual development unless you're sure of both community reactions and your own ability to speak without embarrassment.

Set up the books or give out the lists and, if you've gained enough experience, let the audience call out titles they want to hear about or ask them to tell you any they've already read so that you can match them with a similar story. On the other hand, always be honest and admit when they've stumped you, and never pretend to have read a book you haven't. You'll need to have a talk prepared in case you meet only stolid indifference despite your most artful efforts to stimulate comment.

Be prepared for interruptions by the kids saying "Oooo!" at scary spots and laughing at funny ones. The school PA system usually broadcasts daily announcements once or twice each day, and finding out just when can save you much grief so you're not in the middle of a talk when these come on. There is no way to avoid the more dramatic interruptions, but knowing that they do happen will keep you reasonably calm in all circumstances.

Try never to read to the audience unless in the material you are presenting "the author's style is the important thing and can be communicated in no other way: poetry, some essays, fine writing in general. Even then you would do well to quote rather than to read or know the book so well that you are not bound to it—your eyes can still rove over the group and take cognizance of their enjoyment. Be watchful for signs of disinterest."

Go on to pre-arranged announcements of upcoming library events after you have finished talking. Tell how to get a card or check out a book, invite questions or browsing, distribute additional lists, etc.

Keep track of every class or group you've spoken to for periodic statistical reports which may help justify more staff assistance for your service specialty. Write a brief narrative report so there is a record of what you have done, both for your supervisor and for any possible successors.

Evaluate your success as a booktalker primarily by noting how many people read the books you discussed or come to the library asking for them or to get a card for the first time. You are often successful even when the audience seems indifferent, asleep, or incredibly itchy, although continual responses like these should make you alter your technique. Perhaps the selection wasn't right, or you spoke too long, or over the heads of your audience, or were too monotonal or too dramatic.

1

Getting Along in the Family

During EARLY adolescence there is usually a growing away from the restrictively close bonds of family relationships so important in childhood. In its place there should develop a greater sense of independence and responsibility, while at the same time maintaining close enough ties to receive security and love. This transition period often leads to conflicts concerning parental authority, attitudes toward siblings, and the relative importance of pressure from peer groups. The books in this section describe various aspects of this topic.

William H. Armstrong, *Sounder*
Harper, 1969, $5.95; lib. bdg., $5.79; pap., $1.25 (same pagination)

In his brief preface to this 1970 Newbery Award winner, the author states that he originally heard the story of the coon dog, Sounder, and his master from a gray-haired black schoolteacher who, after school and in the summers, worked for Mr. Armstrong's father. Although the novel is set in the South in the late years of the nineteenth century and deals with a poor black sharecropper and his family, its theme, the endurance and invincibility of people, is ancient. Some critics have accused the author of racial stereotyping, principally because none of the characters are identified by name. But for most readers, the anonymity of the protagonists and the deliberate vagueness of the setting tends to heighten the universality of the theme. The author's sparse, simple style adds to the effectiveness of the work. The book has been enjoyed both by adults and by children from the elementary grades through high school.

Plot Summary

The main characters are a sharecropper and his wife and their four young children, none of whom can read or write. The oldest child, a boy, has tried for two years to walk the eight miles to school, but each year he has been forced to give up when the severe cold of winter has set in. The boy is deeply attached to Sounder, a stray hunting dog who followed the father home one day from the fields. Sounder is a mixture of Georgia redbone hound and bulldog and is well named because of his loud and clear bark.

During the winter months, when the crops have been picked, it is only the sale of the pelts of possum and raccoon, plus the few pennies received for walnut kernels painstakingly picked by the mother from obstinate shells, that keep the family from starvation.

But one cold day in November, despite a disastrous hunting season, the boy sees pork sausages frying in the skillet and smells a ham boiling in the possum pot. He also notices that his mother is humming, a sure sign that she is worried and agitated. That day all of them have good meals, but two days later, a white sheriff and his two deputies arrive and accuse the father of being a "thievin' nigger" who has stolen food from the local smokehouse. The father is handcuffed and thrown into the back of a horse-drawn wagon. Sounder tries to protect his master and has to be restrained by the boy, but as the wagon leaves he pulls himself free and is shot by one of the deputies. The dog drags himself under the house, presumably to die. The boy finds Sounder's ear in the road and, that night puts it under his pillow, making a wish that the dog won't die.

Next morning the mother walks into town to return the remnants of the ham and sausages. The boy tries to find Sounder under the house and discovers that he has gone. When the mother returns that evening, she speculates that the dog has gone into the woods seeking oak leaves to draw out the pus and heal his wound.

By Christmastime there is still no sign of Sounder. The mother bakes a cake and sends the boy into town to deliver it to his jailed father. It is a fearsome trip for the boy, who passes homes festooned with Christmas ornaments. When he arrives at the jail, he is cruelly rebuffed by the keeper, who destroys the cake while looking for a saw or a file. Finally the youngster is allowed to visit with his father, who tells him not to grieve and assures him that he will try to get word to the family through the visiting preacher after the court hearing.

The following day Sounder returns with a shattered shoulder, the use of only three legs, and with only one eye and one ear. He no longer barks, but only emits a dull whine. Despite the dog's state, the boy is overjoyed to welcome him home. Weeks later, the mother learns from townspeople that her husband has been sentenced to a labor gang that works in road camps and quarries.

When summer comes the boy takes his father's place in the fields, but when the harvest is over he sets out wandering from town to town and visiting work camps in the hope of catching a glimpse of his father. When word reaches the family that there has been a terrible explosion in one of the quarries and that 12 men have been killed and many others injured, they are relieved to learn that the father is not one of the dead.

Years pass. The boy continues working during the summer and, when possible, searching for his father. One day, after having been driven away from a work camp by the guard who throws a piece of iron at him and badly injures his hand, the boy finds a book in a trash barrel and, although not able to read it, clings to it as though it were a treasured possession. When he stops at the pump in a school yard to wash the blood from his hand, he meets a kindly schoomaster who tells him that the author of the book is Montaigne. Hearing the boy's story and realizing how desperately he wants to learn, the schoolmaster offers to house and feed him and allow him to attend school during the winter months in exchange for his help with the chores. The mother agrees.

More years pass, and soon the boy is able to share his new knowledge with his younger brother and sisters. One August afternoon when Sounder becomes unusually nervous, the family sees a man in the distance slowly hobbling toward their cabin. For the first time since his return, Sounder barks. His master has come home.

The return is tinged with tragedy, however, because the husband is now a completely broken man. One half of his body is paralyzed from the mine explosion that had killed so many. Within weeks the man dies, and shortly afterward so does Sounder. Although deeply saddened, the boy remembers what Montaigne wrote in one of his essays, "Only the unwise think that what has changed is dead," and he remembers his father walking upright and strong with Sounder barking at his side.

Thematic Material

Although this is an agonizing story of tragedy and pain, it is also one of great dignity and inspiration. The family, although shackled by poverty and ignorance, now has some glimmer of hope because of the boy's new knowledge. The cruelty, loneliness, and injustice suffered by the family is not underplayed, but in their acceptance of tragedy, there is an aura of strength and endurance and a reassurance of survival.

Book Talk Material

With small groups, James Barkely's illustrations, such as his portrait of Sounder (p. 72) and the cabin (facing p. 1), could be used in a book talk.

Specific passages are: a description of Sounder (pp. 4–5); the father being taken to jail (pp. 21–26); the boy's trip to the jail (pp. 55–58); and his visit with his father (pp. 62–64).

Additional Selections

Miller Brody Productions has made available a record (and cassette) based on this book. A black mother tells her children about growing up in the rural South after World War II in Lucille Clifton's *The Times They Used to Be* (Holt, 1974, $4.95; pap., Dell, 95¢). In Milton Meltzer's *Underground Man* (Bradbury, 1972, $6.95; pap., Dell, 95¢), Josh Bowen spends time in prison for helping slaves escape. Martin Duberman chronicles the history of the black man in the United States in *In White America* (pap., New Amer. Lib., 95¢). A young girl's battle with the Depression of the 1930s is told in Phyllis Reynolds Naylor's *Walking through the Dark* (Atheneum, 1976, $6.95). In May McNeer's *Stranger in the Pines* (Houghton, 1971, $4.95), a bitter runaway apprentice finds refuge with a black herb doctor and his wife. A boy and his family help slaves escape to the North in Bianca Bradbury's *The Undergrounders* (Washburn, 1966, o.p.). For a younger audience, suggest Betsy Haynes' *Cowslip* (Nelson, 1973, $5.95; pap., Scholastic, 95¢; new title: *Slave Girl*).

About the Author

Commire, Anne. *Something about the Author.* Detroit: Gale Research Co., 1973. Vol. 4, pp. 11–13.

DeMontreville, Doris and Donna Hill, Eds. *Third Book of Junior Authors.* New York: H. W. Wilson Co., 1972, pp. 20–21.

Ethridge, James M., Barbara Kopala, Carolyn Riley, Eds. *Contemporary Authors.* Detroit: Gale Research Co., 1968. Vols. 19–20, p. 22.

Hopkins, Lee Bennett. *More Books by More People.* New York: Citation Press, 1974, pp. 18–23.

Ward, Martha E. and Dorothy A. Marquardt. *Authors of Books for Young People.* (2nd Edition). Metuchen, N.J.: Scarecrow Press, Inc., 1971, p. 19.

Who's Who in America (39th Edition). Chicago: Marquis Who's Who, Inc., 1976. Vol. 1, p. 97.

Jeannette Eyerly, *The Phaedra Complex*

Lippincott, 1971, $5.50; pap., $1.95 (same pagination); pap., Berkley, 60¢

As in so many of her young adult novels, Jeannette Eyerly has taken a sensitive subject and handled it with delicacy and restraint. This work is a variation on the Greek legend in which a young woman, Phaedra, marries the king of Athens and falls in love with her stepson. Eyerly's story concerns a 15-year-old girl's adjustment to her mother's remarriage. It is enjoyed by girls in the junior high school grades.

Plot Summary

Since the breakup of her first marriage years ago, Charlotte Richards has become a successful career woman and is now a vice-president of a prestigious advertising agency. She and her daughter, Laura, live in a luxury apartment building in New York City. Laura, the narrator, attends an exclusive girls' school, where she is in her junior year. Recently Laura has learned, from an overheard conversation, that her mother married her father only because she was expecting a child.

Now Mrs. Richards announces her plans to marry Michael Barrington, a much-traveled, Pulitzer Prize-winning correspondent. Laura is resentful and apprehensive, partly because she scarcely knows her future stepfather and partly because the marriage will affect her close relationship with her mother. Although Laura declares that she will not attend the wedding, she relents after much persuasion from her best friend, Cricket Clothier. After the wedding, Michael moves into their apartment, and an uneasy peace reigns in the family. Laura finds difficulty in adjusting to this overly solicitous stranger whom she refuses to acknowledge as her stepfather.

During her usual dog-walking trips, Laura often notices an attractive boy slightly older than herself, who walks a variety of dogs. Although they only exchange glances, she begins to look forward to these encounters.

One evening Laura rescues one of the dogs. The young man introduces himself as David Michenor, who is now living with his aunt and uncle so that he can attend a private boys' school in New York. Laura and David begin to date, and gradually they develop a great fondness for each other.

Michael seems overly concerned with this relationship. At Christmastime, when David gives Laura a gold-plated bracelet, Michael presents her with a solid gold one. Laura notices that her mother is becoming edgy and irritable, sometimes acting as though she were jealous of her daughter. Michael persuades Charlotte to give up her job, and the two go to New Hampshire for a few days of skiing. While they are away, Laura and David have an indoor picnic in her apartment, climaxed by the exchange of a few kisses.

When Michael and Charlotte return, Laura becomes alarmed at her mother's increased listlessness and despondency. Michael's frequent absences intensify these periods of depression. One night, after not hearing from her husband for several days, Charlotte takes an overdose of sleeping pills. She is rushed to the hospital and later placed under psychiatric care. Michael returns, and Laura takes over many of her mother's duties, to the exclusion of David. When David warns Laura of the growing danger in these complex family relationships, she becomes so confused about her own motives that she tries to run away. Michael brings her back.

Under the guidance of Charlotte's psychiatrist, the family's tangled relations begin to straighten out. Charlotte resumes her career and Laura begins to call Michael "father." She plans to take her senior year at a boarding school in New Hampshire, near the college that David will be entering in the fall. This arrangement will give her parents time to cement their marriage, and it will enable Laura to keep David's companionship.

Thematic Material

At times, this novel reads like a case history of a triangle in which three people fight their way to understanding and adjustment. Laura's bewilderment and gradual acceptance of her problems are interestingly presented, as is the awakening of her young love.

Book Talk Material

Laura's English teacher explains the Phaedra legend and arouses a violent response in the prologue to the novel (pp. 9–10; pp. 7–8, pap.). Other passages of importance are: Michael is introduced and marriage is discussed (pp. 19–21; pp. 16–18, pap.); Laura meets David (pp. 48–51; pp. 42–45, pap.); and their first date (pp. 81–85; pp. 72–76, pap.).

Additional Selections

After her father's death, Fredrika battles to establish her identity in spite of her cold and ambitious mother, in the Swedish novel, *The Green Coat* (Delacorte Pr., 1977, $6.95) by Maria Gripe. Alice Bach's 11-year-old hero has family problems in *A Father Every Few Years* (Harper, 1977, $5.95). In Florence Parry Heide's *When the Sad Ones Come to Stay* (Lippincott, 1975, $4.95), a heroine is torn between memories of her unsuccessful but loving father and the more prosperous life her mother has offered. An orphaned English girl is adopted by a pioneer farm family in Nova Scotia in Gordon Cooper's *A Second Springtime* (Nelson, 1975, $5.95). In Madeline L'Engle's *Camilla* (Crowell, 1965, $4.95), the heroine learns that her parents are not infallible. Two other suitable novels are: Rosemary Wells' *The Fog Came in on Little Pig Feet* (Dial, 1972, $5.95; pap., Avon, 95¢) and Jill P. Walsh's *Fireweed* (Farrar, 1970, $3.95; pap., Avon, $1.25).

About the Author

Commire, Anne. *Something about the Author.* Detroit: Gale Research Co., 1973. Vol. 4, pp. 80–81.

Ethridge, James M. and Barbara Kopala, Eds. *Contemporary Authors.* Detroit: Gale Research Co., 1967. Vol. 1, p. 303.

Who's Who in America (39th Edition). Chicago: Marquis Who's Who, Inc., 1976. Vol. 1, p. 954.

Earl Hamner, Jr., *You Can't Get There from Here*
Random, 1965, o.p.; pap., Bantam, $1.25

Earl Hamner, Jr., was born and raised in Schuyler, Virginia, the small town that is so lovingly described in *You Can't Get There from Here*. He is best known for his two books about family life during the Depression years in the Blue Ridge Mountains. The first, *Spencer's Mountain* (Dial, 1961, $6.95; pap., Dell, 95¢), is the story of a young boy who reaches maturity; the other is *The Homecoming* (Random, 1970, $4.95; pap., Avon, 95¢), a collection of stories. The title story concerns a Christmas Eve vigil when the Spencer family awaits the arrival of their father. These two books formed the basis of the television series, "The Waltons." *You Can't Get There from Here* is the story of a teen-age boy's day-long odyssey in Manhattan in search of his father. Like Ulysses, he has many adventures and, by recreating his past through remembrances, he learns a great deal about himself. Although originally written for adults, this novel is enjoyed by both junior and senior high school students.

Plot Summary

Sixteen-year-old Wes Scott returns to his Brooklyn Heights home after spending the summer with his grandparents in Schuyler, Virginia. Planning to surprise his parents, he arrives early, but even though it is Saturday, he finds only his stepmother, Meredith, in their small garden apartment. She is upset because Wes' father, Joe had not come home the previous night after being fired from his job as a television scriptwriter.

Joe Scott had been a successful writer for radio, but he has not been able to make the transition to television. A wild and wonderful man, he is an incredible idealist who believes that the only real sin is to harm someone. Unfortunately, he is so affected by other people's hurts that he frequently resorts to heavy drinking. Particularly when intoxicated, he talks about an imaginary village, Shy Beaver, that he is looking for—a village of peace and quiet, his own private Shangri-la, where everyone loves one another. Joe always says that "you can't get there from here," but that if he finds the directions, he'll paint them on the George Washington Bridge in Manhattan.

Meredith is afraid that in his despondency over losing his job, Joe may have become drunk and done something foolish. Wes sets out to try to find him. His first stop is their former Greenich Village apartment. In the past when very drunk, Joe had mistakenly gone there and bedded down in the living room of the new, and very understanding, tenants. Wes was right; Joe was there, but he has already left.

On the street, Wes meets Miss Gregory, who claims she works for the Secret Service and knows where Joe is. Not only is that pure fabrication, but when Wes accompanies her to Macy's department store, he finds that her "secret service" work is really shoplifting. Wes leaves her when she moves on to Gimbels.

When he phones Joe's office at the Continental Broadcasting Company and gets a busy signal, Wes thinks his father must be there. Later the cleaning woman answers, and she notices on Joe's memo pad a scribbled message—*Leave script at Plantation Bar.* Wes tries the bar and is told that Joe was there the night before and that he had been carrying a large amount of cash. Wes decides to try another of Joe's favorite haunts, Halloran's Bar in Rockefeller Center, but on the way he meets a lost youngster who only knows that his mother was taking him to a museum. Eventually Wes gets him to the Museum of Natural History, where he is reunited with his mother.

There is no news of Joe at Halloran's, but there Joe's ex-boss explains that the previous day Joe had received over $2,000 in severance pay. He also speaks highly of this warm and gentle person, and he promises to help get Joe another job. Wes goes to the office and notices that his father's cherished overcoat, a gift from Meredith, is hanging on the rack. While he is there the phone rings. A voice asks for Joe, then says "never mind" because Joe himself has just walked in, and the person hangs up. Wes recognizes the voice as that of Marigold, their former maid who was brought from Schuyler to help the Scott household when Meredith broke her leg. Since then, Marigold has married, had a family of her own, and moved to Harlem. By the time Wes gets the Harlem address, Joe has left, having said something about going back to his office for his overcoat.

Each of these episodes brings back to Wes memories of events involving his beloved father and Meredith. He remembers his father's terrible disappointment when, after working months on the script for the Thanksgiving Day parade, his most important television assignment, the M.C. had ignored it and ad-libbed the entire event. He recalls their close relationship with Marigold and how distressed and lonely Meredith was when she left to be with her husband. When he sees a lost dog on the street, Wes recalls the love they showered on their dog, Greta, who was run over.

Back at the office, Wes discovers that Joe has taken the overcoat and scribbled an address and telephone number on the memo pad. Wes tries the address—it is a closed typewriter store. The number is answered by an old girl friend of Joe's, Prudence Brooks, who lives in a Plaza Hotel suite. Wes visits her, but learns that Joe has already left. She mysteriously alludes to the fact that Joe came to her for help in a surprise he is planning. She reminisces about Joe's first wife, Wes' mother, Ellie, and reveals to Wes that she died at his birth knowing that childbirth could be fatal, but wanting above all to give Joe a son.

Pru says that Joe was off to the jazz palace, the Metropole, to pay his respects to Moses Miles, his favorite drummer. At the Metropole, Miles tells Wes that his father left a short while before, laden down with two large packages, a huge can of paint, and a paint brush. A can of paint! Now Wes knows where his father is.

By the time he gets to the George Washington Bridge, a large crowd, including the police, has gathered because Joe Scott is climbing down the girders at the side of the bridge. He left his two parcels on the bridge. They contain Meredith's most wished-for possession, a leopard skin coat (the help from Pru) and the one thing Wes has really wanted, a typewriter. Wes tries to climb down to his father. He slips, but Joe saves him. As they leave to go back to Brooklyn, Wes sees the beginning of Joe's message in six-foot-high letters. Joe never finished painting the directions to Shy Beaver, but he had completed two words—LOVE IS.

Thematic Material

The close but not cloying family relations are excellently presented. The ideals and principles of the Scott family set a fine example for readers. The author has recreated successfully the color and excitement of life in New York City and the great variety of people found in any large city. Through flashbacks, the reader also has glimpses of a totally different world, the gentle life of a small town in Virginia.

Book Talk Material

The tie-in with "The Waltons" and the author's other books might introduce the story. Suitable passages for retelling or reading are: Wes looks for Joe at the old apartment (pp. 6–8; pp. 3–4, pap.); Wes starts out from Brooklyn (pp. 19–21; pp. 12–13, pap.); Miss Gregory and the Secret

Service (pp. 24–37; pp. 16–24, pap.); the Thanksgiving Day parade script (pp. 50–60; pp. 33–40, pap.); and Wes retrieves an old lady's purse (pp. 82–86; pp. 55–58, pap.).

Additional Suggestions

Bert, rebellious and at times unmanageable, misses his real father when he is placed in a foster home in Mary Calhoun's *It's Getting Beautiful Now* (Harper, 1971, $3.95). Joe David Brown's *Stars in My Crown* (pap., New Amer. Lib., $1.25) is the story of an orphan raised by his grandparents in the rural South. A touching novel of youth and age set in the 1920s is Norman Allan's *Lies My Father Told Me* (pap., New Amer. Lib., $1.50). Also use Vera and Bill Cleaver's *Grover* (pap., New Amer. Lib., $1.25) and Eleanor Clymer's *Me and the Eggman* (Dutton, 1972, $4.95). Two books also set in New York City are Felice Holman's *Slake's Limbo* (Scribner, 1974, $5.95), the story of a disturbed boy who takes refuge and lives in the subway, and Evan H. Rhodes, *The Prince of Central Park* (Coward, 1975, $7.95).

About the Author

Who's Who in America (39th Edition). Chicago: Marquis Who's Who, Inc., 1976.
    Vol. 1, p. 1312.

Norma Klein. *Mom, the Wolfman and Me*
Pantheon, 1972, $4.50; lge-type ed., G. K. Hall, 1973, $5.95; pap., Avon, 95¢

In the few years since the publication of this, her first novel for youngsters, Norma Klein's reputation has grown so that she is now one of the most popular writers of juvenile fiction. In another novel, this one for adults, *Give Me One Good Reason* (pap., Avon, $1.50), she again explores marriageless child rearing. *Mom, the Wolfman and Me* is enjoyed by readers from grades five through nine.

Plot Summary

Although it might be convenient to say that her parents are divorced, when people ask about her father, 11-year-old Brett Levin honestly and bluntly admits that they were never married. The point is that she doesn't miss not having a father because she has a great relationship with her warm and understanding mother, 31-year-old Deborah Levin, a magazine photographer. Deborah is very much a liberated, "with it" woman, who has taught her daughter to be as unpretentious, honest, and forthright as herself. Brett is always consulted before family decisions are made and, although she is given an unusual amount of freedom for her age, it is always tempered with an awareness of responsibility.

Brett and her mother have recently moved from their apartment on a tree-lined street in Greenwich Village to a large high-rise building complete with doormen in uptown Manhattan. The move has meant that Brett can now only occasionally see her close friend and former school-mate, Andrew, but she has made another friend in Evelyn, a highly dramatic and imaginative girl, who lives in the same Manhattan building. Evelyn's parents are divorced and she too is fatherless, but, unlike Brett, Evelyn passionately wants a father—almost as much as her mother wants a husband.

In addition to school and playing with Evelyn, Brett has regular diversions. Deborah usually entertains her boss, Wally, who is separated from his wife, on the Sundays when his two children, nine-year-old Nicky and three-year-old Marshall, are allowed to visit him. Wally often brings with him his movie projector, and the two families watch such old films as *The Wizard of Oz* and *The Yellow Submarine*.

Every Thursday after school Brett visits Grandpa and Grandma Levin in their apartment. Grandma is too staid and conventional to accept fully the nature of Brett's upbringing, but with Grandpa, still a practicing psychoanalyst, there is no problem. An affectionate man, he frequently plays a game with Brett in which she is the analyst and he the patient, a fictitious Mr. Jones, who has problems adjusting to his pet alligator.

Deborah's erratic schedule and exciting assignments intrigue Brett. Sometimes her mother takes her along with her. Deborah has written the same excuse—a dental appointment—so often to Brett's teacher that the girl is convinced everyone at school must think she has terrible teeth. One day she accompanies her mother and an old college friend, Mimi, who runs a menagerie that she trains for television commercials, to a fashion show where Mimi's three bassets are going to be used as props. While alone and tending to the dogs, Brett encounters a man with flaming red hair and beard who has brought along his huge Irish wolfhound to be part of the show. They strike up a conversation, and Brett immediately likes his open and friendly behavior.

A few days later Brett goes on a peace march in Washington with her mother, Wally, Nicky, and old friend Andrew. The Wolfman, as Brett calls him but whose real name is Theodore, joins them. He fits into the group nicely and returns to New York with them.

Two events occur that disturb Brett. First, her Grandpa undergoes a very serious operation. He recovers satisfactorily, but his doctor tells him that he must move to Arizona. Second, Evelyn's mother is rushed to the hospital because of an overdose of sleeping pills. Although the incident might have been accidental, the girls believe it was caused by despondency over the loss of her latest suitor, John.

Theodore, a nightschool teacher, begins seeing Deborah regularly when their schedules permit, and soon he is staying overnight and on weekends. Evelyn tells Brett that this means they are having "sexual intercourse." When asked about this, Deborah admits it but allays Brett's fear of the possibility of her having a baby.

One day Brett confides to the Wolfman that because she fears any change that might upset her family life, she hopes that he will not marry her mother and have a family. She is still trying to get used to her move from the Village and the impending loss of her grandparents. But further change does come when her mother announces that she is going to wed Theodore. Brett loves her Wolfman, but she is apprehensive about all of the new adjustments this will bring, including another move to a larger apartment. She is somewhat soothed by being made part of all the plans for the marriage, including the apartment hunting.

The wedding, a gala affair, is held at Mimi's. Many of the family friends—even Evelyn and Andrew—are present, as well as all of Mimi's animals, including a pet kangaroo named Wilhelmina. After the ceremony, Wally toasts Brett and the wonderful new life that is beginning for her. She hopes he is right.

Thematic Material

This is a novel about families—some conventional, like that of the grandparents, and others like Brett's that have pursued different patterns. It is the participants, not the mode, that determines the amount of happiness derived. Brett's doubts, uncertainties, and fear of change are well developed, as are the many interesting, diverse characters that the author has created. There are several touching relationships depicted in the book, the most important being that between mother and daughter.

Book Talk Material

Brett's fatherless situation is introduced in the opening pages of the novel (pp. 3–5; pp. 13–15, pap.). Other enjoyable passages are: Brett with her Grandpa (pp. 21–24; pp. 35–37, pap.); at Andrew's house (pp. 49–51; pp. 65–67, pap.); and her meetings with the Wolfman (pp. 56–61; pp. 73–77, pap.).

Additional Selections

The effects of divorce on two young people are explored in Norma Klein's *Taking Sides* (Pantheon, 1974, $5.95; pap., Avon, 95¢); also use the author's *It's Not What You Expect* (Pantheon, 1973, $5.99; pap., Avon, 95¢). When her parents separate, Noel-Jennifer begins to fabricate concerning the truth in Anne Alexander's *To Live a Lie* (Atheneum, 1975, $6.95). A boy adjusts to a foster family in Mildred Ames' *Without Hats, Who Can Tell the Good Guys?* (Dutton, 1976, $6.95). Marcia copes with her father's remarriage in Rosemary Wells' *None of the Above* (Dial, 1974, $5.95; pap., Avon, $1.25). Barbara Berson's *What's Going to Happen to Me?* (Scribner, 1976, $6.95) tells how a young boy reacts to his parents' separation. Two other stories involving children living with only one parent are Roald Dahl's *Danny: The Champion of the World* (Knopf, 1975, $5.95) and Barbara Moe's *Pickles and Prunes* (McGraw, 1976, $5.72).

About the Author

Commire, Anne. *Something about the Author.* Detroit: Gale Research Co., 1975. Vol. 7, pp. 152–154.

Kinsman, Clare D., Ed. *Contemporary Authors.* Detroit: Gale Research Co., 1974. Vol. 41, p. 334.

Nicholasa Mohr, *Nilda*

Harper, 1973, $5.95; lib. bdg., $5.79; pap., Bantam, $1.25

Like her young heroine, Nicholasa Mohr was raised in New York City's El Barrio, on Manhattan's Upper East Side—a neighborhood also known as Spanish or Puerto Rico's Harlem—and, like Nilda, she also became interested in art while still a youngster. Several of the author's impressionistic drawings are scattered throughout the text of the hard-cover edition and convey, through words and representational symbols, the mood and spirit of Nilda's world. The work spans a period of four years—from mid-1941 when Nilda is almost 10 until the end of World War II in May 1945. Without resorting to the sensational, the author often includes earthy language and incidents that are a natural part of growing up in the slums. The book is popular chiefly with junior high school students.

Plot Summary

Nilda lives with her family in a crowded six-room, four-floor walkup apartment in El Barrio. In addition to her mother, Lydia, there is aging, somewhat senile Aunt Delia, who delights in playing the numbers and reading news of muggings and murders from the local newspapers, and Nilda's stepfather, Emilio Ramirez, an embittered Spanish Communist with a serious heart condition whose family was killed by the Fascists during the Spanish Civil War. Nilda has four older half-brothers by her mother's previous marriage in Puerto Rico to Mr. Ortega. There is the eldest, Jimmy, who has just quit school; Victor, now 17 and a senior in high school; 15-year-old Paul, Nilda's favorite; and the youngest, Frankie, who is almost 13.

Lydia and Emilio Ramirez have been married only four years, and Nilda secretly suspects that her real father is Leo, a man who lives in the neighborhood with his mistress Dona Concha and who, although estranged from the Ramirez family, is particularly kind to her and her mother when they happen to meet on the street. The guiding force in the family is her mother, a stalwart and courageous woman of great strength and tenderness.

In the steamy, stenchful summer of 1941, Nilda is given the opportunity to attend a summer camp for girls, but the camp is so prisonlike that she prays for a miracle to send her home early. It comes by way of a plumbing failure, and Nilda is happy to return to the streets and her friends, Peter and Marge Lopez and Benjie, a young boy whose family belong to the local Pentecostal church. Nilda's family, with the exception of her atheist father, are Roman Catholic, and she attends Mass faithfully.

Jimmy suddenly disappears, and there is whispered talk of dope and the police. He leaves behind his girl friend, Sophie, who comes to live with the Ramirez family after her parents disown her because she is pregnant. Emilio suffers another heart attack and is unable to work. Without any income, Mrs. Ramirez is forced to undergo a series of humiliating interviews to seek public assistance. They now rely on welfare food, and Nilda is deprived even of a few pennies to buy cookies and milk at school.

Sophie's baby is born. They name him James Ortega, Jr., and Nilda enjoys playing mother whenever Sophie allows her. With her child in her arms and Nilda by her side, Sophie goes to her parents' apartment hoping for a reconciliation, but they refuse to open the door to her.

Nilda, with Peter and Marge, joins Benjie and his family for a service at his Pentecostal church, LaRoca de San Sebastian, Inc. Nilda is amazed at the shouting and writhing when the spirit enters the congregation. The girls are intrigued further when the service in interrupted by drunken Don Justico who comes to retrieve his wife. As a climax to his railings, the man shows his complete disdain by urinating on the altar. Nilda is shocked but fascinated by the experience.

One night, Jimmy reappears and takes Sophie and the baby with him to Hoboken, New Jersey, where he claims he has a job. The family remains apprehensive about his dealings with drugs.

When war is declared, Victor enters the army, and a year later Paul enlists in the navy. For Nilda, one of the highlights of 1942 is a month spent at Bard Manor Camp for Girls. She makes many friends and is able to get her group to accept a pathetic waif, Josie Forest, who had been taunted cruelly. It is a period of enchantment for Nilda and her first introduction to nature outside of Central Park.

Emilio's condition worsens. Nilda's mother resorts to seeking the help of a spiritualist, Dona Tiofila, but, in December 1943, Emilio dies. At the funeral parlor, Mrs. Ramirez, overcome with the death of her husband and her life of hardship, becomes hysterical.

Nilda enters junior high school and is delighted with her new surroundings and friends. Her mother takes a job in a factory, sewing parachutes. The family is now financially more secure, but there is more heartache when they learn that Sophie has married another man and Jimmy has been sent to jail on drug charges.

Frankie has joined a fighting gang, the Lightnings, and on the night of their rumble with the Barons, Nilda witnesses police brutality when a police officer beats up one of Benjie's brothers who is mistakenly thought to be a member of a gang. This incidence of injustice against her people sickens her.

As the war draws to a close, Mrs. Ramirez' health declines. Worn out by years of sacrifice and affliction, she has little resistance left. When she is hospitalized, Nilda's Aunt Rosario comes to take care of the family. Before her death, her mother tells Nilda that she always must be true to herself and that she must try not to repeat the mistakes that have prevented so many people like herself from achieving happiness. She dies on the day that Germany surrenders.

There is no possibility of the family staying together any longer. Aunt Delia will be sent to a home, and Nilda and brother Frankie are to move in with Aunt Rosario's family. With her mother's final words still fresh in her mind, Nilda hopes to overcome this tragedy just as she has coped with other problems in her life.

Thematic Material

This is a novel of grinding hardship and tragedy, endurance and courage. Despite periods of despair and hopelessness, there are also moments of great compassion and joy. Growing up Puerto Rican in New

York City is realistically depicted in great detail. The book stresses a need for solid family relationships and for understanding and open-mindedness between races.

Book Talk Material

The book contains many vignettes that could be used in book talks: Nilda is saved from camp (pp. 15–19; pp. 13–16, pap.); Nilda finds a man who has been stabbed (pp. 35–38; pp. 30–33, pap.); Sophie's trick on Nilda with welfare food (pp. 44–47; pp. 38–41, pap.); Nilda at school (pp. 51–57; 45–50, pap.); and Nilda and her mother at the welfare office (pp. 65–71; pp. 57–63, pap.).

Additional Selections

Nicholasa Mohr has two excellent collections of short stories: *El Bronx Remembered* (Harper, 1975, $5.50) and *In Nueva York* (Dial, 1977, $7.95). Nicky Cruz's true story, *Run, Baby, Run* (Logos, 1968, $4.95; pap., Pyramid, $1.25) is subtitled *The Story of a Gang-Lord Turned Crusader*. A fantasy set in Puerto Rico is Tere Rios' *The Fiftieth Pelican: The Adventures of a Flying Nun* (Hale, 1965, $3.42). In Sharon Bell Mathis' *Listen for the Fig Tree* (Viking, 1974, $6.50; pap., Avon, 95¢), Young Muffin, a blind black girl, and her alcoholic mother have many problems. For a more mature audience, suggest Pedro Juan Soto's *Hot Land, Cold Season*, about an 18-year-old Puerto Rican boy who is torn between two cultures—that of his native land and of the United States. For a younger group, use *Magdalena* (Viking, 1971, $5.95) by Louisa Shotwell, about a young girl and her problems with an elderly Puerto Rican grandmother; and Charles Talbot's *Tomas Takes Charge* (Lothrop, 1966, o.p.); Hila Colman's *The Girl from Puerto Rico* (Farrar, 1961, $6.50); and Frank Bonham's *Viva Chicano* (Dutton, 1970, $5.50; pap., Dell, 95¢).

About the Author

Commire, Anne. *Something about the Author*. Detroit: Gale Research Co., 1976. Vol. 8, pp. 138–139.

Kinsman, Clare D., Ed. *Contemporary Authors*. Detroit: Gale Research Co., 1975. Vol. 49, pp. 379–380.

Robert Newton Peck, *A Day No Pigs Would Die*
Knopf, 1973, $6.95; pap., Dell, $1.25

> 'Tis the gift to be simple
> 'Tis the gift to be free
> 'Tis the gift to come down
> Where we ought to be.

These opening lines of the Shaker hymn "Simple Gifts" describe the honest and wholesome values under which Robert Peck was raised. *A Day No Pigs Would Die* takes us back to a gentler and less complicated period— the locale is rural Vermont and the time is the late 1920s, when Calvin Coolidge was president. The story, as told by Robert, begins when he is a boy of 12 and ends one year later when he suddenly has to assume a man's responsibilities. Its unusual title derives from the last episode in the book, the day of the death and burial of Robert's loving and saintly father, who was the hog butcher in the area. Although originally written for adults, both junior and senior high school students enjoy the humor and touching simplicity of this story.

Plot Summary

One lovely New England spring day, Rob Peck becomes so furious at the teasing he receives because of his plain Shaker clothes that he plays hooky after recess. On his way home he sees Apron, the prize Holstein cow of his neighbor, Ben Tanner, undergoing a difficult labor. Fearful that the calf will choke before being born, Rob tries to help by tying one end of his trouser to a tree and the other around the calf's head, and then beating Apron into motion. It works. The calf is born alive, but suddenly Apron begins choking. Robert reaches into her gullet and yanks out a hard ball of matter. But the cow bites his arm severely and stomps him unconscious.

The ball of matter was really a goiter and its removal saved Apron's life, but young Robert must spend a week in bed recovering. In appreciation, Tanner wants to give him a piglet, but Rob's father insists that it is not the Shaker way to accept gifts for neighborly acts. Tanner then claims it is only a birthday present for Rob, who joyously accepts the gift as the first thing he has really wanted and owned.

Rob spends most of his spare time with his pet, named Pinky, who lives in a nearby unused cow crib. He takes her into the woods with him and together they explore nature. Rob confides to Pinky things he couldn't to a human friend.

While Pinky is growing to maturity, many events take place in the Peck household. One stormy night Rob and his father prevent their neighbor from digging up the body of his illegitimate daughter. Another time Rob witnesses the bloody and brutal matching of a weasel and young terrier in an enclosed barrel. But there are good and humorous times too—Pinky wins a 4H blue ribbon and Aunt Mattie tries to show Rob how to diagram a sentence, but decides it would be easier to teach Pinky. The most tragic happening occurs one night when Rob learns that his father's health is poor and that he will die soon.

After unsuccessful attempts at breeding, Rob realizes that Pinky is barren. The apple crop is bad that fall, and the hunting season brings no meat to the Peck table. On a mid-December morning, with little food left in the larder, his father turns to Rob and says, "Let's get it done." The boy knows his father's meaning. Although his heart is breaking, Rob helps him in killing and dressing his pet. It is the only time that the boy ever saw his father cry.

In late spring, Rob's father dies quietly in his sleep. Rob automatically assumes the responsibilities of heading the household. He arranges for the funeral and digs his father's grave in the orchard. That night, after the service when he is all alone, Robert Peck walks to the orchard to say his last farewell to his father.

Thematic Material

Besides presenting one of the most tender pictures of family life in all young adult literature, particularly of a close father–son relationship, this book movingly re-creates a way of living governed by simple virtues and truths. The passage from boyhood to manhood is also touchingly portrayed. The reader gets a glimpse into Shaker beliefs and the graphic realities of farm life. Other subjects covered are rural American life in the 1920s and the boy's close attachment to his pet.

Book Talk Material

Episodic in form, the book contains many incidents that are complete in themselves, such as: Rob's first encounter with Apron (pp. 3-8; pp. 7-12, pap.); Mr. Tanner gives Pinky to Rob (pp. 21-23; pp. 23-25, pap.); Rob talks with his Papa about baseball and elections (pp. 32-37; pp. 34-39, pap.); and Rob diagrams a sentence (pp. 52-60; pp. 51-59, pap.).

Additional Selections

Robert Peck has followed *Pig* with several other fine books, including *Millie's Boy* (Knopf, 1973, $5.99; pap., Dell, 95¢), about Tit Smith's search for his father in the New England of 1898, and *Path of Hunters* (Knopf, 1973, $4.95; lib. bdg., $5.99) on animal struggles for survival. Doris Faber has written a fascinating history of the Shakers in *The Perfect Life* (Farrar, 1974, $6.95). There is also a section on the Shakers in Leo Rosten's *Religions of America* (Simon & Schuster, 1975, $12.95; pap., $5.95; under the title *Religions in America*, Simon & Schuster, pap., $2.95). Joanna Crawford's *Birch Interval* (pap., Dell, $1.25) is a fine novel about children growing up in a Pennsylvania Amish community as seen through the eyes of a young girl. Barbara Willard has edited *Happy Families* (Macmillan,

1974, $6.95). Those interested in animal stories might enjoy Lois Crisler's *Arctic Wild* (Harper, 1973, $8.95) and Douglas Fairbarn's *A Squirrel Forever* (Simon & Schuster, 1973, $6.95).

Mary **Rodgers,** *Freaky Friday*
Harper, 1972, $4.95; lib. bdg., $4.79; pap. $1.25 (same pagination)

Mary Rodgers, the daughter of composer Richard Rodgers, wrote such hits as *Once Upon a Mattress* for the New York stage before turning to juvenile literature and such delights as *A Billion for Boris* (Harper, 1974, $4.95; pap., $1.25) and *Freaky Friday*. With the latter she scored a success by writing the screenplay for the Disney film version. This delightful novel is enjoyed particularly by girls in upper elementary and junior high school grades.

Plot Summary

One Thursday night, 13-year-old, self-willed Annabel Andrews has another of those persistent disagreements with her mother. As usual, they focus on four subjects: Annabel's appearance (why does she have to wear unsightly braces and what is wrong with having straggly hair?); the tidiness, or lack of it, in her room (why can't she throw apple cores or underpants under the bed and wedge her tights between volumes of the Junior Britannica?); food (why can't she exist on marshmallows instead of eating her mother's nutritious meals?); and, most of all, her freedom (what harm is there in attending kissing parties with her friends in Greenwich Village or walking alone in Central Park?). In short, Annabel is in the throes of a teen-age rebellion against all authority, against the private school she attends, and against her parents and six-year-old docile brother, Ben, whom she has nicknamed Ape Face. Things would be different if she were in her mother's place!

She awakens on Friday to find that a transformation has occurred—she has turned into her mother! Welcoming the idea of a day of freedom and retribution, she awakens her "supercool" father (now, husband) Bill Andrews, an advertising executive, and begins preparing breakfast. Ape Face appears and greets his mommy as usual. Warily, Annabel peers into her room. Who could that marshmallow-chomping, comic-book-reading ogress be? Certainly not her mother—she loathes marshmallows. Without too many incidents, she gets the kids off to school and Bill to work after promising him to buy some liquor for the house and to launder his shirts.

Her quiet is broken by a surprise visit from their neighbor, 14-year-old Boris Harris, who has a severe adenoidal condition, and has "cub to returd a collander his buther" had borrowed. Annabel has an unrequited crush on Boris and can't resist, in her mother's guise, making a few complimentary remarks on her behalf.

When Boris leaves, she starts the laundry. She overloads the machine with both clothes and detergent, and soon the kitchen is awash with water and soap suds. At this point Mrs. Rose Schmauss, their cleaning lady, arrives. But when Rose begins lecturing her employer about what a pig her daughter is and falsely accuses Annabel of drinking the family gin (actually Mrs. Schmauss is the tippler), they argue and Annabel, in a fit of self-righteous wrath, fires her.

To calm herself, Annabel goes to the liquor store and on her way home meets Ape Face returning from nursery school. She tries to call him Ben and feeds him a lunch of cold macaroni she has found in the fridge. Ben confides to her that he really loves and admires his sister and wishes she would be kinder to him. In spite of her callous exterior, Annabel is touched by her brother's love.

The phone rings. It is Mr. Andrews who tells his wife that he is bringing home for dinner two clients, Mr. and Mrs. Philip Frampton of the Francie's Fortified Fish Fingers account. He also reminds her that she has an appointment that afternoon at Annabel's school to discuss her scholastic record. In desperation, Annabel calls Boris, who very graciously not only consents to act as babysitter while she goes to the Barden School, but also to prepare a "beetloaf" dinner.

Before meeting with the principal and other school personnel, Annabel learns from her classmates that her double has played truant. Where could she be? The officials begin discussing Annabel's dismal record at school, and one teacher breaks down and weeps at her failure to help such an intelligent girl with immense potential. At first Annabel is on the defensive but when the school psychiatrist suggests that the problem may lie in the girl's home life, she stoutly defends the Andrews and sincerely promises to change Annabel's attitudes and work habits.

Back home she finds Boris still in the kitchen, but Ben is missing. The boy claims that a "beautiful chick" rang their bell and took Ben with her. Annabel can think only of kidnapping. She calls the police but so garbles the story that they call her a "fruitcake." In a short time a man and woman come to the apartment, and she believes momentarily that it is help in the form of plainclothes police officers. Wrong! It's the Framptons. Dismayed and despairing, she rushes to her bedroom and begs for the spell to be broken. Suddenly her mother is sitting beside her and she is the real Annabel again. Her mother had spent the day as her daughter having her hair fixed, buying some snappy clothes, and getting their orthodontist to remove her braces. Annabel is the "beautiful chick" that attracted Boris.

Ben is back, the Framptons are appeased, and Annabel has a wonderful time with Boris eating his beetloaf. She even finds out that his name is really Morris—it's those adenoids again. Although she has learned many valuable lessons by this experience, she never finds out how her mother was able to produce such a "freaky Friday."

Thematic Material

Many have asked for the opportunity to see themselves as others see them, and Annabel has this rare experience. On the surface this is a delightful, often hilarious fantasy, but it also makes some valid points about the generation gap and family relationships. Youngsters will identify with both Annabel's rebelliousness and her growing sense of responsibility and compassion.

Book Talk Material

A brief description of the role change between mother and daughter can be used to introduce the book. Passages that also could be used in a book talk are: the transformation (pp. 1-2); breakfast (pp. 11-14); Boris appears (pp. 27-30); and Ben talks about his love for Annabel (pp. 56-59).

Additional Selections

A genie is freed from captivity in a carpet in George Seldon's book for a slightly younger audience, *The Genie of Sutton Place* (Farrar, 1973, $5.95). The young heroine of Stella Persher's *Call Me Heller, That's My Name* (Seabury, 1973, $5.95) causes trouble when she tries to live up to her nickname. A girl's adjustment to her divorced mother's suitors is the story of Kin Platt's *Chloris and the Creeps* (Chilton, 1973, $4.95; pap., Dell, 95¢). A girl spends a complex summer on eastern Long Island in M. E. Kerr's *Love Is a Missing Person* (Harper, 1976, $5.95; pap., Dell, $1.25). An elevator ride takes Susan Shaw back in time in Edward Ormondroyd's *Time at the Top* (Parnassus, 1963, $5.95). Also use Paula Danzinger's *The Cat Ate My Gymsuit* (Delacorte Pr., 1974, $5.95; pap., Dell, 95¢); W. E. Butterworth's *Susan and Her Classic Convertible* (Four Winds, 1970, o.p.); and Ethelyn Parkinson's *Rupert Piper and Megan, the Valuable Girl* (Abingdon, 1972, $4.95).

About the Author

Commire, Anne. *Something about the Author.* Detroit: Gale Research Co., 1976.
Vol. 8, pp. 167-168.
Kinsman, Clare D., Ed. *Contemporary Authors.* Detroit: Gale Research Co., 1975.
Vol. 49, p. 463.

Barbara Wersba, *Run Softly, Go Fast*
Atheneum, 1972, $7.95; pap., Bantam, $1.25

Perhaps at no time in our history was the conflict between generations more apparent than in the late 1960s, largely over the battle in Vietnam. This novel describes the division between a father who is materialistic, garish, and financially successful and his pampered, rebellious son, both trying to love and retain respect for each other, but neither able to bridge the ever-widening gap that separates them. It is intended for mature eighth and ninth graders and senior high school students.

Plot Summary

The central character, 19-year-old David Marks tells the story through his journal. Two years before, he left his parents' luxury apartment in New York City to seek his own life in the less "posh" side of town. Davey remembers many happy incidents from his childhood, as well as the awe and affection he felt for his crude but generous father, Joe. With his brother Ben, a gentle, scholarly bachelor who now works at the Library of Jewish Studies, Joe immigrated to the United States to escape persecution. Forced to quit grammar school to find a job, Joe rose steadily, with hard work and long hours, to a position of importance in the wholesale clothing business. He is determined that his only child will receive all of the advantages that he himself was denied.

When the boy is nine, his father takes him to the Lower East Side to show him the neighborhood where he grew up. He tells Davey stories of the grueling poverty he suffered and that everything he has planned in life is for his son. Embarrassed and bewildered, Davey does not respond, which Joe takes as a sign of rejection and hostility.

His father expects Davey to develop into an athletic, social, all-American boy who will take over the business some day. Instead, Davey is introspective, overly sensitive, and interested in reading, writing poetry, and drawing. The boy feels more in common with thoughtful Uncle Ben than with his own father.

One night while his mother is asleep, Davey witnesses an intimate scene between his father and one of his buyers. The boy's attitudes of detachment and remoteness toward his father turn to contempt and loathing.

Although Davey often goes out on dates, his feelings about sex are filled with anxiety and guilt. Quarrels between father and son increase in frequency and intensity. Whether they discuss Joe's ruthless business deals, race relations, or the war in Vietnam, there is no common ground between them.

In Davey's senior year at his exclusive private school, he meets Rich Heaton, an intelligent, knowledgeable young man who shares many of

Davey's interests and attitudes. They begin to visit galleries and museums, go to the theater, and pool reading experiences. Their close friendship gives Davey encouragement and direction in his painting and drawing. However, one night Joe comes into Davey's room and finds the two young men wrestling on the bed. Misinterpreting the situation, he calls Rich a "lousy little queer" and orders him out of the house. Outraged, Davey packs his bags and moves to the East Village apartment of his old friend, Marty Brooks.

Davey completes his senior year and increases his painting activities while living off his savings account and family checks. Any attempts at reconciliation, usually through his mother or Uncle Ben, only make the estrangement worse.

Rich visits Davey and tells him that, under pressure from his family, he has decided to enter the army. Davey dismisses him as another sellout. Several months later, Rich is killed in Vietnam, and Davey is filled with remorse and guilt.

Slowly Davey sinks further and further into the hippie life of the East Village, experimenting with pot, acid, and speed. He becomes sickened by this life and his own excesses. Then he meets Maggie Carroll at a party and falls in love. Davey moves to her loft. She is able to arrange a one-man show of his paintings in the gallery where she works. It is a modest but encouraging success. However, Davey is disappointed when, of his family, only his mother and Uncle Ben attend the opening.

Toward the end of his second year of independence, Davey's mother visits him and begs him to visit Joe, who is in the hospital dying of cancer. Reluctantly, Davey agrees, but during the visit Joe insists that Davey cut his hair and wear decent clothes if he intends to come back to the hospital. Another quarrel follows, and Davey leaves, swearing never to return. Weeks pass, and Davey's conscience prods him into another visit. But it is too late. Joe is now so sedated that he does not recognize his son. At the funeral, Davey cannot feel pity or sorrow. His only thought is "he was a bastard and you hated him."

Several days later, as Davey is making his last entry in his journal, he softens somewhat and hopes that in time his memory of his father will become less filled with guilt and rancor, and that someday he will be able to see events from Joe's point of view. For the present, it is a consolation that Joe has found peace at last.

Thematic Material

The seamy sides of the materialistic, often hypocritical values of the middle class and frequently unrealistic, sentimentalized idealism of the hippie culture are brilliantly portrayed in this grim, often depressing novel. Also powerful is the description of the gradual deterioration through lack of understanding and communication of a father-son relationship. Although sympathetic with Davey, the astute reader can also detect his flaws of self-indulgence, impatience, and inability, because of stubbornness, to reach compromises. These, when placed in conflict with his father's faults, produce the tragedy of the book.

Book Talk Material

Because the novel consists chiefly of introspective remembrances rather than straightforward narration, perhaps a description of the father-son conflict might be the best way to introduce this book. Some isolated passages for study are: Davey at Joe's funeral (pp. 3-5; pp. 1-3, pap.); a lake incident from childhood (pp. 12-16; pp. 8-12, pap.); Joe takes Davey to the Lower East Side (pp. 23-26; pp. 17-20, pap.); and the conflict of father and son (pp. 59-61; pp. 46-48, pap.).

Additional Selections

Bridie is devastated by the death of her father and must make a difficult adjustment in Mollie Hunter's *Sound of Chariots* (Harper, 1973, $5.49; pap., Avon, $1.25). A 17-year-old girl becomes a member of a Boston hippie group in Lee Kingman's *The Peter Pan Bag* (Houghton, 1970, $5.95; pap., Dell, $1.25). Mac's father labels him a "hippie" because he doesn't conform in Elizabeth Baker's *This Stranger, My Son* (Houghton, 1971, $4.50). The generation gap is also explored in Nat Hentoff's *I'm Really Dragged but Nothing Gets Me Down* (Simon & Schuster, 1968, $5.95; pap., Dell, 95¢) and Peter Hamill's *The Gift* (Random, 1973, $4.95). Other novels of adolescent crises are: Paula Fox's *Blowfish Live in the Sea* (Bradbury, 1970, $6.95; pap., Dell, 95¢); Paul Zindel's *I Never Loved Your Mind* (Harper, 1970, $5.95; pap., Bantam, 95¢); and Maia Wojciechowska's *Don't Play Dead Before You Have To* (Harper, 1970, $4.79; pap., Dell, 95¢).

About the Author

Commire, Anne. *Something about the Author.* Detroit: Gale Research Co., 1971. Vol. 1, p. 224.

DeMontreville, Doris and Donna Hill, Eds. *Third Book of Junior Authors.* New York: H. W. Wilson Co., 1972, pp. 298-299.

Kinsman, Clare D. and Mary Ann Tennenhouse, Eds. *Contemporary Authors.* Detroit: Gale Research Co., 1972, Vol. 29, pp. 674-675.

Ward, Martha E. and Dorothy A. Marquardt. *Authors of Books for Young People.* (2nd Edition). Metuchen, N.J.: Scarecrow Press, Inc., 1971, p. 544.

2

Developing Lasting Values

To REPLACE THE rigid, authoritative value system imposed on children from outside, the adolescent must try to understand the various gradations of formal and informal value systems. He or she must make wise decisions in developing a value system that will work and meet the needs of both the individual and society. Each of the books in this section explores situations in which a central character's ethical and moral nature is challenged or needs redefinition.

John Christopher, *The Lotus Caves*
        Macmillan, 1969, $4.95; pap., Collier, 95¢

The métier of the English writer, John Christopher, is the realm of science fiction. Immediately before *The Lotus Caves,* he wrote a highly successful trilogy about a boy, Will Parker, and his two friends who struggle during the twenty-first century to free the world from possible domination by the Tripods. The boys' flight to freedom in Switzerland is described in the first book, *The White Mountains* (Macmillan, 1967, $5.95; pap., Collier, $1.25). In the second, two of them enter *The City of Gold and Lead* (Macmillan, 1967, $4.95; pap., Collier, $1.25), the dreaded headquarters of the Tripods. In the third, *The Pool of Fire* (Macmillan, 1968, $5.95; pap., Collier, $1.25), they meet with ultimate triumph. All of these novels are enjoyed particularly by boys in the junior high school grades.

Plot Summary

The year is 2068, and the setting a lunar colony enclosed in a hemispheric plastic dome known as the Bubble. Marty has spent all of his 14 years in the Bubble. What little he knows of the planet Earth he has received through construct films in school and from his parents, both

25

Americans who still have to complete six years of their 25-year employ-
ment contract before they return to Earth. Life is not unpleasant in the
Bubble. Marty attends an electronically equipped high school; he has
access to a huge recreation center with swimming pool, library, and movie
theater; he can even venture out of the Bubble to the eight-mile limit via
jitney-type vehicles called crawlers. His major foe is boredom. The meals
of processed food are monotonously the same; movements are limited; and
the claustrophobic unnatural environment often creates strain and
tension.

When Marty's best friend is suddenly sent to Earth for medical treatment,
Marty begins to chum with Steve der Cros, a lonely, somewhat rebellious
youth whose parents were killed in a landing pad accident when he was
only a child. As a prank, the boys release some balloons in the Bubble, after
having painted on them caricatures of their school principal, Mr. Sherrin.
The principal is not amused, and, as punishment, bans them from the
recreation center for a month.

Out of boredom, the boys decide to take out a crawler, which they
discover not only has a key in the control panel that will enable passage
through the eight-mile limit, but is also well stocked with food. Perhaps it
had been prepared for a trip by one of the official geological teams. Ready
for any new adventure, Steve persuades Marty to take advantage of the
situation and explore an abandoned space station some 300 miles away.
Because they have almost 12 days of lunar light left before nightfall and
plenty of provisions, Marty consents, but reluctantly. They transmit a de-
layed message at the eight-mile limit to the Bubble detailing their plans.

By alternating driving and sleeping, the boys reach First Station in 48
hours. The small bubble had been abandoned 70 years before, when three
of the men stationed there died while trying to locate the fourth member,
Andrew Thurgood, who had mysteriously disappeared. In their space
suits, the boys explore the deserted station. Wedged under one of the bunks,
Marty finds Thurgood's log in which he reports sighting a gigantic flower,
yards wide, growing out of a rock crevice. The boys set out to explore, but at
the location specified in the log the crawler suddenly plunges forward into
an opening and the two find themselves in a large cave. A whirring sound
around them signals an avalanche of leaves, which covers the cave
opening. The cave, filled with luxurious vegetation and oxygen-rich air, is
bright with light from the phosphorescent moss that covers the cave floor.
They find the wreck of an ancient crawler and identify it as Thurgood's.
The entrance leads to a network of gigantic caves, each filled with
magnificent trees and foliage, all swaying as though alive. A fantastic
orchard in one cave is filled with every kind of fruit tree and berry bush,

many of which the boys had read about but never tasted. They eat and are resting by the shores of a huge lake when they notice that the cave is gradually darkening. As though under a spell, they fall asleep. When they awaken, it is light again and a stranger is standing before them.

The stranger is Thurgood, who appears as young as the day he disappeared. Gradually he explains that all of the verdure is part of a mystical power, known as the Plant, which exists through the absorption of solar radiation by huge flowers similar to the one he had seen many years ago. The hours of darkness are the Plant's period of meditation. Thurgood remembers little of the past, nor does he seem curious about or interested in the outside world. Gradually the boys realize that he, like the lotus eaters in the *Odyssey*, has been dulled into forgetfulness by the fruits that the Plant supplies.

The Plant summons the boys, and they are conveyed by a raft of lily pads far into the lake, where they are confronted by a pillar of fire pulsating like a heart and emitting a golden radiance. The Plant's thoughts are conveyed by telepathy; the boys speak in their normal language. After questioning them, the Plant says that they can never return home, but all their wants and needs will be satisfied. Steve asks for a tree from which to dive into the lake. Like a speeded-up film, a tree grows at the lakeside. The boys notice that Thurgood actually worships the Plant as his god and has fallen so deeply into its power that he is able to communicate with it completely through telepathic processes.

Realizing that they too are gradually losing their will and are slowly becoming slaves of this superintelligence, Marty and Steve try to eat little of the cave's food. Instead, during the periods of the Plant's meditation, they return by flashlight to the crawler and to their fast-dwindling supply of Earth food.

Over a period of several days and under a barrage of constant questioning, Steve forces Thurgood to remember his past and the location of the fissures in the cave through which the crawler could pass. The three make their escape, but once back on the moon's surface, the drawing power of the Plant is so strong that Thurgood jumps from the crawler and returns to the cave. For Thurgood's sake, Marty and Steve decide not to tell the people in the Bubble of their adventures, but when they think of him in his Eden-like existence, they experience a feeling not unlike envy.

Thematic Material

People have always dreamed of a Shangri-la where time stands still and worries cease, but the boys discover that reality, although often difficult, is preferable. The glimpse of a futuristic lunar colony and its problems is both exotic and informative. The boys' bravery and resourcefulness in withstanding the Plant's brainwashing is another important theme.

Book Talk Material

A description of life in the Bubble will interest readers, as will any of the following episodes: the great balloon crime (pp. 22-25; pp. 30-34, pap.); the boys take out the crawler (pp. 30-33; pp. 41-46, pap.); Thurgood's log (pp. 54-58; pp. 73-79, pap.); and the scenes in the cave (pp. 74-76; 102-105, pap.).

Additional Selections

Two novels set in the future in Britain, written by another English writer of science fiction, Peter Dickinson, are *The Devil's Children* (Little, 1970, $5.95) and *The Weathermonger* (Little, 1969, $5.95). Interplanetary mail service is the subject of André Norton's *Postmarked the Stars* (Harcourt, 1969, $5.95), and intergalactic trade in gems is dealt with in her equally recommended *The Zero Stone* (Viking, 1968, $4.50). Two fine collections of short stories are Ray Bradbury's *S Is for Space* (Doubleday, 1966, $3.95) and Ben Bova's *The Many Worlds of Science Fiction* (Dutton, 1971, $5.95). Also recommended is John Christopher's second trilogy, which deals with English life in the twenty-first century after a volcanic disaster produces a new feudal culture: *The Prince in Waiting* (Macmillan, 1970, $4.95; pap., Collier, 95¢); *Beyond the Burning Lands* (Macmillan, 1971, $4.95; pap., Collier, $1.25); and *The Sword of the Spirits* (Macmillan, 1972, $4.95; pap., Collier, $1.95). Franklyn Branley, George Gamow, and Herbert Kondo have each written good nonfiction descriptions of our Earth's satellite (each is called *The Moon*).

About the Author

Townsend, John Rowe. *A Sense of Story*. Philadelphia and New York: J. B. Lippincott Co., 1971, pp. 48-53.

Robert Cormier, *The Chocolate War*
Pantheon, 1974, $5.95; pap., Dell, $1.25

One day Robert Cormier's son brought home from school some boxes of chocolates to sell. When the boy was asked if he really wanted to sell the chocolates, he replied that he didn't, and his father returned them to the school without incident. But, what if . . . this started the germ of an idea for this novel, which created a sensation when it appeared in 1974. The book begins with three words, "They murdered him." Although the reader soon learns that this refers to the beating that the 14-year-old protagonist takes at a school football practice, the words gain greater significance and portent as the novel progresses. It is recommended for mature readers in the junior and senior high school years.

Plot Summary

The power structure at Trinity, a New England parochial day school for boys, involves two elements: Brother Leon and the Vigils. Brother Leon is the Assistant Headmaster, on the surface ingratiating and overly cautious, but underneath a venomous, sinister man who is fiercely ambitious. At present, because of the Headmaster's prolonged illness, Brother Leon is in charge. If possible, he intends to make this appointment permanent.

The Vigils is the powerful secret society composed of the student elite. Its real power lies with Archie Costello, the Assigner, the officer who conceives and assigns the various hazing tasks that are given to non-members. Archie is intelligent and imaginative, but he is also completely heartless and cynical. His ability to make up outrageous assignments is diabolically clever. Archie has as his muscleman or enforcer, Emile Janza, the school bully.

Each year under the direction of Brother Leon, the students sell boxes of chocolates to raise money for the school. This year Brother Leon has overextended himself by buying twice the number of boxes for sale as in the past years, using funds earmarked for other purposes. With 20,000 boxes of chocolates to be sold and only 400 boys in the school, each student will have to sell 50 boxes, a stiff quota. Leon asks Archie for his support in the sale, but both know that he really is asking for the support of the Vigils. Archie plays a cat-and-mouse game with Brother Leon, but he finally agrees to help.

Two freshmen come before the Vigils for assignments. The first is Roland Goubert, nicknamed The Goober, whose assignment is to loosen everything held together by screws in Brother Eugene's classroom. (Brother Eugene later suffers a nervous collapse from this incident.) Before the assignment becomes official, Archie must undergo the black box test. He is handed a box containing six balls, five white and one black. If Archie draws the black ball, he must fulfill the assignment himself. In his three years as Assigner, Archie has been phenomenally lucky. Once again, he draws a white ball.

The other assignee is Jerry Renault, a spunky, well-liked boy, but something of a loner, particularly since his mother's death from cancer a few months before. Jerry lives alone with his father, a dispirited, unassertive man, who, unlike Jerry, accepts unquestioningly whatever life offers.

Everyone knows that Jerry has received his assignment, but no one knows what it is until, on the day the chocolates are distributed, Jerry refuses to accept his quota. Through threats and bribery, Brother Leon learns from a student that Renault's refusal was a Vigil assignment. It will last only 10 days and then Jerry will accept his 50 boxes. On the tenth day, however, Jerry's answer is still negative. In his locker is a poster with T. S. Eliot's words on it, "Do I dare disturb the universe?" Somehow, and without thought of the consequences, Jerry has answered that question with a resounding "Yes."

Renault's refusal to sell begins to slow the momentum of the chocolate sales. Several students openly sympathize with Jerry, and sales figures begin to drop. Realizing that his tenure at Trinity depends on the success of the project, Brother Leon becomes desperate. He once more speaks to Archie and demands that the Vigils make Jerry sell the chocolates.

Jerry is summoned to appear before the Vigils to receive his new assignment—accept the chocolates. Again, he refuses. Archie now realizes that it is not just the authority of Brother Leon, but his own authority and that of the Vigils that is being challenged. This calls for sterner measures, organized harassment. Jerry receives anonymous telephone calls throughout the night; his locker is ransacked and school assignments stolen; and finally he is beaten by Emile Janza and a group of neighborhood thugs. In the meantime, the Vigils have taken over the management of the chocolate sales, using threats and other tactics. Once more, the sales figures begin to rise.

Still intent on breaking Jerry's rebellion, Archie promises him the possibility of a fair fight to avenge himself on Janza. He tricks Jerry into coming to the school athletic field. Unknown to Jerry, the students have assembled there to witness a raffle that Archie has organized for the last 50 unsold boxes of chocolates. The rules of the raffle are simple; for each ticket purchased the student not only gets a chance at the chocolates but also has the opportunity of calling a punch for either Janza or Renault.

Until the black box is suddenly presented to Archie, he has forgotten that one of these two assignments could be his. Will his luck continue to hold? He draws once for Janza—a white ball—and once for Renault—another white! The raffle goes on as scheduled. Archie is sure that the crowd is sufficiently anti-Renault, that Jerry will be beaten up, and, at the same time, be the unwitting salesman of his quota of chocolates.

The fight gets out of hand, and, ignoring the rules, Janza begins beating Jerry to a pulp. Brother Leon witnesses the spectacle from a hilltop, but does nothing to stop it. Fortunately, another Brother happens along and intervenes, but Jerry is in very bad shape. As the ambulance approaches to take him to the hospital, he thinks that no matter what the poster says, he should never have tried to disturb the universe. He has lost much more than a chocolate war.

Thematic Material

The major theme of *The Chocolate War* is the direct opposite of the usual upbeat young adult book. The message is one of despair and hopelessness—one should not question or oppose the Establishment even when justice and right are on one's side. "One cannot fight City Hall and win." Instead, the comfortable goals of conformity, acquiescence, and personal security are the realistic goals in life. The corrupting influence of power, its misuse, and the premise that the end justifies the means are subthemes. Jerry's ordeal is also another example of an adolescent journey to maturity.

The jacket of the hard-cover edition shows a young boy casting a shadow much larger than himself. Perhaps this could signify that Jerry's sacrifice was not in vain and that his actions might be a positive influence in someone like him in the future.

Book Talk Material

There is a Miller-Brody recording of sections from *The Chocolate War*, No. YA 405 (disc, $6.95; cassette, $7.95). Some interesting episodes from the book are: Goober receives his assignment (pp. 30–35; pp. 28–31, pap.); Brother Leon shows his true colors in class (pp. 38–45; pp. 34–39, pap.); the destruction of Brother Eugene's classroom (pp. 68–72; pp. 57–59, pap.); Jerry's first refusal (pp. 80–83; pp. 65–68, pap.); and Archie's trick on Brother Jacques (pp. 125–129; pp. 99–101, pap.).

Additional Suggestions

A revolution led by an Archie-like person in a summer camp for boys gets out of hand in *The Butterfly Revolution* by William Butler (pap., Ballantine, $1.50). Another adult novel with a somewhat similar theme is William Golding's *Lord of the Flies* (Coward, 1962, $6.95; pap., Putnam, $1.50). In William Huntsbury's *The Big Wheels* (Lothrop, 1967, $4.95; condensed in *Introducing Books*, Bowker, 1970), a group of boys are narrowly foiled in their attempt to take over the power structure of their school. The humorous side of school politics is explored in Sidney Offits' *The Adventures of Homer Fink* (St. Martin's, 1966, $3.95; pap., Scholastic,

85¢) when the wackiest kid in school runs for president. Beryl and Sam Epstein write about a number of people like Ralph Nader who have been able to beat the system in *Who Says You Can't* (Coward, 1969, $6.95). A young boy fights the mysterious power of a stranger in John Rowe Townsend's *The Intruder* (Lippincott, 1970, $5.50); also recommended is Townsend's *Hell's Edge* (Lothrop, 1969, $4.95).

About the Author

Ethridge, James M. and Barbara Kopala, Eds. *Contemporary Authors*. Detroit: Gale Research Co., 1967. Vols. 1–4, pp. 205–206.

T. Degens, *Transport 7-41-R*

Viking, 1974, $5.95; pap., Dell, 95¢

This novel is set in Germany during the grim days following World War II. The time is 1946, and both the land and people have been ravaged by war. Food and clothing are scarce, but corruption and black marketeering thrive. The story is seen through the eyes of a 13-year-old girl, never identified by name, who lives through a harrowing journey by boxcar from the Russian sector to the city of Cologne, now under British control. This is a trip that should take only a few hours but stretches into five nightmarish days. The author grew up in eastern Germany during this time and, in 1956, immigrated to the United States. The book is read chiefly by students in the junior high school grades.

Plot Summary

The girl has been sitting close to the open door of the boxcar for almost seven hours, waiting for the train to move. She is surrounded by other war refugees, all crowded like cattle, clinging to a few meager possessions, in an area where there is scarcely room to sit down. Each had been evacuated during the war from the Cologne area and has received permission, usually through illegal means, to return home. The girl's case is different. She has never been to Cologne, but by bribery and forgery her parents obtained the necessary visa so that she can leave the Russian zone and attend a boarding school in the western sector. Secretly, she has rejected the idea of attending school, but plans to strike out on her own and, she hopes, locate her older brother, Jochen, who was last heard of two years ago from a military hospital in Cologne.

Although she is sullen and speaks to no one, the girl is soon able, through overheard conversations, to identify some of her traveling companions. There is Frau Hasselmann and her young son, Rudi, and Frau Warnke and her three children. Others she identifies only by such characteristics as the Fat Woman (she wonders how anyone could find enough food in Germany to maintain that weight); Rabbit Coat because of what she is wearing; and the Captain, obviously a former army officer, now minus a leg. All of them show hostility and resentment toward an elderly, sickly couple, Mr. and Mrs. Lauritzen, because the woman's wheelchair, to which she is confined, takes up a large amount of room in the boxcar.

After finally moving, the transport suddenly stops in the countryside and, without explanation, the engine is uncoupled, leaving them stranded for the night. Against her better judgment, the girl promises to help Mr. Lauritzen nurse his ailing wife. Together they lower the wheelchair out of the boxcar to give the invalid some fresh air. He tells the girl stories of their happy former life in Cologne where they operated a small grocery store. The girl wonders if Mrs. Lauritzen will live long enough to see her home again, because she cannot speak or eat and breathes with great difficulty. During the second night in the boxcar, Mrs. Lauritzen dies. Her husband tells the girl that he has promised his wife to bury her next to their only daughter in Cologne's Central Cemetery. Knowing that they would be removed from the train if the death were discovered, he begs the girl for her help. The two begin an elaborate charade to deceive their fellow passengers: they talk to the old lady; pretend to feed her soup and tea; and make sure she is always heavily covered with blankets.

In the morning, an engine rescues them and the trip begins again. There are more delays and detours, and a third night is spent on the transport. The food supply that the passengers brought with them is either gone or dangerously low. Despair bordering on panic spreads through the group.

The following day, the transport is once again halted, and the group is herded into an empty elementary school now used as an evacuation depot. The girl finds an unused closet in which she and the Lauritzens remain undisturbed by the other travelers. The group is told that the border to the British zone is temporarily closed and that they must wait indefinitely until it reopens.

The girl wanders into town and meets a group of youngsters who promise to smuggle Mr. and Mrs. Lauritzen and herself across the border the next day. They give her food to take back to the school. Illegal entry proves unnecessary, for the next morning they are loaded onto trucks and sent across the border. There is a tense moment when a medical officer begins to examine each of the passengers. The girl is quick to tell him that her "grandmother" becomes violent when others touch her and that recently she had bitten off the finger of the last doctor who tried to examine her. The wheelchair is allowed through without examination.

They spend a fifth night in another internment camp. Conditions are even worse, and the girl is forced to steal both food and blankets to keep the old man alive.

The next morning, another train, and at last Cologne, now a mass of rubble. The body is wheeled to the cemetery, and, after bribing the attendant with the Lauritzen's wedding rings, the girl's leather boots, and the wheelchair, they purchase a coffin and fulfill Mrs. Lauritzen's final wish. After the simple ceremony, the girl and the old man leave the cemetery. Perhaps together they can sort out their lives and begin again.

Thematic Material

This is not only a fast-moving suspense story, but also a valuable historical document. The aftermath of war, its stark tragedy, and the effects of misguided nationalism, whether in peace or war, are well depicted. The transition of the girl from disillusionment and fierce independence to a rekindling of idealism and a desire to help others is also a major theme. The journey of the girl and the old man is a moving illustration of courage, initiative, and determination.

Book Talk Material

A little historical information about the four Germanys that existed after World War II could be given as an introduction. The girl's situation and Mrs. Lauritzen's death are sure to arouse interest. Specific passages are: the transport leaves (pp. 9–11; pp. 5–7, pap.); the engine deserts them (pp. 30–32; pp. 25–27, pap.); the girl's home life (pp. 39–43; pp. 34–38, pap.); and the death of Mrs. Lauritzen (pp. 58–61; pp. 51–53, pap.).

Additional Selections

Boris by Jaap Ter Haar (Delacorte Pr., 1970, $4.50; pap., Dell, 95¢) is the story of a young boy's life during the siege of Leningrad in 1942–1943. Life in occupied Norway during World War II is the situation in Aimée Sommerfelt's *Miriam* (pap., Scholastic, 75¢). The story of a refugee German family in Germany after World War II is told in Margot Benary-Isbert's *The Ark* (Harcourt, 1953, $6.50; pap., 95¢; condensed in *Juniorplots*, Bowker, 1967) and its sequel, *Rowan Farm* (Harcourt, 1954, $4.25). Other recommended World War II stories are Elliot Arnold's *A Kind of Secret Weapon* (Scribner, 1969, $5.95); Jane Gardam's *A Long Way from*

Verona (Macmillan, 1972, $4.95; pap., Collier, $1.25); and Martha Stiles'
Darkness over the Land (Dial, 1966, o.p.).

M. E. Kerr, *Is That You, Miss Blue?*
Harper, 1975, $6.50; lib. bdg., $4.79; pap., Dell, $1.25

M. E. Kerr burst on the world of juvenile literature in an unconventional
novel with the attention-getting title, *Dinky Hocker Shoots Smack!*
(Harper, 1972, $4.95; pap., Dell, 95¢). Before youngsters realized the
innocence of the title, they were hooked on M. E. Kerr. Since then, there has
been a string of hits, all of which are read by children in upper elementary
grades through high school.

Plot Summary
Fourteen-year-old Flanders Brown is on her way by train from New York
City for the fall term at Charles School, an Episcopal boarding school for
girls in Virginia, where she has been enrolled by her father as a sophomore.
Her change of schools has been caused by the breakup of her parents'
marriage. Flanders blames her mother completely because the reason for
the divorce was her mother's affair with a graduate student 14 years her
junior, who had been Mr. Brown's research assistant. Flanders has rejected
her mother and even refused to call her before leaving for Charles.

On the train, Flanders meets Carol Cardmaker, a returning sophomore,
who gives her a rundown on the horrors of life at Charles. Carol's
personality matches her unkempt physical appearance—she is unconventional, sassy, imaginative. Much later, Flanders is to realize that some of
Carol's bravado and scornful attitude is because she hasn't the clothes,
money, or popularity to participate in the school's major activities.

Flanders finds the school difficult to adjust to, but not quite as exotic or
demented as Carol promised. Carol's assessment of the faculty seems not
too far off the mark, however. The headmistress is Annie P. Ettinger, a
huge, tough woman whose monogram is appropriately APE; and some of
the faculty are Miss Sparrow, who makes eyes at the married Reverend
Cunkle; Miss Mitchel, who makes eyes at the music teacher, Miss Able; and
the vain Miss Balfour, who makes eyes at herself.

Because of her asthma, Flanders is given a private room in the dormitory,
known as Little Dorrit, where she shares the bath with Miss Blue, the
science teacher, who immediately hangs on the wall a picture of Jesus. Miss
Blue, whom Carol claims is a religious fanatic, refers to Jesus as her
"buddy."

The other resident of Little Dorrit is Agnes Thatcher, a beautiful freshman who is deaf and also afflicted with a severe speech impediment. But she is far from the withdrawn type one might expect. Instead, she hates pity and demands that her acquaintances learn to translate her statements into clear English. Unfortunately for Flanders, she also snores.

Flanders gradually settles into the routine at Charles—she attends a dismal formal dance with a cadet and, although she is not invited to join the school's secret society, ELA (only members know what the letters stand for, but Carol, a nonmember, calls them Extra Lucky Asses), she makes a few friends. Flanders also tries to sort out her personal life, and through conversing with her father and seeing him on a television show, she begins to wonder if he was in truth blameless in the marriage breakup.

Fortune, however, takes a downward turn for both Miss Blue and Carol Cardmaker. Miss Blue becomes more withdrawn; when not locked in her room chanting Bible verses, she sits for hours in a hallway gazing at a picture of Mary Queen of Scots. The APE has begun an investigation of Miss Blue's mental competency. Through a series of misadventures, Carol gets into trouble and has most of her privileges suspended. To show her defiance, she forms a secret society, the AAAC (Atheists Against All Cruelty). She gains a convert in Agnes, a recent recruit of ELA, and soon the school learns the great secret—ELA means Episcopal Library Association.

Immediately before the Christmas vacation, events reach a climax. Miss Blue is dismissed and Carol is so upset at this action that she recruits Flanders, Agnes, and another friend into a scheme to help make Miss Blue's parting less painful. They steal the painting of Mary Queen of Scots, forge a note from APE to Miss Blue giving her the picture, and leave both at her door just before her departure. Unfortunately, Miss Blue is so touched that she drops a thank-you note to APE, who immediately suspends the privileges of the entire student body until the culprits are found. The four girls decide to confess. Each is assessed $250 to pay for the painting, but Carol knows her father hasn't the money and, therefore, accepts the alternate punishment—expulsion.

During the Christmas vacation, Flanders is reconciled with her mother. In her remaining days at Charles and later at college, she tries to remain in touch with Carol Cardmaker and her other prep school friends, but gradually the ties are broken. In her daydreams, Flanders often imagines seeing on the street the person she remembers most from Charles School. In her dreams, she approaches and says, "Is that you, Miss Blue?"

Thematic Material

As in her other novels, the author's protagonists are facing problems involving loneliness, establishing identities, and relating to values and authority figures in the adult world. In this novel, there is the added dimension of trying to determine what constitutes acceptable adult emotional behavior. The distinguishing qualities of the book are the depth of characterization and its many wildly funny, although often despairing, episodes. Agnes Thatcher is one of the few portrayals of the physically handicapped in juvenile literature that is not one of a goodie-goodie.

Book Talk Material

Some episodes that could be used in a book talk are: Carol Cardmaker talks about the students at Charles School (pp. 5-11; pp. 12-18, pap.); on her second night at school Flanders assesses the situation (pp. 20-23; pp. 28-31, pap.); Agnes is introduced (pp. 39-45; pp. 46-51, pap.); and Flanders has lunch with a student's father and friend (pp. 81-84, pp. 86-89, pap.). Any of M. E. Kerr's other titles also could be used in book talks.

Additional Suggestions

A mystery story set in a girl's boarding school is Lois Duncan's *Down a Dark Hall* (Little, 1974, $5.95; pap., New Amer. Lib., $1.25). Also recommended are Frances Gray Patton's *Good Morning Miss Dove* (Dodd, 1954, $5.95; pap., Pocket Bks., 75¢) and Eleanor Craig's *P.S. You're Not Listening* (Barron, 1972, $5.95; pap., New Amer. Lib., $1.75), an account of a year the author spent teaching a class of five disturbed children. There are also many fine books about youngsters adjusting to divorce: Norma Klein's *Taking Sides* (Pantheon, 1974, $5.99; pap., Avon, 95¢), the story of 12-year-old Nell, whose life is split between her mother and father; and Honor Arundel's *A Family Failing* (Nelson, 1972, $5.95; pap., Scholastic Book Service, 75¢), about Joanna's struggle to accept her parents' divorce. Three others are Ruth M. Arthur's *The Dark Little Thorn* (Atheneum, 1971, $5.25); Rose Blue's *A Month of Sundays* (Watts, 1972, $4.90) for younger audiences; and Judy Blume's *It's Not the End of the World* (Bradbury Pr., 1972, $5.95; pap., Bantam, 1973).

Robert C. O'Brien, *Z For Zachariah*

Atheneum, 1975, $6.95; lge. type ed., G. K. Hall, $8.95; pap., Dell, $1.25

Robert C. O'Brien, a Newbery Award winner for *Mrs. Frisky and the*

Rats of NIMH (Atheneum, 1971, $6.95; pap., $1.95), died before completing *Z For Zachariah*. The last few chapters were written by his wife and daughter from the notes he left. This is the story, told in diary form by a 15-year-old girl who believes that she is the sole survivor of a nuclear war, of the four months that elapse between sighting a stranger in her valley and their final confrontation. The winner of an Edgar Award from the Mystery Writers of America, this novel is popular with junior high school students.

Plot Summary

Immediately after the atomic holocaust, Ann Burden's family, along with Mr. and Mrs. Klein, proprietors of the local grocery story and gas station, leave the girl alone in their secluded valley close to Amish country in the northeastern United States, to hunt for survivors. They never return, and, as the radio stations leave the air one after another, Ann realizes that the world's population has been destroyed by radiation and she is perhaps the last survivor. Although very lonely, she has managed well in the year since the war ended. She has supplemented the supplies, provisions, and clothing she uses from Klein's store with fresh milk and eggs from the family's cows and chickens and with fruit and vegetables from her tiny garden. Although the river, Burden Creek, that runs through the valley is contaminated, there is still a freshwater pond that she uses for fishing, washing, and drinking water.

One day, through her binoculars, she sees smoke from a campfire on a hill nearby. Fearful that whoever is approaching her valley might cause harm, she leaves her home and erases every evidence of life by uprooting the garden and setting the animals free. With an ample supply of provisions, she retreats to a cave on a mountain slope to await the stranger.

Soon a man emerges from the woods by her house wearing a strange green plastic suit and pulling a wagon covered with the same material. Through her glasses, Ann sees him explore the area carefully with a geiger counter. Satisfied that it is not radioactive, the man removes his suit, erects his tent, and begins to settle in. The next day he is joined by Faro, Ann's dog, who has amazingly reappeared at the homestead after a year. Then the man makes a mistake by taking a bath in Burden Creek. In the next few days he becomes visibly ill and finally crawls into his tent. Fearing that he might die, Ann, carrying her gun, cautiously approaches the tent. The man is delirious and continually calls out for someone named Edward. In order to nurse him, she returns to the house.

When the man regains some of his strength, she moves him into an unused bedroom. His name is John R. Loomis, age 32, a chemist from

Cornell University. He had been working on a secret government project to perfect a plastic material impervious to radiation. At the point when he was successful and the first suit of the material was made, the war broke out. Since then he has been wandering in his safe suit using his supply of processed foods protected from contamination on his wagon. He also tells Ann that the second more dangerous stage of his radioactive sickness is about to begin, and, depending on the extent of his exposure, he may die.

The next week is a horror for both of them. Loomis sinks into a trance coupled with a high fever. Through his mutterings, Ann pieces together the story of his hours in the lab when the bombs were dropping. To prevent his colleague, Edward, from leaving the lab in the safe suit, Loomis shot him. Ann sees that the front of the suit contains three tiny patches that cover the bullet holes. Although shaken, she never mentions the incident to Loomis.

During her vigil at the man's bedside, she sometimes slips away to pray at their little church for the man's recovery. She remembers her Biblical ABC book from childhood that begins "A is for Adam" and ends "Z is for Zachariah." If Adam was the first man, she has always presumed that Zachariah must be the last.

Under Ann's constant attention, the crisis passes, but Loomis is so weakened by his ordeal that it is days before he is able to stagger from his bed. During his recovery, Ann plays hymns for him on the piano and reads poetry from her precious stock of books. He seems unmoved, and, instead of showing gratitude, he is brusque and overbearing. He talks often of how they must plan scientifically for the future and that it is their responsibility to start a new colony.

One night shortly after Ann's sixteenth birthday, Loomis comes into her room and tries to make love to her. She fights him off and escapes to the cave. A few days later, she returns, hoping to work out a compromise, but it is obvious that he is no longer sane. He shoots his rifle at her, wounding her in the heel, and padlocks the store in an effort to starve her into submission. As he regains his strength, he tries unsuccessfully, with the use of Faro, to find her hiding place. Although hunted like a wild animal, Ann refuses to give in. During one of the chases, Faro jumps into the creek and later dies of radiation poisoning.

Ann realizes that her only hope of escape is to gain possession of the safe suit and leave the valley. She tricks Loomis into leaving the house unguarded for a few moments. However, her sense of honesty and integrity does not allow her to leave under such circumstances. In the safe suit, she confronts Loomis and tells him that to stop her from leaving he will have to shoot her as he did Edward. Shaken by this reminder of his guilt, Loomis allows her to go. Pulling the wagon behind her, the girl sets out alone, hoping to find another valley where there may be other survivors.

Thematic Material

This is not only a chilling glimpse of what could result from a nuclear war, but also an inspiring, suspenseful story of a girl fighting to retain her set of values. In it, Ann's wholesomeness and honesty are pitted against another's self-interest.

Book Talk Material

A retelling of the story until the arrival of the stranger will interest readers. Some passages from the diary that could be used are: Ann and her journal (pp. 3–6; pp. 10–13, pap.); Loomis explores the house and bathes in the creek (pp. 24–31; pp. 25–30, pap.); Ann leaves the cave to help Loomis (pp. 45–49; pp. 41–43, pap.); Loomis' past (pp. 59–62; pp. 51–53, pap.); and his quarrel with Edward (pp. 114–118; pp. 91–94, pap.).

Additional Selections

In a time warp, 14-year-old Zan Ford is transported from a New York City park to the same spot during the Stone Age in Norma Fox Mazer's *Saturday the 12th of October* (Delacorte Pr., 1975, $6.95). The beautiful planet of Pern is the dominion of science fiction/fantasy writer Anne McCaffrey. For junior readers she has written *Dragonsong* (Atheneum, 1976, $7.95) and for adults, *Dragonflight* (Ballantine, 1975, $1.50) and *Dragonquest* (Ballantine, 1975, $1.50). There is a futuristic view of English society in John Rowe Townsend's *Noah's Castle* (Lippincott, 1976, $6.95), and the plight of survivors after the death of civilization is described in André Norton's *No Night without Stars* (Atheneum, 1975, $6.95). Also use Ben Bova's "Exiled" trilogy, which ends with *End of Exile* (Dutton, 1975, $7.95), and Ursula K. LeGuin's *The Farthest Shore* (Atheneum, 1972, $6.95; pap., Bantam, $1.75).

About the Author

Kingman, Lee, Ed. *Newbery and Caldecott Medal Books, 1966–1975*. Boston: Horn Book, Inc., 1975, pp. 79–92.

Hans Peter Richter, *Friedrich*

Holt, 1970, $4.50; pap., Dell, 95¢

Friedrich is truly a horror story of two boys—one Jewish, the other Aryan—growing up in Nazi Germany. It is told in episodes that span the years 1925 to 1942. Since its original publication in Germany in 1961, it has been translated into several different languages and has received many honors, including the Mildred L. Batchelder Award. It is read by youngsters in grades five through nine. The young man who narrates the story is identified only as "I." Therefore, for the purposes of the plot outline, he is given the same first name as the author, Hans.

Plot Summary

Hans and Friedrich are born in 1925 to two families that live in the same small apartment house owned by the downstairs tenant, cantankerous Herr Resch. Friedrich Schneider's parents are middle-class Jews. Herr Schneider is a civil servant who works for the post office. Hans' family is very poor. It is the middle of the post-World War I depression in Germany, and Hans' father is unemployed. They exist on gifts from Hans' stern, Jew-hating grandfather and the little money his mother earns taking in laundry.

As the two boys grow up together, they become close friends and so do their families. Hans spends a great deal of time upstairs in the Schneiders' apartment. He learns to love Friedrich's kind and gentle parents and to respect their religion although their observances seem strange to him at first.

After the boys' first day at school, the Schneiders want to celebrate. They reluctantly persuade Hans' family to accompany them to an amusement park—reluctantly, because Hans' father has practically no money. He becomes increasingly uncomfortable and embarrassed at the money Herr Schneider spends on them. At the end of the day, however, he is able to pay to have two photographs taken of the group as remembrances.

Early in 1933, the first signs of jew-baiting occur. Friedrich's doctor has "Jew" painted in large red letters across his wall plaque, and there are other similar incidents. By decree, all Jewish civil servants are forced to retire, and Herr Schneider takes a job as head of a toy department in a large department store. The only minor victory during this period is that a court judge does not allow Herr Resch to evict the Schneiders solely on the basis of their Jewishness; it is still only 1933.

Conditions rapidly worsen. Friedrich is forced to leave Hans' school and attend a Jewish school. The Schneiders' maid, an Aryan, is forbidden by law to work for Jews. Friedrich, with Hans watching, is forcibly evicted from a public swimming pool. But there are still a few moments of joy as when Friedrich celebrates his Bar Mitzvah.

To obtain a job and security, Hans' father joins the Nazi party. However, he still tries to help the Schneiders. He begs Herr Schneider to take his family and leave Germany. Schneider's answer is that Germany is their homeland and things are bound to get better.

They don't. Late in 1938, Goebbels issues a decree that allows the German people to inflict their own form of revenge on the Jews for the assassination of a German diplomat in Paris by a Jew. Mobs form; there is mass pillage and looting of Jewish establishments. Even Hans gets carried away by the frenzy of the time and participates in the destruction of a school for Jewish apprentices.

Shortly after Hans arrives home ashamed of his actions, the mob attacks the Schneiders' apartment. They savagely beat Frau Schneider, break their china, slash their pictures, and throw their furniture and valuables out into the street. A doctor is called to tend to Friedrich's mother, but later that night she dies.

Herr Schneider is once more forced out of his job, Friedrich leaves school, and the two begin a lamp repair business in the apartment. In spite of all, the boy remains cheerful and idealistic. He and a non-Jewish girl, Helga, fall in love, but Friedrich realizes that she risks being sent to a concentration camp each time they meet, so he stops seeing her.

It is now 1941. All Jews must wear an identifying Star of David on their clothing and the large-scale deportation begins to concentration camps. One night when Hans delivers a few potatoes to the Schneiders, he learns that they are hiding a rabbi sought by the Nazis in their apartment. Shortly afterward the police arrive and arrest Herr Schneider and the rabbi. Later that night Friedrich returns to the apartment and finds the landlord Herr Resch busy stealing what is left. Friedrich goes into hiding.

Early the next year, a gaunt and dirt-encrusted Friedrich appears at Hans' apartment. He has come to ask, as a remembrance, the picture of his parents taken many years ago in the amusement park. Then the air raid siren wails, and Hans and his family leave Friedrich to go to the shelter. Their district is heavily hit. Friedrich becomes so frightened that he leaves the apartment and begs to be let into the shelter, but Herr Resch, the warden, refuses. After the raid, they find Friedrich's body. Herr Resch cynically remarks that Friedrich is lucky to have died *this* way. Perhaps, for once, Herr Resch is right.

Thematic Material

The gradual destruction of Friedrich and his family give a microcosmic view of the full horror and tragedy of the holocaust. It also makes readers search their own lives for signs of prejudice and its effects. The simplicity and directness of a youthful narrator of Friedrich's age add impact and power to the story. The characterizations, particularly of gentle, idealistic Friedrich, will remain with the reader long after the book is read.

Book Talk Material

The author has appended a chronology of German edicts and decrees against the Jews from 1933 to 1945. A reading of a few of these could be used as an introduction. Specific passages are: at the amusement park (pp. 20–25; pp. 27–32, pap.); the first sign of persecution (pp. 27–31; pp. 34–38, pap.); the Jungvolk (pp. 32–38; pp. 39–45, pap.); the lesson by Herr Neudorf, the boys' teacher (pp. 59–64; pp. 66–71, pap.); and Herr Schneider explains why he will not leave Germany (pp. 71–74; pp. 79–81, pap.).

Additional Selections

Hans Peter Richter's *I Was There* (Holt, 1972, $5.95) tells from a young boy's point of view, about everyday life in Nazi Germany. The trek home for a 12-year-old boy from a concentration camp to Denmark is the story told in Anne S. Holm's *North to Freedom* (Harcourt, 1965, $5.95). Jack Kuper's *Child of the Holocaust* (Doubleday, 1968, o.p.) tells how nine-year-old Jankel tries to survive disguised as a Christian in wartime Poland. In Judith Kerr's *When Hitler Stole Pink Rabbit* (Coward, 1962, $5.95; pap., Dell, $1.25), a young girl and her family are forced to flee Nazi Germany. Its sequel is *The Other Way Around* (Coward, 1975, $7.95). Good nonfiction accounts are Louis Snyder's *Hitler and Nazism* (Hale, 1961, $3.72); Burton Wolfe's *Hitler and the Nazis* (Putnam, 1970, $4.97); and William L. Shirer's *The Rise and Fall of Adolf Hitler* (Random, 1961, $4.39).

About the Author

Commire, Anne. *Something about the Author*. Detroit: Gale Research Co., 1974. Vol. 6, pp. 191–192.

Kinsman, Clare D., Ed. *Contemporary Authors*. Detroit: Gale Research Co., 1974. Vol. 45, pp. 472–473.

William Sleator, *House of Stairs*
Dutton, 1974, $5.95; pap., Avon, 95¢

It is ironic that Harvard, William Sleator's alma mater, should be the university where B. F. Skinner conducted his experiments on behavior modification through conditioning responses in animals and birds. It is ironic because this novel deals with the horrifying results of similar experiences, but this time with human subjects. It is an excellent science fiction novel, particularly for junior high school students.

Plot Summary

Shy, withdrawn Peter is the first to arrive. He remembers being called into the office at the orphanage, being blindfolded and transported by car, and then being left in this place where there are no walls, ceilings, or windows. There are only flights and flights of stairs rising in various directions and at strange angles above and below him. These narrow, white stairs, all without banisters, seemingly stretch to infinity, but they often intersect with occasional small landings.

Peter is joined by Lola—brash, outspoken, and aggressive. While exploring their strange surroundings, they come upon a girl on one of the landings. She is hovering over a small red dome with diamondlike facets. The girl is Blossom—fat, selfish, and ultimately divisive. Blossom quite naturally is the one who has discovered the food machine. She has also found out, after much trial and error, that the machine only disgorges its pellets of delicious synthetic food when she sticks out her tongue. She grudgingly shares a few food cylinders with Lola and Peter.

Soon they are joined by Abigail, a naive, impressionable girl of great beauty, and by Oliver, a boy of more ego and bravado than substance. There are now five of them, and although each is very different in character and personality, there are certain similarities: each is 16, an orphan, and has been brought to this place of stairs under the same mysterious circumstances.

Lola discovers, on a precariously narrow bridge between two flights of stairs, a water supply and bathroom facilities, but the food supply no longer operates on Blossom's behavior. The signals are there; the penetrating red glow in the dome and soft whispering voices, but no food. The five try various responses, and just as they are becoming desperate, the machine gives food to what seem to have been random movements. However, they learn to repeat these movements and modify and refine them when necessary. This develops into a ritualistic dance for survival.

The stressful environment, where a fear of falling off the stairs makes even sleep difficult, causes all sorts of tensions and strains in the young people's adjustments. Blossom is particularly difficult. She dislikes Lola and in subtle ways tries to turn the group against her. Oliver is attracted to Abigail, who returns his affection, but the boy is so unable to give or receive genuine feelings that he alternately accepts and rejects her love. Peter slowly but increasingly is escaping into dreamlike dazes.

The red machine again begins to deny them food. But after a bitter argument during which Blossom openly accuses Lola of malicious gossip, their weird dance activates the machine. Once again the machine spews out pellets when the dance follows a bitter argument, this time between Oliver and Abigail. The truth is suddenly evident; they are being programmed to hate and distrust, and their reward for attacking and brutalizing one another will be survival.

Lola refuses to accept these as conditions for living. She convinces Peter that it is better to starve than become subhuman, and the two leave the security of the landing with its red machine.

Blossom, Abigail, and Oliver alone cannot get food and so they beg Lola and Peter to return, but the two remain adamant. Suddenly their visits stop, and, after a few days, overcome with curiosity, Lola and Peter weakly creep back down to the landing and find the others healthy and well-fed. When it appeared that Lola and Peter would not return, the machine began giving food on the basis of acts of cruelty among the remaining three. The various forms of behavior that they have devised to satisfy the machine constitute a horrifying chronicle of mental and physical abuse. Now, in their efforts to find a new and effective variation, they turn on the half-starved pair.

Even when Peter and Lola return to their perch, the others follow to torment them, committing physical violence. Lola realizes that she is about to die. She whispers to Peter that her will to live is stronger than a total loss of humanity and she wishes to give in to the machine. Peter would rather die, but he remains loyal to his friend and agrees to accompany her back to the machine. At that moment, elevators appear to take them away. The experiment is over.

After recuperation in the hospital, Peter and Lola are joined by Abigail, Blossom, and Oliver. All five are taken to Dr. Lawrence. He explains that they have been at a reinforcement center undergoing extensive conditioning as part of a plan to supply the president of the country with a group of young people who will obey him without question. The group will be used for international spying missions and, domestically, as directors of concentration camps and interrogation centers. Dr. Lawrence considers the experiment only partially successful because just three have passed the initial steps and are ready for further conditioning. The other two, Peter and Lola, are to be sent to the outside world as misfits. The doctor will never know how close he was to complete success.

The briefing over, Blossom, Abigail, and Oliver leave and cross the hospital grounds. They see a blinking traffic light and immediately begin to dance.

Thematic Material

The misapplication of scientific theories and practices to control and change human behavior is an important theme. Peter's conduct demonstrates that the seemingly weak can often amass the greatest amount of inner resources. As happens to many who undergo severe emotional ordeals, Peter and Lola emerge stronger and more confident. The interaction of five very different people in an enclosed and forced situation makes a fascinating character study.

Book Talk Material

An explanation and discussion of the concept of behavior modification might precede an introduction to the situation and characters in this book. Some interesting passages are: Chapter I with Peter alone in the house of stairs (pp. 3-6; pp. 9-11, pap.); Lola and Peter find Blossom (pp. 19-23; pp. 24-28, pap.); they get the machine to work (pp. 61-64; pp. 62-64, pap.); and performing the dance (pp. 68-69; same pagination, pap.).

Additional Selections

In addition to William Sleator's other novels for young people, such as *Blackbriar* (Dutton, 1972, $5.95; pap., Avon, 95¢), there is good science fiction in Jean and Jeff Sutton's *The Programmed Man* (Putnam, 1968, $5.95), an espionage story about the race to a crashed space destroyer to rescue military secrets, and Ben Bova's *The Dueling Machine* (Holt, 1969, o.p.), a thoughtful science fiction novel about overpopulation and a unique peace-keeping invention. Bova's *The Weathermaker* (pap., New Amer. Lib., 95¢) is an exciting story of the efforts of two friends to control the weather. A boy's interplanetary search for his father is told in Lester Del Ray's *The Infinite Worlds of Maybe* (Holt, 1966, $3.59). Some excellent titles by Robert Heinlein are *Starman Jones* (pap., Ballantine, $1.50); *Starship Troopers* (Putnam, 1960, $6.50; pap., Berkley, $1.50); and *Citizen of the Galaxy* (Scribner, 1957, $5.95; pap., Ace Bks., $1.25; condensed in *Juniorplots*, Bowker, 1967).

About the Author

Commire, Anne. *Something about the Author*. Detroit: Gale Research Co.,1972. Vol. 3, pp. 207-208.
Kinsman, Clare D. and Mary Ann Tennenhouse, Eds. *Contemporary Authors*. Detroit: Gale Research Co., 1972. Vol. 29, p. 585.

Paul Zindel, *Pardon Me, You're Stepping on My Eyeball!*
Harper, 1976, $6.95

In this, Paul Zindel's fourth novel for teen-agers, he returns to the same setting, Staten Island, and the same situation, two distressed teen-agers trying to cope, that he used in his first book, *The Pigman* (Harper, 1968, $4.95; pap., Dell, 75¢). Like its predecessor, this novel is suitable for mature junior high school students and up.

Plot Summary

Louis "Marsh" Mellow is a 15-year-old junior whose favorite pastime is compiling lists of the things he hates most. These usually involve various aspects of school life, the governmental or business establishment, and anything he considers phony or pretentious. Also figuring prominently in these lists is his mother, whom he calls Schizo Suzy, a slatternly woman who gets drunk every night and verbally abuses him. Apart from not having any friends, Marsh has two other hang-ups—his compulsive lying and his father. He adores his absent, iconoclastic father, nicknamed Paranoid Pete, and constantly reminisces—half in fantasy, half in truth—about the good times they had together in the past visiting bars and Pete's other favorite haunts, drinking and talking with his father's eccentric friends.

A few rooms away in the same school, Mr. Meizner, the school psychologist, is holding a joint conference with Mr. and Mrs. Shinglebox and their daughter, Edna. The girl, also 15 and a junior, is a passive, disturbed loner, who would like to be as social and popular as her vulgar, overly protective parents would like her to be. But she is too modest and self-effacing to assert herself.

Mr. Meizner begins a group therapy experience (GTE) class for eight of the school's misfits. Edna is one, and so is Marsh Mellow, who has recently been trying to strike up conversations with her. Marsh brings his constant companion to the classes, a baby pet raccoon he has rescued. Another member of the group is Edna's coworker on the school newspaper, Jacqueline Potts, daughter of extremely wealthy parents, who believes, and rightly so, that many of her friends, including her boyfriend, Butch Ontock, are using her for her money. In their first class on sensitivity training, the kids are blindfolded and must touch the person next to them. Edna's partner is Marsh, and as she gently strokes his face, she feels a tear run down his cheek.

After class, Marsh shows Edna a letter from his father. It supposedly is written from a mental institution where Pete has been illegally imprisoned by the FBI, CIA, and high government officials including the president, in an attempt to silence him. That evening Marsh dates Edna (Mrs. Shinglebox is ecstatic!) and drives her to a sleazy roadhouse where he feeds her three Harvey Wallbangers. Afterward he takes her to his room and shows her a three-stage rocket, a present from Pete, and forces her to read another rambling diatribe from Pete written just before his mysterious enemies caught up with him. It is another indictment of all the forces that work against truth and justice and, like the first, ends with, "Don't let them step on your eyeball." When he is alone, Marsh recalls a mad drunken spree with his father in Los Angeles, but something refuses to let him remember all that happened on their last day together after Pete staggered out of a bar drunk.

Edna has recognized that both letters are in Marsh's handwriting and, back at school, publicly denounces him as a liar. She is, however, consumed with curiosity about the real fate of Paranoid Pete, and that evening, when she is sure Marsh will be away, she pays a visit to his mother. Under questioning, the drunken woman drags Edna to Marsh's room supposedly to meet her husband. She brings out an urn from under Marsh's bed. It contains Pete's ashes. While drunk in Los Angeles a year ago, Pete was killed by a bus as he was crossing the street to rejoin his son.

Confused and panicky, Edna flees, and on her way home stops by the house of Miss Aimée, who has gained a local reputation as a clairvoyant and palm reader. Edna blurts out her story, and for $10 the old woman says that Marsh must not only be made to believe his father is dead, but also he must perform some symbolic act to show his acceptance of that fact. Edna is now determined to help Marsh, but because he is still humiliated and hurt by her recent accusations, he rebuffs her.

The entire GTE class, along with Butch Ontock and a few others, are invited to a party at Jacqueline Potts' supermod mansion while her parents are away. At the Potts', things get out of hand with the arrival of many party crashers, plus some candle-carrying hippies who are members of a religious commune. The party is becoming an X-rated, pot-polluted, drunken orgy when, in a freak accident, newspapers in the kitchen are ignited by the candles. Soon the entire house is ablaze. Edna and Marsh, along with the others, escape, but the raccoon dies in the fire.

On their way home, Marsh tells Edna that he has heard again from his father: in 72 hours Pete is scheduled for a lobotomy. Will she drive across the country with him to prevent the operation? Realizing this might be her chance to help him, Edna consents. They pack bags and leave.

They drive through the night and reach Washington by 4 A.M., but the car careens out of control and crashes down an embankment. Both are dazed but unhurt. Fearing police intervention, they leave the car and begin walking over one of the Potomac River bridges. Halfway across, Edna notices the urn inside Marsh's torn luggage. Slowly, and without any protests from him, she slips it into the river.

They wander into Arlington Cemetery and sit close to the Kennedy gravesite. Edna sees that Marsh has also brought the rocket with him. She assembles it and suggests that they attach a message of the things they hate most in the world. Hers is "I hate not being able to tell you I want to touch you," and Marsh's is "I hate that my father is dead." As the rocket flies into the sky, Edna thinks it is like the departure of a ghost now sent to rest.

Thematic Material

This novel reveals how two estranged young people, through their agonizing experiences, learn to reach out to each other and to handle honestly their personal problems. Acceptance of death and alienation of many of the present generation are important subthemes. With accuracy and often great humor, the author has captured the mores and life-style of today's teen culture.

Book Talk Material

In addition to an introduction to Marsh, the reader is given one of his lists of hates on pp. 1-3. Edna and her parents visit Mr. Meizner on pp. 4-9. Other interesting passages are: Marsh's talk with Mr. Meizner, (pp. 24-27); the sensitivity training session (pp. 46-48); and Edna's reading of the first letter (pp. 53-56).

Additional Selections

In addition to Zindel's other novels, one could use Mildred Lee's *Fog* (Seabury, 1972, $5.95; pap., Dell, $1.25), in which Luke must adjust to his father's death, and Robert Nathan's story of how a drowning accident robs Joanna of her joy and love, *Long after Summer* (pap., Dell, 95¢). Albert Scully, self-proclaimed failure, meets an aging actress in Barbara Wersba's *The Dream Watcher* (Atheneum, 1968, $5.25; pap., 95¢). In Bianca Bradbury's *Red Sky at Night* (Washburn, 1968, o.p.), a young girl learns to accept her mother's death. Also use M. E. Kerr's *If I Love You, Am I Trapped Forever?* (Harper, 1973, $4.95; pap., Dell, 95¢). In the nonfiction area are John Langone's *Death Is a Noun* (Little, 1972, $5.95; pap., Dell, 95¢) and David Hendin's *Death as a Fact of Life* (pap., Warner Bks., $1.25).

About the Author

Ward, Martha E. and Dorothy A. Marquardt. *Authors of Books for Young People.* Metuchen, N.J.: Scarecrow Press, Inc., 1971, pp. 573–574.
Who's Who in America (39th Edition). Chicago: Marquis Who's Who, Inc., 1976. Vol. 2, p. 3496.

3

Understanding Social Problems

As ADOLESCENTS mature, they are able to project themselves more easily into situations that require understanding of and identification with the problems facing contemporary society. In this section, problems such as poverty, class struggles, racial discrimination, and the generation gap are explored.

Frank Bonham, *Chief*
Dutton, 1971, $5.95; pap., Dell, 95¢

Frank Bonham's first successful novels for young people, such as *Burma Rifles* (Crowell, 1960, $4.95; condensed in *Juniorplots*, Bowker, 1967), were primarily war stories, but more recently, as in this novel, he has concentrated on fiction about youngsters from minority groups and their struggles against poverty and prejudice. *Chief* is read mainly by students in the junior high school grades.

Plot Summary

Orphaned Henry Crowfoot, the hereditary leader of 87 Santa Rosa Indians, has left his reservation, one hour's drive by freeway, to live in Harbor City and attend Metropolitan High School where he is a senior. Without any means of support, Chief, as he is called, lives as a guest at a halfway house, operated by kindly Velma Taylor, for young parolees like his cousin, 16-year-old Tony Acosta with whom Chief shares a room. Chief occasionally gets money from his uncle, Joseph Whirlwind Horse, once a young idealistic college student, but now, at 40, a drifter and wino who lives in a transient house on Skid Row. Between disability pension checks, Uncle Horse gets drinks from sailors on leave by showing off his pet rattlesnake, Captain. Although Chief is titular head of the Santa Rosas and, therefore, the keeper of their historical documents, the actual leaders are

Tom Cachora and their wise old medicine man, Doctor Charlie. Chief hopes to go to law school, not only to assist his people, but also to help right some of the wrongs inflicted on all Indians.

Hoping to help himself and his people, Chief is trying, in chemistry lab at school, to perfect a glue formula that he has partially learned from Uncle Horse. One night he breaks into the school to continue his experiment. He accidentally upsets a jug of acetone, which ignites. Although the fire is put out by the sprinkler system, Chief is caught by the night watchman and spends the rest of the night in jail.

Released in his uncle's custody, Chief is given the name of a court-appointed lawyer, Barton Shackleford. The lawyer is a has-been and reformed alcoholic whose law career declined after his wife's sudden death. Nevertheless, Chief goes to his office where he is greeted by Jenny Shackleford, an attractive young girl of Chief's age who acts as her father's secretary after school. When he meets Shackleford, Chief realizes the man is an idealistic antique who not only acts but also dresses like his hero, Clarence Darrow.

The real purpose of Chief's visit is to ask Shackleford to peruse the document signed in 1855 by his great, great, grandfather, Chief Buffalo-boy, which deeded to the white man the property on which Harbor City was built. Shackleford discovers that only part of this land was actually sold and that the rich downtown area, now controlled by real estate multimillionaire Whitney Wolfert (a descendant of one of the original signers) really belongs to the Santa Rosa Indians. Shackleford offers to take the case on a contingency fee basis, and Chief gets a grudging assent from his clan to proceed.

At a prearranged meeting at Treaty Oak in the city square where the original document was signed, Shackleford and Chief, along with Horse and Tony Acosta, confront Wolfert and his lawyer, Louis Podesta, with the evidence. Podesta briefly shows them another document that deeds all of the land and is, he claims, the only legal binding agreement. Chief is shattered, but Shackleford is convinced that Podesta is trying to bluff them. Knowing that Wolfert could delay for several years having a civil case brought to court, he decides that a speedier criminal case will force the issue.

Hoping to get arrested, Chief and Tony one night build a shack on the city square, claiming it is their rightful property. The plan works, but Wolfert gets the boys released without trial. Shackleford is convinced now that the wealthy landowner is deliberately avoiding a confrontation in the courts. The boys try again, by "fishing" over a manhole, thus stopping traffic at a crowded intersection. This time, after arrest, a trial date is set, but on the day everyone is scheduled to appear in court, the trial is postponed because Shackleford suffers a nervous collapse and reverts completely into his role of Clarence Darrow. The lawyer is taken to the reservation by Chief and put into the hands of Doctor Charlie, who places the man in a trance and applies ancient Indian remedies. When Shackleford awakens, he is once more lucid and clear-thinking.

In the two weeks before the trial, Shackleford does some intensive research through local and state archives, old newpaper files, and eyewitness accounts. He discovers that, although there was an agreement drawn up giving away all the land, the Indians had refused to comply and had argued for better terms. The document that Chief owns is the only binding agreement signed by both sides. The case is dismissed and the boys freed, but Shackleford knows that when Wolfert is forced into a settlement of the land claim, it will mean several million dollars to the Santa Rosas. Chief is now aware that his impossible dream to help his people live in dignity and respect will become a reality.

Thematic Material

Through Chief's eyes, the reader is able to experience the struggle of the exploited modern-day Indian in finding a rightful and just place in society. The Indians' plight is realistically portrayed without sermonizing or condescending, although many of the characters express a natural bitterness and disillusionment with the values of present-day America. Many of the characters, particularly boozy Uncle Horse and the enterprising hero, are very well drawn.

Book Talk Material

Some passages suitable for a book talk are: Chief in his crash pad (pp. 1–3; pp. 5–7, pap.); the laboratory fiasco (pp. 21–24; pp. 25–27, pap.); Shackleford first looks at the document (pp. 40–41; pp. 42–46, pap.); the lawyer gets the Indians' support (pp. 91–95; pp. 91–96, pap.); and confrontation at Treaty Oak (pp. 130–134; pp. 128–132, pap.).

Additional Selections

Lon Miller, raised in Vietnam, encounters bigotry in a small American town in Paige Dixon's *Promises to Keep* (Atheneum, 1974, $6.95). R. R. Knudson's *Fox Running* (Harper, 1975, $5.95) is the story of a young Indian girl in training for the Olympics. An explanation of Black-Indian cultures is part of Virginia Hamilton's complex but compelling novel, *Arilla Sun Down* (Morrow, 1976, $7.95). An Indian kidnaps a young white boy in a novel for older readers about conflicting cultures, Frank Herbert's *Soul Catcher* (Putnam, 1972, $7.95; pap., Bantam, $1.25). *Hatter Fox* (Random, 1973, $7.95; pap., Bantam, $1.50) by Marilyn Harris is the harrowing story of a 17-year-old Navajo girl. Other books with Indians as principal characters are: Molly Cone's *Number Four* (Houghton, 1972, $4.95); Betty Baker's *And One Was a Wooden Indian* (Macmillan, 1970, $4.95), and Nathaniel Benchley's *Only Earth and Sky Last Forever* (Harper, 1972, $4.95; pap., $1.25).

About the Author

Commire, Anne. *Something about the Author.* Detroit: Gale Research Co., 1971. Vol. 1, pp. 30–31.

DeMontreville, Doris and Donna Hill, Eds. *Third Book of Junior Authors.* New York: H. W. Wilson Co., 1972, pp. 42–43.

Hopkins, Lee Bennett. *More Books by More People.* New York: Citation Press, 1974, pp. 41–47.

Kinsman, Clare D. and Mary Ann Tennenhouse, Eds. *Comtemporary Authors.* Detroit: Gale Research Co., 1974. Vols. 9–12, pp. 96–97.

Ward, Martha E. and Dorothy A. Marquardt. *Authors of Books for Young People.* (2nd Edition). Metuchen, N.J.: Scarecrow Press, Inc., 1971, p. 53.

Alice Childress, *A Hero Ain't Nothin' but a Sandwich*
Coward, 1973, $5.95; pap., Avon, 95¢

Alice Childress' experience as playwright and actress is revealed in the brilliant characterization and dialogue in *Hero*, essentially the story of a 13-year-old black boy, Benjie Johnson, and his near-fatal brush with permanent heroin addiction. It is told honestly in the vital, but strong, street idiom of Harlem by several people close to Benjie, and by Benjie himself. While each monologue is part of the story, it also presents a different point of view and helps to develop a gallery of memorable characters. This book is read by students in junior high school.

Plot Summary

Some of the main characters are:

Rose Johnson Craig, Benjie's hard-working and devoted mother, who after her husband walked out shortly after Benjie's birth, was left to support herself, an aging mother, and her son. Four years ago, she met and fell in love with Butler Craig, who has become her common-law husband.

Butler Craig, Benjie's more-or-less stepfather. As a youth in Georgia and later in New York, he wanted to become a jazz saxophonist, but the need for a steady income forced him to become a janitor in a downtown office building. He is strong, unselfish, and dependable. He genuinely loves Rose, whom he calls "Sweets," and tries hard to be a father to Benjie, but he knows the boy resents his presence in the house.

Mrs. Ransom Bell, Benjie's grandmother. Aging, despondent, and increasingly afraid because she has already once been robbed and beaten on the streets, Mrs. Bell relies increasingly on her old-time Baptist religion as a salvation and comfort. The daughter of a Mississippi sharecropper, she has had a tough life and at one time even worked as a dancer in a speakeasy. While Rose was still a child, Mrs. Bell's beloved husband died. She still misses him.

Jimmy-Lee Powell, Benjie's friend. Jimmy-Lee and Benjie were once the best of friends, but Jimmy-Lee's warning to Benjie about his increasing drug use only produces resentment because, as Jimmy-Lee says, "friendships begin to split when one is caught in a habit and the other not."

Bernard Cohen, Benjie's teacher. Somewhat bitter and defensive about being a white teacher in an all-black school, Cohen tries to cling to his middle-class liberal values, but at the same time is basically hostile to the black liberation movement. However, at least his students learn to read.

Nigeria Greene, another seventh-grade teacher, a militant black nationalist and an extremely popular teacher. But sometimes, for example when he attends a dinner or testimonial for black causes, he thinks perhaps that he gradually might be adopting, or at least giving in to, the values he professes to hate.

And there is Benjie himself, the boy everyone likes, with a wonderful disposition and friendliness, but for whom something is missing, the sense of really belonging and being somebody. He feels enclosed in his tight family circle and feels that Butler Craig has taken his mother's love. School has become a drag, and he sees very little hope for the future of a black kid growing up in Harlem. His environment has destroyed what small seeds of idealism might have grown, and he now feels that "a hero ain't nothin' but a sandwich." He is ready for some form of escape.

Benjie's life on drugs begins with a few joints of pot smoked with Jimmy-Lee and another friend, Carwell. Under Carwell's influence, Benjie begins to cut class and go to Tiger's place, a comfortable apartment where the kids hang out when Tiger's aunt is out working. Tiger runs a little business on the side in candy, hot dogs, and soft drinks, but mostly in pot and heroin. To prove he isn't chicken, Benjie tries his first needle. Soon his trips to Tiger's place become so frequent that Jimmy-Lee is convinced he is hooked and tries desperately to get Benjie to swear off. Benjie says that he can take it or leave it, but now to supplement what he gets from Tiger, he uses the services of Walter, a pusher, and even steals from his grandmother to feed his habit.

It is Nigeria Greene who alerts Bernard Cohen about Benjie's constant nodding in class. They see the principal, and social workers are called in to inform the family and arrange for treatment. Benjie is sent to a detoxification clinic for a week. Back home, everyone tries to help him, but he senses feelings of tension and stress always in the background. One night when Butler and Rose go to a movie, leaving Benjie alone, he steals Butler's suit and overcoat to get money for a fix.

When Butler finds out, he decides that to keep peace in the family, he will move from the apartment and visit Rose only when Benjie is out. He rents a vacant room downstairs from Emma Dudley, who begins making advances that Butler discourages.

Unhappy at Butler's absence, Rose clutches at straws to help rehabilitate Benjie. She visits a spiritualist, who sells her a bottle of indigo-blue that, when placed in bath water, is supposed to exorcise the bather. Of course, it doesn't work. Soon after, Butler catches Benjie in Miss Dudley's kitchen trying to steal her toaster. He chases him to the roof of the building. Benjie tries to jump across the shaft to the next building, but he slips. Butler grabs him by one arm. As he dangles six stories above the cement, Benjie begs Butler to drop him because he wants to die. Instead, Butler drags him to safety and cradles him in his arms.

Benjie now knows that Butler really loves him. To help himself through a terrible case of the shakes, he writes over and over again, "Butler is my father." Benjie learns of his friend Kenny's death from an overdose, and he and his mother go to the funeral.

This time Butler feels that there are many encouraging signs that Benjie is going to pull through—he has been faithful in his trips to the parole office; he has been trustworthy with money given him and has resumed his friendship with Jimmy-Lee; but, best of all, he has started to call Butler "Dad."

Thematic Material

Hero is not just a family of blacks and their problems: it deals with themes and experiences that are universal, such as rejection, love, the importance of family ties, poverty, and the problems of growing old. It also depicts the frustration and despair of lives warped by discrimination and want; at the same time showing that people must believe in themselves. Lastly, it is a horrifying picture of the effects of dope that make a fine boy become an enemy in his own home.

Book Talk Material

A complimentary cassette of Alice Childress reading from *Hero* is available from Avon Books' education department. Many parts of *Hero* are written in street jargon that might be difficult to reproduce, but some passages that could be used are: Benjie introduces himself (pp. 9–10, both editions); Butler tells about his youth (pp. 17–18; pp. 17–19, pap.); Grandma tells her story (pp. 31–33, both editions); Tiger's place and Benjie's first fix (pp. 66–68; pp. 67–69, pap.).

Additional Selections

Readers who like *Hero* will also enjoy Ronald L. Fair's *Hog Butcher* (Harcourt, 1966, $6.95) or, as it was renamed for the film and paperback edition, *Cornbread, Earl and Me* (pap., Bantam, $1.25). Also use Nat Hentoff's *In the Country of Ourselves* (Simon & Schuster, 1971, $5.95) and John H. Griffin's *Black Like Me* (Houghton, 1961, $5.95; pap., New Amer. Lib., $1.25). A story of three black brothers in the inner city is in Sharon Bell Mathis' *Teacup Full of Roses* (Viking, 1972, $4.95; lg. type ed., G. K. Hall, $5.95). Girls enjoy Elizabeth Kata's *A Patch of Blue* (pap., Popular Library, $1.25) and Gretchen Sprague's *A Question of Harmony* (Dodd, 1965, $4.50).

About the Author

Commire, Anne. *Something about the Author*. Detroit: Gale Research Co., 1974. Vol. 7, pp. 46–47.

Kinsman, Clare D., Ed. *Contemporary Authors*. Detroit: Gale Research Co., 1974. Vols. 45–48, p. 93.

Who's Who in America (37th Edition). Chicago: Marquis Who's Who, Inc., 1972. Vol. 1, p. 556.

Lorenz Graham, *Whose Town?*
Crowell, 1969, $5.95

Whose Town? is the continuation of two other books about David Williams and his family—*South Town* (Follett, o.p.; pap. New Amer. Lib., 95¢) and *North Town* (Crowell, 1965, o.p.; condensed in *Introducing Books*, Bowker, 1970). The latest installment is *Return to South Town* (Crowell, 1976, $6.50). All four novels are suitable for upper elementary and junior high school grades.

Plot Summary

It is now more than two years since the Williams family left the oppressive discrimination of blacks in South Town and moved north. Since that time the family has prospered. A machinist at the Iron Works, Mr. Williams earns enough to enable the family to move from their squalid apartment in the ghetto to a comfortable two-story brick house in a partially integrated section on the west side of town. Their two children also have thrived; Betty Jane is now 12 and David, 18, is a senior with hopes of going to medical school.

One wintry evening David borrows the family car and returns to his old neighborhood to hear an address by an Ethiopian minister, sponsored by a group known as the Black Brotherhood. The man speaks about exploitation by the white man through the centuries and calls for a united black movement to restore glory and dignity to the black race.

David and the entire audience are impressed by the man's eloquent words, but David's excitement is dampened when, back home, he learns that his father, along with 4,000 other workers, has been laid off for an indefinite period. David's Saturday job at the hardware store takes on added importance even though the pay is small.

The next day David talks over the previous night's lecture with the only other black employee at the store, John Bowman. John repeats the message that action and force, not the evolutionary process, are needed to correct the inequality that exists between the races. He invites David to a meeting of the Black Brotherhood that evening, but David is taking his girl friend, Jeannette Lenoir, to Maybelle Reed's party.

At the party they are greeted by Maybelle's parents; her father is a police officer. The party is a lot of fun, and afterward David and Jeannette, with a group in Jimmy Hicks' car, go to a drive-in for hamburgers. David goes in for the food and is first taunted and then jostled by a group of white youths. He drops the tray, and the gang begins beating him up before he can escape to the car. The white youths follow David's group in two cars, and soon a wild chase begins through town. A police car stops them, but the white boys convince them that the blacks started the fight at the drive-in. David and his friends go down to police headquarters. They are booked, but Sgt. Reed gets them released. They return to the car to find all the windows and the headlights smashed. The garage attendant is obviously lying when he claims not to know who did it.

David doesn't tell his father at first, but Mr. Williams hears about it from the police. He is unjustly shocked and disappointed in David. However, he does hire a lawyer in case legal action proves necessary.

A formal complaint is lodged, and, to make things worse, Mrs. Hicks thinks that David should pay for damages to her car. One night, the three boys who were involved—David, Jimmy Hicks, and Lonnie Webster—talk things over. Lonnie is particularly bitter. He claims that North Town is a white man's land where blacks have no rights or power. Even David begins to wonder whose town it really is. Lonnie insists that they go to question the garage attendant, but David refuses. However, when David is driving the boys home, Lonnie grabs the wheel when they pass the service station and forces the car in. The same attendant is on duty. When Lonnie steps out of the car, the man panics, pulls out a gun, and shoots the boy. The attendant claims he shot in self-defense. David is arrested and spends two days in jail before the lawyer, Mr. Taylor, can get him released.

Things get worse. David's principal tells him that any more incidents will mean expulsion without graduation. Mr. Williams, still without work, becomes increasingly depressed, particularly when his wife is forced to become a cook and cleaning lady for white people to help pay the bills. The lawyer gets the complaint against David dropped. But the jury at Lonnie's inquest decides the homicide was justifiable. This prompts the Black Brotherhood to take up the cause; there is mounting tension and fear in North Town.

David graduates in June. But, during the summer, racial conflict erupts in town because of a bizarre accident; some white boys playfully push a black child into the public swimming pool, and he drowns. The Brotherhood arouses the black community, and there are riots, cars overturned, and a rash of fires and looting.

The National Guard is called, and peace is restored. The following day, Sunday, the residents of North Town attend church as the town officials requested. David hears his minister say that hatred and destruction, regardless of cause, can only accelerate division and discord. He calls on all the people of North Town—black and white—to work together to rebuild their city and correct the injustices that produced this tragedy. After church the Williams family learns that the Iron Works will be rehiring. The next day, when David goes to the hardware store to help clean up, his employer philosophically tells him: "Sometimes just living through your trouble is success." David agrees.

Thematic Material

As in his other "Town" novels, the author stresses the debilitating effects of discrimination and the need for courage and restraint in facing problems involving racial inequality. He emphasizes that extreme measures rarely achieve their purpose, but instead often aggravate the situation. The solid relationships in the Williams family are well portrayed, as are David's positive and admirable values and loyalties.

Book Talk Material

A brief introduction to the Williams family through other books in the series should arouse interest in this volume, or perhaps only a brief explanation of the significance of the title is necessary. Some important passages are: John's thoughts on black unity (pp. 28–30); at the drive-in (pp. 38–41); at the police station (pp. 43–47); and Lonnie's death (pp. 77–78).

Additional Selections

A 17-year-old Harlem boy goes south to play baseball in Donald Honig's *Johnny Lee* (Dutton, 1971, $4.95). A young girl is bused to an all-white school in Betty Baum's *Patricia Crosses Town* (Knopf, 1965, $5.39). A black family loses an apartment and finds difficulty in getting a new home in Natalie Savage Carlson's *Marchers for the Dream* (Harper, 1969, $3.50). Other novels dealing with black/white relations are Florence K. Randall's *The Almost Year* (Atheneum, 1971, $5.95; pap., Scholastic, $1.25); Ester Wier's *Easy Does It* (Vanguard, 1965, $4.95); David Westheimer's *My Sweet Charlie* (pap., New Amer. Lib. $1.25); and Frank Bonham's *The Nitty Gritty* (Dutton, 1968, $5.95; pap., Dell, 95¢; condensed in *Introducing Books*, Bowker, 1970).

About the Author

Commire, Anne. *Something about the Author.* Detroit: Gale Research Co., 1971, pp. 122–123.
DeMontreville, Doris and Donna Hill, Eds. *Third Book of Junior Authors.* New York: H. W. Wilson Co., 1972, pp. 108–109.
Ethridge, James M., Ed. *Contemporary Authors.* Detroit: Gale Research Co., 1964. Vol. 9, pp. 180–181.
Hopkins, Lee Bennet. *More Books by More People.* New York: Citation Press, 1974, pp. 193–199.

S. E. Hinton, *The Outsiders*
Viking, 1967, $4.95; pap., Dell, 75¢

The Outsiders is a novel about three brothers growing up in the shadow of a gang culture and street rumbles. When is was first published, it created a sensation for a number of reasons. It ushered in a new realism in young adult fiction. Never before had anyone written with such bite and passion of the raw and violent world of street gangs. It is one of the few adolescent novels actually written by a teen-ager. S. E. Hinton was 17 when *The Outsiders* was published. The "S" in S. E. Hinton stands for Susan, a surprising fact considering the subject matter and predominance of male characters in her novels. *The Outsiders* is popular with junior and senior high school students.

Plot Summary

The novel begins on a violent note. Fourteen-year-old Ponyboy Curtis, who tells the story, is returning home when he is attacked by five members of a gang called the Socs (for Socials). His screams for help bring members of his own gang, who drive away the Socs. Ponyboy's gang is the Greasers—the hoods, poor kids from the wrong side of the tracks who have long, well-greased hair and wear jeans and leather jackets. Their rivals and dread enemies, the Socs, are the "haves," who dress well, drive around in expensive cars, and have lots of money.

Ponyboy's only family is two older brothers. His parents were killed in a car accident, and the court allowed the three brothers to stay together "as long as they behaved," a condition they find harder to maintain each day. Ponyboy's brothers are very different. Twenty-year-old Darry is quiet, thoughtful, and very intelligent. He has had to become a manual laborer and give up the prospect of a college education to support the family. Ponyboy regards Darry's frequent lectures and his sullenness as signs of dislike and hostility. By contrast, 16-year-old Soda is outgoing, always joking, and a great pal to Ponyboy. Soda is a school dropout now working in a garage.

All three Curtis boys are Greasers. In fact, it is generally considered that Darry is the gang leader. The other gang members are Two Bit Mathews; Steve Randle; Dally Winston, the most dangerous and violent member, who already has a long police record; the pathetic Johnny Cade, who looks to the Greasers for the only love and attention he has ever received.

The most memorable night in Ponyboy's life begins innocently enough when he, Johnny, and Dally meet two Soc girls, Cherry Valance and her friend Marcia, at a drive-in. In spite of initial hostility, Ponyboy has a long talk with Cherry. They discuss their differences and finally agree that, rich or poor, growing up in today's world is a tough business. While taking the girls home, they have a narrow brush with the Socs, but manage to avoid violence. Because Ponyboy is late getting home, Darry, who has been worried about his safety, becomes angry and, in the ensuing argument, strikes him. Now convinced that Darry really dislikes him, Ponyboy runs out into the night. He meets Johnny in a park and while they are talking, the same five Socs they met earlier that evening drive up. They grab Ponyboy and shove his head into a fountain, holding him under until he passes out. When he comes to, he is by the fountain next to Johnny, who is clutching his switchblade. Beside him is the body of a dead Soc, Bob Sheldon. To save Ponyboy, Johnny drove off the gang by murdering their leader.

The boys panic. They seek out Dally, who gives them some money and directions to a hideout in an abandoned church in a rural area many miles away, but accessible by freight train. To disguise themselves, each gives up his most prized possession and status symbol—they cut each other's hair. After almost a week, Dally shows up to check on them. By this time, Johnny has decided to give himself up. As they are about to leave, fire breaks out in the church, trapping some schoolchildren who have been playing inside. The three risk their lives and save the children, but during the rescue all three are injured. Johnny is hurt critically when a flaming timber falls on him and breaks his back.

They return home as celebrities. The emotional greeting he receives from Darry convinces Ponyboy that his brother really loves him. But news from the hospital is bad—the doctors give little hope for Johnny's recovery.

The Socs want a fight to avenge their leader's death. The Greasers win the skin rumble—fists, no hardware—but are battered themselves. Dally and Ponyboy rush to the hospital to tell Johnny the news, but while they are with him, he dies.

Dally goes beserk at Johnny's death and robs a grocery store. The gang tries to help him, but reach him just as he is shot down by police. Dally's death wish has been answered.

The deaths numb both gangs, and there are indications that some members want an end to the senseless violence. Ponyboy is cleared of charges concerning Bob Sheldon's death and is not sent to a foster home as he feared. The brothers return home stronger and more united as a result of these ordeals.

Thematic Material

Without preaching or moralizing, *The Outsiders* explores the causes and consequences of a gang culture and the changes in the different personalities who join. It examines the effects on youngsters who live surrounded by violence. The author also touches on the differences in economic classes and on how they influence youngsters growing up. Despite the amount of brutishness and terror in *The Outsiders*, such positive themes as loyalty to friends and the importance of family ties are also present.

Book Talk Material

A selection from the recording of the Broadway musical *Grease* might set the mood. To introduce the differences in each gang's point of view, Cherry cites the Soc's case well (p. 46; p. 36, pap.) and Ponyboy explains what it means to be a Greaser (p. 140; p. 116, pap.). Ponyboy's narrow escape from the Socs (pp. 12-15; pp. 7-10, pap.) will be of interest, as well as the park incident that results in Bob's death (pp. 61-65; pp. 49-52, pap.).

Additional Material

In S. E. Hinton's *Rumble Fish* (Delacorte Pr., 1975, $6.95; pap., Dell, $1.25), 14-year-old supertough Rusty James finds tragedy in trying to be like his brother, Motorcycle Boy. Another novel of gangs by this author is *That Was Then, This Is Now* (Viking, 1971, $4.95; pap., Dell, 95¢). Scott O'Dell's *Child of Fire* (Houghton, 1974, $6.95; lge. type ed., G. K. Hall, $8.50) is about a Chicano gang leader out on parole, and Frank Bonham's *Durango Street* (Dutton, 1965, $6.95; pap., Dell, 95¢) deals with gang warfare in a big city ghetto. Also interesting are David Wilkerson's *Cross and the Switchblade* (pap., Pillar, $1.50) and its sequels. James Haskins' *Street Gangs, Yesterday and Today* (Hastings, 1974, $6.95) is a serious, nonfiction account of the history of street gangs from colonial times to the present.

About the Author

"Readers Meet Authors," *Top of the News*, Vol. 25 (November 1968), pp. 26-39; (January 1969), pp. 194-202.

Annabel and Edgar Johnson, *Count Me Gone*
Simon & Schuster, 1968, o.p.; pap., Archway, 95¢

The Johnsons are most closely associated in juvenile literature with outdoor adventures and wilderness romances. They have, however, written one other popular novel about a teen-aged boy trying to find himself— *Pickpocket Run* (Harper, 1961, $5.95; condensed in *Juniorplots*, Bowker, 1967). Both books are suitable for junior and senior high school audiences, particularly boys.

Plot Summary

The story is told from a hospital bed to the family lawyer by 18-year-old Rion Fletcher, a recent high school graduate who is recovering from an accident in which his car went out of control and crashed down an embankment. He is also facing charges for disorderly conduct, striking an officer, and resisting arrest. The lawyer wonders how a fine, upper-middle-class boy with every advantage could get into such a scrape.

Rion's immediate trouble began a week before when he suddenly arrived home after being fired from his job as a counselor in a summer camp. But this is only the climax of a problem that has been growing for the past two years. In his junior year, he began questioning the values of his family and friends. His life suddenly seemed without direction or purpose, and the constant platitudes and bromidic advice from Mr. White, his guidance counselor, did not help. He had quit his last summer's job as a mailroom clerk because of the monotony, dullness, and conformity that surrounded him. Since then he has been hanging out in pool halls and has made friends with people he considers to be real and nonartificial, like Nick, a professional gambler who is now serving a term in prison.

Rion barely made graduation, and, in an effort to straighten him out, his parents arranged for the job at the camp and made plans to send him to a military academy in the fall, against his wishes. The camp job was another fiasco—to teach real woodsmanship, Rion had deliberately gotten his troop lost so they could learn to forage for food and shelter. The camp director was furious, and Rion was fired.

Back home, he finds that his parents have gone on an ocean cruise and that only his 22-year-old brother, Doug, and Doug's fiancée, Shirli, are there. Rion had always worshipped his brother's looks, brains, and charm, but since his last year in college, Doug has grown more conservative and conventional. He plans to do graduate work, not for love of learning, but for the increased job opportunities and greater security it will bring. Shirli is the opposite—disillusioned, bitter, and rebelling. Although Doug hopes to convert her into a model suburban housewife, Rion soon realizes that he has slipped onto a battleground of incompatibility. While Doug lectures Rion on the need for responsible attitudes and a good education, Shirli ridicules Doug's resignation to life and his lack of daring. Rion does not care for Shirli, yet she insists on backing him and even makes an overt pass when his brother isn't looking.

Aggravated by Shirli, the rift between the brothers grows through increasingly bitter arguments in which Doug accuses Rion of being shiftless and indolent. Rion tries to get a job—any job—but is unsuccessful. Doug invites over an old friend, Norman Ashburn, who has entered the business world, to talk sense into Rion. The night is a dismal failure. Norman gets drunk and rambles on.

The following evening there is another argument. Shirli again tries to defend Rion, and the boy notices that Doug's remarks are now tinged with jealousy. After trying to calm down, Rion steals out for a ride, but he finds Shirli in his car. She refuses to leave, so he takes her for a drink, at a roadhouse operated by Nick's girlfriend, Jo Duncan. Shirli begins flirting with another customer, and Rion takes her out of the bar. But the would-be suitor follows. A fight starts, and someone grabs Rion from behind. Thinking he is being jumped, the boy turns and knocks down a policeman, who has come to break up the fight. Rion is booked on several charges and spends the night in jail. The following morning he is bailed out, not by his brother as he expected, but by his friend, Jo Duncan. He goes home and finds that Shirli has told Doug lies about the incident. Disgusted with his brother's disloyalty. Rion packs his bag to leave home. On the highway, his car goes out of control, crashes, and he is sent to the hospital.

Within two weeks, he is dismissed from the hospital and the lawyer has had the charges dropped. Although his parents are now at home and the misunderstanding with Doug has been cleared up, Rion knows that he must strike out on his own and make some sense of his life. Once more he packs his bag. He leaves a note for his parents explaining the situation. It ends, "Count me gone. I'll be O.K."

Thematic Material

This novel successfully depicts Rion's alienation from his family and their code of values, from its beginnings to the breaking point. The young man's confusion and lack of direction are well drawn, as are the growing conflicts between the brothers. The use of Rion as narrator, with his authentic speech and expressions, adds realism and power to the story.

Book Talk Material

A brief introduction to Rion and his problems will interest readers. Passages of importance are: Rion and the camp fiasco (pp. 165–169; pp. 149–153, pap.); Doug and Shirli quarrel (pp. 25–28; pp. 16–19, pap.); Shirli makes a pass at Rion (pp. 59–61; pp. 50–52, pap.); the evening with Doug (pp. 111–114; pp. 98–102, pap.); and the brothers quarrel (pp. 138–143; pp. 124–128, pap.).

Additional Selections

At the Naval Academy, a young boy bristles under discipline in Kurt Schmidt's *Annapolis Misfit* (Crown, 1974, o.p.), and young Pat is sent to a military school where he is told to *Shape Up, Burke* (Nelson, 1976, $6.50) in Richard Shaw's novel. Mary Calhoun's *It's Getting Beautiful Now* (Harper, 1971, $3.95) tells how Bert wants to run away when he is arrested on drug charges. Mike and his father rarely agree in Ella Thorp Ellis' *Riptide* (Atheneum, 1969, $4.95; pap., 95¢). Other suitable titles are: Carolyn G. Hart's *Danger: High Explosives* (Lippincott, 1972, $4.95) and Mildred Lee's *Fog* (Seabury, 1972, $5.95; pap., Dell, 95¢). In Nat Hentoff's *In the Country of Ourselves* (Simon & Schuster, 1971, $5.95), some self-styled revolutionaries, mostly high school students, challenge the school board.

About the Author

Commire, Anne. *Something about the Author.* Detroit: Gale Research Co., 1971. Vol. 2, pp. 156–158.

DeMontreville, Doris and Donna Hill, Eds. *Third Book of Junior Authors.* New York: H. W. Wilson Co., 1972, pp. 150–152.

Kinsman, Clare D. and Mary Ann Tennenhouse, Eds. *Contemporary Authors.* Detroit: Gale Research Co., 1974. Vol. 9, pp. 435–438.

Ward, Martha E. and Dorothy A. Marquardt. *Authors of Books for Young People.* (2nd Edition). Metuchen, N.J.: Scarecrow Press, Inc., 1971, p. 268.

Robert Lipsyte, *The Contender*

Harper, 1967, $4.95; lib. bdg., $4.79; pap., Bantam, 95¢

The Contender is the story of a teen-age high school dropout growing up in Harlem. He is a decent, deserving boy trying to remain on the straight path, but beset by influences that could easily cause his undoing. The title comes from a conversation with the boy's boxing coach and promoter, who tells him, "Everybody wants to be a champion. That's not enough. You have to start by wanting to be a contender, the man coming up, the man who knows there's a good chance he'll never get to the top, the man who's willing to sweat and bleed to get up as high as his legs and his brains and his heart will take him." The novel asks, "If Alfred cannot be a champion in life, will he be content to be a contender?" The author effectively has used his experience as a sports reporter for the *New York Times* in his re-creation of the behind-the-scenes boxing world. The novel was the winner of the 1967 Children's Book Award of the Child Study Association of

America. It has been a consistent favorite, particularly with boys in junior and senior high school grades.

Plot Summary

Alfred Brooks is growing up in a Harlem tenement apartment with his Aunt Pearl Conway and her three young daughters, plus more than the usual requisites of roaches, rats, and drug addicts getting fixes in the stairwell. He has a full-time job as a stockboy in a grocery store run by the three Epstein brothers. Alfred's best friend, James Mosely, has also dropped out of school, but he is jobless and hanging out with some very tough characters.

One Friday evening while looking for James, Alfred finds him with his friends, Sonny, Major, and Hollis, in their clubhouse. The boys taunt him and call him an Uncle Tom working for tight-fisted Jews. In defending the Epsteins, Alfred says they are very religious, and he lets slip that they don't even touch the money in the cash register on Fridays after sundown because it is the Sabbath.

In spite of Alfred's protests, the boys, eager for quick cash, decide to rob Epstein's grocery. After they leave, Alfred remembers with horror that recently a silent burglar alarm has been installed in the store. But it is too late to warn James. Out on the street, Alfred hears the wail of police sirens. Knowing where James would seek refuge, he rushes into the local park to a secret cave that James and he had discovered years ago. But James doesn't come. On his way home, his fears are confirmed when he meets the rest of the gang, who tell him that James was caught. For revenge, Major, Sonny, and Hollis beat and kick Alfred into unconsciousness.

Alfred recovers slowly and returns to work. Because the Epsteins know that James was Alfred's best friend, the situation is rather awkward, but gradually the tension eases.

Through Henry Johnson, the crippled janitor at Donatelli's Gym, Alfred is urged to come to the gym and try boxing. After meeting and talking with Donatelli and others, the boy decides to go into training. Soon he becomes part of the friendly people that hang out there.

After James is released, Alfred searches for him at the clubhouse. Suddenly forgetting the constraints of his training schedule, he begins drinking and smoking pot. He also notices that James is into heroin. This episode ends for Alfred with a narrow escape from the police when he is found in a stolen Cadillac. At first he is so ashamed of his behavior that he stays away from the gym, but gradually he gets back into training.

At last it's time for his first fight—three rounds of two minutes each at Amateur Boxing Night. For Alfred, it is the chance of a lifetime. He wins by a unanimous decision. In his second fight, he knocks out his opponent, but Donatelli notices that in both fights Alfred has shown a basic distaste for inflicting pain. Donatelli tells him that he lacks the "killer instinct" and advises him to give up the idea of professional boxing. Alfred, however, insists on going through with his third fight. It is a disaster, and Alfred is severely beaten. It is then that he decides he has neither the real ability nor the temperament to be a champion.

But during this period, there are many subtle influences that have been giving Alfred's life greater direction than he realized. Spoon from the gym has persuaded him to complete his high school education at night. The examples of his sometimes preachy Uncle Wilson, who lives in middle-class comfort in Queens, and Wilson's son, Jeff, who went through college on a scholarship, also have shown Alfred that there is hope even for oppressed blacks. He thinks seriously of teaching at the new community recreation project; it might lead to a career in social work.

By contrast, James' life continues on the skids. His heroin habit is beginning to control his life. One night he again attempts a robbery of Epstein's store and, in escaping, jumps through a store window. Alfred sets out to hunt for him and, as expected, finds him in the secret cave in the park. James is bleeding profusely. In a poignant scene, Alfred persuades him to give himself up and promises to dedicate himself to James' complete recovery. Alfred has his first case.

Thematic Material

The Contender portrays the dilemma faced by most black youngsters growing up in ghettos—the desire to live productive lives in conflict with the negative pressures of the environment. It also shows a youngster's need for direction by understanding adults, who can serve as models and can give guidance. Such virtues as loyalty in friendship, sportsmanship, and the need for self-discipline are depicted as still relevant today. Although the book gives a bleak picture of slum life, it also shows that it is possible to change those conditions.

Book Talk Material

A brief introduction to Alfred and his problems could serve to interest readers. The story also could be introduced by relating one of several incidents: Alfred innocently causes the Epstein robbery (pp. 1–6; pp. 1–4, pap.); Alfred first goes to Donatelli's Gym (pp. 20–21; pp. 15–16, pap.);

Alfred attends his first fight (pp. 61-66; pp. 46-50, pap.); and has his first fight (pp. 136-141; pp. 101-105, pap.).

Additional Suggestions

Among Mr. Lipsyte's other books on sports is *Assignment Sports* (Harper, 1970, $3.95), a collection for young readers of his articles on the world of sports. Readers interested in boxing might like some nonfiction titles, such as Peter Heller's *In This Corner* (Simon & Schuster, 1973, $10), in which 40 boxing champions tell their stories; Ocania Chalk's *Pioneers in Black Sports* (Dodd, 1975, $7.95), which also includes coverage on baseball, basketball, and boxing; or John Durant's *The Heavyweight Champions* (Hastings, 1976, $7.95). There are also many individual biographies about such boxers as Sugar Ray Robinson and Muhammed Ali. In the fiction area, recommended titles include Kristin Hunter's *Guests in the Promised Land* (Scribner, 1973, $5.95), stories of young blacks growing up in the ghetto; Matthew Skulicz's *Right On, Shane* (Putnam, 1972, $5.95), a Harlem boy's search for respect; and Louis Tanner's *Reggie and Nilma* (Farrar, 1971, $4.50), a New York City story about an interracial friendship that involves drugs.

About the Author

Kinsman, Clare D., Ed. *Contemporary Authors*. Detroit: Gale Research Co., 1976.
Vols. 17-20, p. 449.

Adrienne Richard, *Pistol*

Atlantic Monthly Pr. (Little, Brown), 1969, $5.95; pap., Dell, 95¢

In this, her first book, Adrienne Richard tells, in the first person narrative, the story of Billy Catlett, from June 1930, when he is 14 and spends his first summer on a cattle ranch, to September 1934, when, at 18, he strikes out on his own. It is also the story of how the Great Depression changed this country, as well as the lives of the Catlett family. The novel is popular with both junior and senior high school students, particularly boys.

Plot Summary

Billy and his brother, Conrad, who is three years older, remember their childhood as a series of Montana towns where their father pursued one unsuccessful business venture after another. Finally, in Great Plain, a ranching town, their mother, usually submissive and resigned, rebels and forces her husband to settle down. He works at first in a wool house and later becomes manager of a small meat-packing plant which processes wild horse meat.

During his fourteenth summer, Billy is offered a job as horse wrangler and general handyboy at Sam Tolliver's cattle ranch; Conrad goes to a much larger ranch operated by the Kincaids. At first, Billy is apprehensive about his ability, but his honesty and eagerness to learn soon help him win the acceptance of the rough-and-ready ranchmen.

Tom Driscoll, the taciturn but dependable leader of the ranchmen, becomes Billy's mentor and nicknames him Pistol. He helps Billy break in a horse that Tolliver has given him, a little sorrel maverick that Billy names Sundance. Soon the boy is participating in all of the ranch activities. One evening they all attend a wild country dance at the town of Sunshine. Billy dances several times with Allison Mitchell, a girl he has seen at school. She is the daughter of a wealthy English gentleman farmer. Although both are shy and reserved, they enjoy each other's company.

In the fall, after such a wonderful summer, a return to school is a great anticlimax for Billy and Conrad. But the monotony is relieved by Billy's increased friendship with Allison.

The next summer he again goes to the ranch, but two summers of bad drought plus a terrible winter have brought great losses. There are other tragedies—a prairie fire and the death of old Seth, one of the ranchmen, in a cattle drive. But Billy is able to spend all his free time with Allison.

In the fall, this happy life comes to a shattering end. The full impact of the Depression hits when the local bank fails and all of the townspeople lose their savings and investments. The meat-packing plant goes bankrupt, and the Catlett's furnishings, except a few necessities, are taken for nonpayment of loans.

Because Conrad blames his father for their situation, Mrs. Catlett sorrowfully sees her family torn apart by accusations and bitterness. Billy suffers an additional loss when Allison is sent to a private school in Chicago. Conrad takes a job as a dishwasher, and Billy, unable to find full-time work, stays in school and pumps gas at a local filling station. Mr. Catlett, broken and despondent, stays at home.

One night their father deserts them, leaving a note that says he is going elsewhere to try to find work. The remaining Catletts struggle to survive, and that summer there is no ranch job for Billy because Tolliver has sold out and moved.

In the spring, Mr. Catlett returns and joyously tells the family that there is work in northeastern Montana at a federal project to build a huge dam on the Missouri River (now known as Fort Peck Dam). The family moves, but at the dam site they find a wide-open frontier shanty town populated mainly by dislocated single men and general riffraff. Conrad works on the dam with his father; Billy takes a job as a shoe salesman; and the family moves into a tarpaper-covered shanty without electricity.

After several months of work, the family is once again solvent. But Billy notices that his mother is gradually crumbling under the strain of the hardship and drudgery of this primitive life. Bill, as he is now called, confronts his father and demands that, for his mother's sake, he move back to Great Plain where it is rumored that the wool house is about to reopen. His father agrees, but Conrad decides to stay.

After he helps his parents resettle into their former home, Bill knows it is time for him to leave and seek his own life. With his savings of $150, he takes a job on a cattle train bound for Chicago, hoping for a better life, perhaps with Allison.

Thematic Material

The effects of economic depression are told harrowingly, but with honesty, in this novel. Although terrible in its overall consequences, Billy's sudden change of status becomes his bridge between adolescence and manhood. The author has created many believable characters, together with an authentic description of Montana life and a telling picture of a trying period in our history.

Book Talk Material

This powerful novel can be introduced through a general description of the period, setting, and principal characters. Some interesting passages from the first part of the book are: Billy tries to capture an escaped steer (pp. 31–33; pp. 32–33, pap.); Tom and Billy break in Sundance (pp. 46–51; pp. 44–47, pap.); the dance at Sunshine (pp. 60–67; pp. 54–59, pap.); and Billy returns to Sundance (pp. 100–104; pp. 83–87, pap.).

Additional Selections

A young boy works as a clerk during the Great Depression in Hilary Milton's *November's Wheel* (Abelard Schuman, 1976, $6.95), and in Phyllis Naylor's *Walking through the Dark* (Atheneum, 1976, $6.95), a 14-year-old girl must make adjustments when her family is hit by the Depression. In 1933, 17-year-old Vic Martin strikes out on his own in Tom E. Clarke's *The Big Road* (Lothrop, 1964, $7.50; condensed in *Juniorplots*, Bowker, 1967). Vera and Bill Cleaver's *Dust of the Earth* (Lippincott, 1975, $6.95) is the story of Fern Drawn and her family's fight for a livelihood as sheep farmers. Other recommended stories are Edward Fenton's *Duffy's Rocks* (Dutton, 1974, $5.95), A. E. Hotchner's *Looking for Miracles* (Harper, 1975, $8.95), and Eleanor Clymer's *Luke Was There* (Holt, 1973, $4.95; pap., Archway, 95¢).

About the Author

Commire, Anne. *Something about the Author.* Detroit: Gale Research Co., Vol. 5, pp. 157-158.

Kinsman, Clare D. and Mary Ann Tennenhouse, Eds. *Contemporary Authors.* Detroit: Gale Research Co., 1972. Vol 29, p. 512.

Mildred D. Taylor, *Roll of Thunder, Hear My Cry*
Dial, 1976, $7.95

This Newbery Award winner, whose title comes from a black spiritual, is the second in a projected series of books about the Logans, a black family in rural Mississippi. The first, *Song of the Trees* (Dial, 1975, $4.95), for younger readers, was also much praised. This novel spans a year—fall 1933 through summer 1934—in the lives of the narrator, nine-year-old Cassie, and her family. The book is intended for upper elementary and junior high school readers.

Plot Summary

The Logan family consists of mother and father; grandmother, who is called Big Ma; Cassie; and her three brothers, Stacey, Christopher-John, and Clayton, the baby of the family who is nicknamed Little Man. It is the height of the Depression. High taxes and the mortgage on their house and land has forced the father to take a job away from home on the railroad. They make ends meet with his salary, plus what Mrs. Logan earns as a schoolteacher, and the small amount they get from their cotton crop.

In many ways, the Logans are more fortunate than their sharecropper neighbors, who work on the plantation owned by Harlan Granger and who are enslaved by debt to the local store, operated by the three redneck Wallace brothers and controlled by Granger. The black adults live in economic and social slavery, and in constant fear of night riders, usually led by the Wallaces. The most recent raid, on the Berry property, left one dead and two others badly burned.

The children also suffer discrimination and prejudice—they must walk to their run-down, segregated school while white children ride on a bus to the attractive, well-equipped Jefferson Davis school. The black children receive only outdated textbooks, and their school year is shortened so they can be sent to work in the cotton fields.

During one of his stays at home, Mr. Logan brings with him a giant of a man, Mr. Morrison, to work for them and help protect the family. He is quickly welcomed into the warm family circle.

Although they know that Granger is anxious to own their property, the Logans courageously decide to help the sharecroppers by putting up their land as collateral to establish credit so their neighbors can buy supplies at lower interest in the city of Vicksburg. A liberal white lawyer and friend, Mr. Jamison, knows this will make them vulnerable to a takeover by Granger. Instead, he volunteers to underwrite the credit note. Soon the Logans have organized 30 families in the cooperative venture, and each week they take orders and travel to Vicksburg to do their buying. When the white establishment hears of this, the harassment begins.

T. J. Avery, one of the sharecropper's sons, is a pupil in Mrs. Logan's seventh-grade class. His cheating and bad behavior constantly get him into trouble. When he fails his first–term examination, he tells everyone at Wallace's store that the cause is Mrs. Logan's poor teaching. Granger uses this as an excuse to have her fired.

Through eviction and foreclosure threats, families are forced to drop out of the cooperative. Finally, only seven families remain. But Mr. Logan, along with Morrison and Stacey, decide to make the trip by horse and wagon to Vicksburg. One of their enemies has tampered with the wagon, and, as a result, Mr. Logan's leg is broken. They are attacked and shot by night riders, but Morrison drives them off. In a final effort to get the Logans, Granger arranges to foreclose on their mortgage, but an appeal to Mr. Logan's brother in Chicago brings a visit from Uncle Hammer and the necessary cash.

In the meantime, Cassie is fighting her own battles. She is publicly humiliated by being forced unjustly to apologize to a spiteful white girl, Lillian Jean Simms, for an imagined slight. Cassie then gains the confidence of Lillian Jean, who tells her about her boy friends and all the local gossip. One day Cassie forces an apology from Lillian Jean by threatening to tell all the girl's secrets. Revenge is sweet for Cassie.

Ignored by the black children because of his role in Mrs. Logan's dismissal, T. J. begins to associate with two cynical white boys, R. W. and Melvin, Lillian Jean's brothers. The three make a robbery attempt on a local store. When it fails and the owner and his wife are beaten, the boys blame T. J. A lynch mob arrives at the Averys. To save T. J. and divert the crowd, Mr. Logan sets fire to his own cotton fields. Fearing the fire will spread, the men rush off to fight it, and T. J. is whisked off to jail. When the fire is put out, Mr. Logan has lost one-quarter of his crop, but their homestead has been saved and another crisis has passed.

Thematic Material

In the brief preface, the author tells how she learned from her family to respect both her own heritage and her people, who, although not free, would not allow their spirits to be enslaved. These qualities of indomitability and dignity pervade the novel. The reader will also enjoy meeting the wonderful Logan family, particularly the courageous Cassie.

Book Talk Material

A description of the period, setting, and the Logan family will serve to introduce the novel. Some representative passages are: Little Man receives his first textbook (pp. 22–25); the school bus incident (pp. 50–55); Cassie is humiliated (pp. 114–116); Mr. Jamison backs the credit note (pp. 160–165); and Stacey tells of the attack on the wagon (pp. 214–217).

Additional Selections

A black girl grows up during the 1950s in a warm, neighborly atmosphere in a small Georgia town in Brenda Wilkinson's *Ludell* (Harper, 1974, $5.95). Walter Dean Myers' *Fast Sam, Cool Clyde and Stuff* (Viking, 1975, $6.95) tells of three young boys in Harlem and their encounters with sex, drugs, and the police. A 14-year-old black girl questions life's value in John Steptoe's *Marcia* (Viking, 1976, $7.95). Shane Stevens' *Rat Pack* (pap., Pocket Bks., $1.25) tells of four black ghetto youths and a night of violence. In the nonfiction area, try Leonard A. Stevens' *Equal! The Case of Integration vs. Jim Crow* (Coward, 1976, $5.86), Marcella Thum's *Exploring Black America: A History and Guide* (Atheneum, 1975, $10.95), and Lucille Clifton's beautiful tribute to her family, *Generations* (Random, 1976, $5.95).

4

Developing an Understanding of the Past and Other Cultures

Primarily through indirect experience, adolescents increase their knowledge of diverse past and present cultures and deepen their understanding and appreciation of the historical development of various countries, including their own. The books in this section range historically from the beginning of the Christian Era to life during World War II. Geographically, the settings span a good part of our globe—from the North American continent to Europe and the Holy Land.

Joan Aiken, *Midnight Is a Place*
    Viking, 1974, $6.95; pap., Pocket Bks., $1.50
Many critics have compared Joan Aiken's writing to that of Dickens. Certainly like Dickens, she is a storyteller, who, through her suspense-filled novels and memorable characters, has re-created nineteenth-century England with great accuracy. This book is popular with both adults and young readers from the sixth grade up.

Plot Summary
    It is 1842, and for the past year, since both his parents died of smallpox in India on a cotton-buying expedition, 13-year-old Lucas Bell has been living in a decaying mansion, Midnight Court, with his crusty, usually drunk guardian, Sir Randolph Grimsby. The house overlooks the grimy, squalid Yorkshire city of Blashburn, which is dominated by the belching smokestacks of the Murgatroyd Carpet, Rug and Matting Manufactury, otherwise known as Midnight Mill. Mr. Oakapple, Lucas's somewhat brittle tutor and general factotum at Midnight Court, explains that before making the late Mr. Bell a partner, Grimsby had won the Mill in a bet,

which many believe was rigged, from the scion of the Murgatroyd family, Denzil.

According to his father's will, Lucas must live with Sir Randolph and learn the carpet-making business. On his first trip to the Mill with Mr. Oakapple, he is sickened at the appalling, inhuman working conditions, where even eight- and nine-year-old children daily face death or maiming in the press room when they dart out to gather balls of fluff from newly finished carpets before the murderous press claps shut. On subsequent trips, Lucas notices that the employees are further terrorized by a gang of ruffians lead by a Mill worker, Bob Bludward, who squeezes protection money from the workers to prevent "accidents" on the job by operating a pseudo-union, ironically called the Friendly Society. Lucas helps to save one worker, Sam Melkinthorpe, from a vat of glue where he had been thrown by Bludward's gang for nonpayment of dues.

In addition to his other faults, Sir Randolph is a compulsive gambler and is now facing the loss of either the Mill or the house for nonpayment of back taxes. The serving staff is reduced to a bare minimum, when suddenly there is a new mouth to feed. It is eight-year-old Anna-Marie Murgatroyd, whose father, Denzil, died penniless in Calais. Lucas is hoping that she will cure his loneliness, but instead the girl, who knows no English, is stubborn and arrogant.

Mr. Gobthorpe, the tax collector, and Mr. Throgmorton, Sir Randolph's crafty lawyer, continue to warn him of impending financial collapse. However, before any action can be taken, Grimsby dies in a fire that destroys Midnight Court. Lucas and Anna-Marie escape unharmed, but Mr. Oakapple is severely burned and sent to a hospital in town.

The two young waifs are penniless and homeless. An appeal to Throgmorton leads only to a cold dismissal. They rent lodgings in town at a run-down waterfront rooming house, run by penny-pinching Mrs. Tetley, a sister of one of their former servants, and set out to get work. Under her veneer of pride and disdain, Anna-Marie, who learns to speak English, proves a most enterprising and resourceful young girl. She collects discarded cigar stubs, rolls them into new ones, and sells them in a small rented space in the market stall operated by Elias Hobday, seller of junk.

One of Hobday's sources of merchandise is Tom Gudgeon, a "togher"— a man who fishes through the slime and filth of Blashburn's underground sewers for lost and discarded valuables. Lucas becomes Gudgeon's apprentice, and with a long pole descends through a manhole into the mire and stench of the cavelike tunnels. He must not only face the danger of rising tides, huge rats, and attacks from a pack of wild pigs that have bred in the sewer, but also Gudgeon's evil moods, which Lucas learns might be responsible for the unexplained deaths of several former apprentices. The boy is lucky on his first day underground—he uncovers a jewel-studded saddle and a packet of legal papers.

As the weeks pass, the two youngsters are able to collect enough money to pay for their lodging and food and meet the hospital bills of Mr. Oakapple, whom they visit regularly.

Beds are needed in the hospital, and Mr. Oakapple, although far from well, is discharged. They desperately need larger rooms, and Anna-Marie remembers a circular icehouse at the edge of Sir Randolph's property. They discover a comfortable dwelling, which is already occupied by a sweet old lady, who identifies herself as Mrs. Murgatroyd, Anna-Marie's grandmother. Under the name Minitti (because Murgatroyd is a hated name in town), she earns a meager living sewing and giving music lessons. She invites the children to stay with her. When they tell her of Mr. Oakapple, her face brightens. As a young boy, Julian Oakapple had been in the Murgatroyd's employ and had been particularly devoted to her son, Denzil. There is a joyful reunion when Mr. Oakapple is brought from the hospital, during which he explains that he became Lucas' tutor only to discover the whereabouts of the remaining Murgatroyds.

Harassment from local toughs causes Anna-Marie to give up her cigar business, and she takes a job in the carpet factory cleaning the combs that clog the wool. There she incurs the wrath of Bludward and his gang by refusing to pay fees and by devising a simple gadget that increases her productivity. Lucas narrowly escapes death in the sewers, and he too finds work in the factory. To make amends for the boy's harrowing experience, Mr. Hobday arrives at the icehouse with a gift of money (actually Lucas' rightful share for the sale of the saddle) and the packet of papers, which Hobday states deal with the fortunes of the Bells and Murgatroyds. They begin trying to decipher the documents.

To rid himself of Anna-Marie, who constantly challenges his authority, Bludward has the girl transferred to the press room as a fluff catcher. Then he oils the press so heavily that it will descend even faster and crush her. Sam Melkinthorpe, whose life was saved by Lucas months before, tells the boy of the scheme. Lucas rushes to the press room, pushes a huge wooden drum under the press, and pulls the girl to safety. Incensed at Bludward's evilness, a coworker challenges him to a duel with pistols. While trying to escape, the villain drowns in an ice-filled lake.

The papers show that Grimsby had illegally rigged the wager between

Denzil and himself. The Murgatroyd property must now be returned to its rightful owners. Although the factory has already been bought by a new company, Mrs. Murgatroyd knows the new owner and is assured that Lucas will enter the training program as his father wished. Lucas hopes that someday he will be able to improve working conditions in the Mill, but for now it is comforting to know that his adopted family is safe and secure in their new home.

Thematic Material

The author uses the familiar mystery themes of coincidence, mistaken identity, and forgotten family secrets to produce a novel of suspense, melodrama, and unexpected twists of plot. The plight of the factory workers and the dismal living conditions during the Industrial Revolution are memorably re-created. The strength and fortitude of the children in their struggle for survival is also an important theme.

Book Talk Material

A verse from one of Denzil's songs reads "Nights' winged horses/No one can outpace/But midnight is no moment/Midnight is a place." An explanation of this in the context of the novel could be used as an introduction. Some interesting passages are: Lucas sees the press room (pp. 27-29; pp. 20-22, pap.); he meets Anna-Marie for the first time (pp. 38-39; pp. 30-32, pap.); the history of the wager (pp. 52-58; pp. 44-50, pap.); and in the sewers (pp. 150-154; pp. 141-145, pap.).

Additional Selections

Try any of the gothic novels of Victoria Holt, such as *Lord of the Far Country* (Doubleday, 1975, $7.95; pap., Fawcett, $1.95), about the amazing adventures of an orphan named Ellen, and also those of Mary Stewart, who has had a series of successes since her novel about an endangered governess, *Nine Coaches Waiting* (Morrow, 1959, $9.95; pap., Fawcett, $1.50). Witchcraft and superstition mingle in the novel set in the Channel Islands during the seventeenth century, Margaret Greaves' *Stone of Terror* (Harper, 1974, $4.95). Other good mysteries are: Leon Ware's *Delta Mystery* (Westminster, 1974, $5.50); Lois Duncan's *I Know What You Did Last Summer* (Little, 1974, $5.95; pap., Archway, 95¢); Gretchen Sprague's *Signpost to Terror* (pap., Tempo, 95¢); and Jane Edwards' *What Happened to Amy?* (pap., Scholastic, 75¢). Also use Joan Aikens' many novels, which include the trilogy that begins with *The Wolves of Willoughby Chase* (Doubleday, 1963, $4.95; pap., Dell, $1.25; condensed in *Introducing Books*, Bowker, 1970).

About the Author

Commire, Anne. *Something about the Author*. Detroit: Gale Research Co., 1971. Vol. 2, pp. 1-2.

DeMontreville, Doris and Donna Hill, Eds. *Third Book of Junior Authors*. New York: H. W. Wilson Co., 1972, pp. 4-5.

Ethridge, James M., Ed. *Contemporary Authors*. Detroit: Gale Research Co., 1964. Vol. 9, pp. 11-12.

Jones, Cornelia and Olivia R. Way. *British Children's Authors: Interviews at Home*. Chicago: ALA, 1976, pp. 3-10.

Townsend, John Rowe. *A Sense of Story*. Philadelphia and New York: J. B. Lippincott Co., 1971, pp. 17-23.

Ward, Martha E. and Dorothy A. Marquardt. *Authors of Books for Young People*. (2nd Edition). Metuchen, N. J.: Scarecrow Press, Inc., 1971, p. 7.

James Lincoln Collier and Christopher Collier, *My Brother Sam Is Dead*
Four Winds, 1974, $6.50; pap., Scholastic, $1.25

With *My Brother Sam Is Dead*, the Collier brothers made a particularly auspicious debut as a writing team. The novel received a Newbery Honor Award in 1975. James Lincoln Collier is a professional writer who already had many juvenile titles to his credit; his brother, Christopher, is a professor of history whose area of specialization is the same period as this novel, the American Revolution. In an interesting postscript to the book, the authors state that, although the Meeker family as depicted in the book is fictitious, most of the other characters and events are real. A later book by the Colliers, *The Bloody Country* (Four Winds, 1976, $6.95), uses the same theme of divided allegiances during the Revolution, but the setting is Pennsylvania rather than southern Connecticut. Both novels are suited to junior high school students or better readers in the upper elementary grades.

Plot Summary

Eleven-year-old Tim Meeker is confused about his loyalties in the gathering crisis that later becomes the long and bloody American Revolution. His parents, Eliphalet (nicknamed Life) and Susannah Meeker, operate a small tavern in an area of Tory sympathizers, the southern Connecticut town of Redding, some 10 miles north of the Long Island Sound. Although his parents do not feel great dedication to George III, they are furiously opposed to the war, knowing what disruption and tragedy it could bring to people's lives. However, Tim's brother, 16-year-old Sam, carried along on the wave for liberation and independence encountered as a student at Yale, has joined the rebel army with several of his colleagues and is serving under Capt. Benedict Arnold.

One Saturday in April 1775, Sam visits his home. Almost immediately he and his father begin arguing about the war. Over chores, Sam tells Tim that the real reason for his return is to arm himself by taking his father's musket, Brown Bess. Tim, who loves and admires his only brother, is shocked but cannot dissuade him from his plan. That evening there is another bitter disagreement between father and son. Mr. Meeker orders Sam out of the house, and, as he leaves, Sam secretly takes the gun with him.

After church service the next day, Tom Warrups, the only Indian in town, tells Tim that his brother is hiding in Tom's shack on the property of Colonel Reed and his family, known patriot sympathizers. The boy visits his brother, who is with his girl friend, Betsy, Colonel Reed's granddaughter and a devout rebel. Knowing that the loss of Brown Bess will leave his father defenseless in an emergency, Tim begs his brother to return the gun, but Sam is adamant. Tearfully, the boy bids his brother good-bye.

In the fall, Betsy gets word to Tim that Sam has slipped away for a day and is in Tom's shack. Before Tim can visit him, a squad of rebel troops arrives at the tavern demanding that Life turn over his musket. Unwilling to believe the story about the gun's disappearance, they become abusive and slash Mr. Meeker's cheek with a bayonet. Tim runs to get Sam's help, but by the time the two return to the tavern the troops have gone. Sam once more leaves without a reconciliation.

When Mr. Heron, a respected townsman of dubious allegiance, asks Tim to deliver by hand a letter to the coastal town of Fairfield, Mr. Meeker, fearful that the letter might contain political information, denies the boy permission. Eager for excitement, Tim steals away. On the way, he is intercepted by Betsy Reed, who demands to know the letter's contents. She breaks the seal, but the cryptic message reads only "If this message is received, we will know the messenger is reliable." The boy creeps home knowing that his career as a secret agent has been a dismal failure.

In the fall of 1776, Mr. Meeker and Tim set out to trade some cattle and pigs for provisions at Verplanks Point, south of Peekskill on the Hudson River in New York. Although the trip is only about 25 miles, it is through disputed territory, where there are gangs of marauding cowboys who take advantage of the confused situation and prey on weary travelers. The trip is successful in spite of a narrow brush with a gang of cowboys, who are driven off by a posse. On the way back, there is a severe snowstorm and Mr.

Meeker rides ahead of the ox team to make sure that the road is clear. When his father doesn't return, Tim becomes alarmed. He leaves the ox cart and walks ahead through the blinding snow. He soon recognizes signs of a struggle. It appears that his father has been taken prisoner. The boy returns to the wagon and continues his journey alone. He is once more stopped by three cowboys, but tricks them into believing that a posse is on its way. They scatter and Tim arrives home safely with the provisions but with no news of his father.

In the spring, British troops raid the town, killing rebel sympathizers and burning their homes. Later the family learns that Mr. Meeker has died of cholera on a prison ship. Tim becomes sickened by the war and the wanton destruction and death it has brought.

At the end of 1778, Sam's regiment is sent to Redding for winter encampment. One evening he steals away from his post to visit his family. A noise is heard in the barn. Sam runs out and intercepts two soldiers trying to steal the cattle. Afraid of the consequences if caught, the soldiers take Sam prisoner and accuse him of being the cattle thief. He is court-martialed and sentenced to death. In spite of personal pleas to General Putnam by both Mrs. Meeker and Tim, no reprieve is granted, and Tim witnesses his brother's execution by a firing squad.

Years later, when Tim has become a successful merchant in Pennsylvania, he looks back at all of the tragic events of the Revolution and how it destroyed his family. He speculates that there might have been a way besides war to achieve the same ends. But now it is too late; all has become history.

Thematic Material

From this novel, readers gain a different perspective on the Revolution than history texts convey. Through Tim's experiences, war becomes a senseless, destructive force that brings tragedy regardless of allegiances. Besides the futility of aggression, the book graphically portrays, through one family's misfortunes, the agony of a country divided against itself. The authentic details of colonial life add immediacy and realism to the story. Tim's courage and perseverance form an important subtheme.

Book Talk Material

The basic conflict between Sam and his father is revealed in conversations on pp. 3-7 (pp. 3-8, pap.) and pp. 20-22 (pp. 23-25, pap.). Other important episodes are: Tim tries to save his father from the rebels (pp. 52-60; pp. 60-70, pap.); Tim tries to deliver Mr. Heron's letter (pp. 77-

84; pp. 89-98, pap.); the first brush with the cowboys (pp. 93-98; pp. 108-114, pap.); and Tim tricks them on the homeward journey (pp. 123-126; pp. 143-147, pap.).

Additional Selections

A recording and cassette based on this book are available from Miller-Brody Productions. Richard F. Snow's novel of the American Revolution, *Freelon Starbird* (Houghton, 1976, $7.95) has the subtitle, "Being a Narrative of the Extraordinary Hardships Suffered by an Accidental Soldier in the Beaten Army during the Autumn and Winter of 1776." A farm boy is transformed into a patriot during the final years of the Revolutionary War in the Carolinas in John and Patricia Beatty's *Who Comes to King's Mountain?* (Morrow, 1975, $5.95). Four other recommended novels of the period are: Jean Fritz's *Early Thunder* (Coward, 1967, $6.95); Esther Forbes' perennial favorite, *Johnny Tremain* (Houghton, 1943, $6.95, pap., Dell, $1.50); James Forman's *The Cow Neck Rebels* (Farrar, 1969, $3.95); and Leonard Wibberley's *John Treegate's Musket* (Ariel, 1959, $4.50) and its many sequels.

About the Author

Commire, Anne. *Something about the Author.* Detroit: Gale Research Co., 1976. Vol. 8, pp. 33-34.
Ethridge, James M., Ed. *Contemporary Authors.* Detroit: Gale Research Co., 1964. Vol. 9, p. 94.

Paula Fox, *The Slave Dancer*
Bradbury, 1973, $6.95; pap., Dell, $1.25

Since the publication of *Maurice's Room* (Macmillan, 1966, $4.95; pap., Collier, 95¢), Paula Fox has written numerous books for young people. Many of them, like *The Slave Dancer*, the 1974 Newbery Medal winner, have been singled out for various honors and awards. In her Newbery acceptance speech (*Horn Book*, August 1974), the author traces the genesis of this novel to a footnote in a forgotten history book, which stated that often, to preserve the physical health of their wretched cargo, the crews of slave ships kidnapped young street musicians to serve as slave dancers. Better readers in grades six through the junior high school years will find this novel both engrossing and harrowing.

Plot Summary

Jessie Bollier is a 13-year-old boy who earns a few pennies each day playing his fife on the docks of New Orleans for the amusement of sailors and passersby. He lives with his widowed mother, a seamstress, and a nine-year-old sister, Betty, in abject poverty in the Vieux Carré, now called the French Quarter. It is 1840 and slavery is still legal, but by law no American ship may engage in this odious practice.

One evening Jessie is sent to his Aunt Agatha's to borrow some candles so that his mother and Betty can work into the night on a special sewing assignment. On his way home he is grabbed from behind by two men, and a canvas bag is thrown over him. He is first transported by wooden raft to a marshy area and then the three walk to a small sailboat. When the canvas is removed, he recognizes his captors, Claudius and Purvis, as part of the group he had entertained that afternoon. They soon arrive at their destination, a many-masted sailing ship, *The Moonlight*. The boy is brought before Captain Cawthorne, a cruel, corrupt man who, in his characteristic sarcastic way, nicknames the boy Bollweevil. With satanic coldness, he explains that the ship is bound on a four-month voyage to the Bight of Benin in Africa to purchase slaves and later sell them to a Spanish contact in Cuba. There they will purchase molasses and then return to Charleston. Jessie realizes with horror that he has been press-ganged onto a slaver.

He finds life on the ship filled with misery and hardship and is amazed at the indifference and cruelty of the crew, even toward each other. There are 13 crew members—an unfortunate number—aboard, including the brutal Captain Cawthorne and his equally hated and feared mate, Nicholas Spark. Jessie soon gets to know them all. At first he is mistakenly deluded by the friendliness of one seaman, Ben Stout, but soon finds that Stout is even more calculating and cunning than the rest. Clay Purvis is the most enigmatic—moody, unpredictable, taciturn—but in time Jessie realizes he is the only one to be trusted. Because of the menial jobs he is given, Jessie often also works with the cynical ship's carpenter, Ned Grime, and the cook, Adolph Curry.

One night, Stout steals an egg from the Captain's stores. Purvis is falsely accused and, without protesting his innocence, he is publicly flogged before being hung on the shrouds for the night. Jessie finds this lassitude and stoicism incomprehensible, but he is filled with loathing and disgust for Stout.

At the Bight of Benin, the ship is harassed by a British naval vessel whose crew destroys the barracoon, or compound where the slaves were imprisoned while awaiting the arrival of *The Moonlight*. Captain Cawthorne makes new deals with the local slave brokers, and in the dead of night the human cargo, shackled and terrified, is brought to the ship and herded in the hold. Cawthorne, who is known as a "tight packer," squeezes almost 100 slaves in before the ship leaves Africa.

Jessie now learns his real function on the journey. Each day the slaves are exercised and fed on the deck. He must play the flute while the seamen prod the hapless prisoners into a macabre dance to keep their muscles strong. Jessie watches the slaves carefully and is particularly intrigued by a quiet wide-eyed boy of his own age.

The homeward journey is a nightmare of degradation, hardship, and death. Several of the slaves develop a fever and, while still alive, are pitched overboard. Stout is the only one who seems to thrive on these conditions. Fed up with the bestiality and horror of the situation, Jessie rebels and refuses to play his pipe. Under Captain's orders, he is flogged into submission.

The mate, Nicholas Spark, takes pleasure in tormenting and abusing the slaves. After one strikes out against him, the mate has the black man flogged unmercifully and then shoots him in the back. The Captain has Spark thrown overboard, not to serve justice but because the mate had destroyed a valuable piece of cargo.

Stout, who takes Spark's place, turns his sadistic nature against Jessie, the one crew member who has openly shown his scorn and loathing. He steals Jessie's flute, drops it into the hold and forces the boy to clamber among the half-dead slaves to retrieve it. The wide-eyed boy finds it for him, but in spite of this kindness, Jessie begins to hate even the slaves because it is they and their plight that are slowly eroding his sense of conscience.

They reach Cuba, and the night before the slaves are to be taken ashore, the Captain holds his customary "farewell party." He brings the slaves on deck, feeds them rum, and dresses them in strange costumes and bits of finery for a final dance. Both slaves and sailors become drunk, but panic breaks out when an American naval ship is spotted on the horizon lowering landing boats. Fearful of being caught with evidence aboard, the seamen begin flinging the slaves into the ocean. Jessie and the wide-eyed boy hide in the hold. Before a landing can be made, a tropical squall develops and for hours, perhaps days, the terrible storm batters the ship. When the ship begins to list badly, the boys emerge and find the entire crew dead or missing. They grab a piece of boom and attempt to swim to safety.

They are successful and come ashore on the coast of Mississippi, close to the cabin of an escaped slave, Daniel, who befriends and nurses them, makes arrangements to have Ras, the black boy, sent north via the

Underground Railroad, and gives Jessie food and directions for his journey home to New Orleans.

In a postscript, Jessie tells how, after spending some time at home, he travels north and becomes an apothecary in Rhode Island. He survives service in the Civil War and three months in Andersonville prison. Throughout his later life, he tries to blot out the memory of the events of 1840 but is only partially successful. Whenever he hears music, he often thinks of the slaves, their joyless dances and the clanking of their chains.

Thematic Material

This is a graphic, realistic picture of one of the most shameful aspects of our history. Although the story is grim and often horrifying, it is never sensationalized to exploit the material. In the self-hatred and abhorrence that the crew feels for each other, one realizes that slavery diminishes the oppressors as well as the oppressed. Jessie's character is well developed, and one feels both the physical and mental agonies he suffers, particularly in his outburst against the slaves (p. 91; p. 69, pap.) when his conscience can no longer bear the burden of his guilt and shame.

Book Talk Material

An explanation of the title plus the "History" page (p. 1; p. 6, pap.) could be used to introduce the book. Also use Eros Keith's dark and forbidding illustrations in the hard-cover edition. Specific passages are: Jessie is kidnapped (pp. 11-14; pp. 13-15, pap.); he meets Captain Cawthorne (pp. 24-26; pp. 21-24, pap.); Purvis is flogged (pp. 52-56; pp. 41-44, pap.); and the first slaves arrive (pp. 72-75; pp. 54-57, pap.).

Additional Selections

In *Slavery* (Regnery, 1970, $6.50; pap., Dell, $1.75), Milton Meltzer traces its history from the rise of Western Civilization until today. The years 1619 to 1865 are covered in Volume One of Robert A. Liston's *Slavery in America* (McGraw, 1970, $5.95). Also use Julius Lester's *To Be a Slave* (Dial, 1968, $5.95; pap., Dell, 95¢) and *Long Journey Home* (Dial, 1972, $5.95; pap., Dell, 95¢). A much different view of slavery in which the heroine, a slave, becomes a princess in London society is told in *Sophia Scrooby Preserved* by Martha Bacon (Little, 1968, $6.95; pap., Dell, $1.50). Audrey Beyer's *Dark Venture* (Knopf, 1968, $5.69) tells the moving story of a chieftain's son forced into slavery. Also use *Freedom Trail* (Putnam, 1973, $5.95) by Jeanne Williams and, for a slightly younger audience, Marcia M. Mathews' *The Freedom Star* (Coward, 1975, $4.39).

About the Author

Townsend, John Rowe. *A Sense of Story: Essays on Contemporary Writers for Children.* Philadelphia and New York: J. B. Lippincott Co., 1971, pp. 89–96.
Who's Who in America (39th Edition). Chicago: Marquis Who's Who, Inc., 1976. Vol. 1, p. 1050.

Leon Garfield, *The Sound of Coaches*
Viking, 1974, $5.95; pap., Popular Library, $1.75

In any list of the best English authors currently writing children's books, Leon Garfield's name would appear. His historical novels—usually set, as this book is, presumably around the end of the seventeenth century in England—attract a steadily increasing audience of both adult and juvenile readers. Evidence of his appeal is that *The Sound of Coaches*, originally intended for good readers in junior high school and up, became a selection of a major adult book club.

Plot Summary

One dark, stormy night, the stagecoach from Chichester to London, called The Flying Cradle, carries, along with the driver, Mr. Chichester, and his wife, who rides as guard, five passengers—four men and one quiet young woman who clutches a metal box. They stay the night in Dorking at the Red Lion, an inn and tavern operated by Mr. and Mrs. Roggs. After the woman has gone to her room and the men are drinking by the fire, screams of pain come from the woman's room. The bumpy ride has brought on premature labor, and a baby boy is born. The woman dies. She leaves no identification, only the metal box, labeled Arundel, which contains a cheap pewter ring and a pistol with a beautifully carved handle.

Mr. and Mrs. Chichester, who are childless, decide to adopt the child, whom they name Sam. Everyone, including the male passengers and the potboy, Joe, contribute to a collection to help support the child.

As Sam grows up, he spends his time at the Red Lion or riding with his parents on The Flying Cradle. Every birthday, presents arrive from the four passengers.

When he is seven, Sam learns from Joe that the Chichesters are not his real parents. Mr. Chichester tells him the full story and gives the boy his "inheritance," the untouched money collected for his upbringing and the metal box. When Sam sees the pistol, it becomes his talisman. He carries it everywhere, and he often dreams that his real father was a dashing highwayman or perhaps a gentleman of great means.

When Sam is 10, a terrible misfortune occurs. On a London run, the coach is stopped by a man with a pistol, and Mr. Chichester is shot. The man escapes into the woods. Mr. Chichester recovers, but he is completely paralyzed from the waist down. Money is raised by friends to help the invalid and hire a substitute coachman until Sam is old enough to take over. The Chichesters take up permanent residence at the Red Lion.

When he is 16, Sam becomes coachman of The Flying Cradle. But on his first trip, while trying to impress young Caroline Stacey with his abilities, he causes an accident that demolishes the coach. Already embittered by his own misfortune, Mr. Chichester disowns Sam and orders him to leave.

With his savings of over 50 pounds and the metal box, Sam leaves for London. He first visits one of his long-ago benefactors, Dr. Bratsby, but he is too ashamed to tell this kindly gentleman of the problems he has caused. Sam takes lodgings at The Bunch of Grapes and later falls in love with Jenny, a young maidservant there. Together they often visit a tavern in Covent Garden called The Shakespeare's Head, where Sam meets an aging actor, Daniel Coventry, who offers to teach Sam the art of acting for the price of 30 pounds. Sam joins Coventry's traveling acting company. The old charleton is more addicted to booze than the Bard, but Sam grows to love the theatrical life and slowly becomes more than a competent actor.

One night Coventry sees Sam's pistol for the first time. With great excitement, he drags the boy into his room and shows him its twin. The actor had given the pistol to a young woman from Arundel whom he had seduced many years before while acting with a theatrical company in Chichester. Sam realizes with sickening disappointment that his real father is Mr. Coventry. But their relationship changes Coventry, and he begins to drink less and to take a fatherly interest in the boy.

Through a letter from Jenny, Sam learns that his beloved Chichesters miss him terribly and are eager for a reconciliation. Coventry manages to schedule a performance for the acting company at the Red Lion Inn in Dorking. There is a joyful reunion, and Sam excels in the part of Ariel in *The Tempest*.

Coventry seems unaccountably disturbed when he sees crippled Mr. Chichester, but inwardly both men know why. Coventry was the man who shot Chichester on the highway. Not wishing to place Sam in conflict with his real father, Chichester remains silent. There is another happy reunion at the Red Lion when Jenny arrives from London. Sam, now certain of his identity and his profession, looks forward to his next great adventure, marriage.

Thematic Material

This is a headlong adventure story filled with coincidence and an exciting plot theme reminiscent of *Tom Jones*. Readers will find appeal in the boy's search for identity. The author has captured the lusty, bawdy atmosphere of eighteenth-century England, filling the pages with a wonderful cast of heroes and villians, including the resourceful, adventuresome central character, Sam.

Book Talk Material

The story can be introduced by describing the peculiar circumstances of Sam's birth. Some exciting passages are: Sam is adopted and named (pp. 18–22; pp. 20–24, pap.); Joe tells Sam of his true origin (pp. 38–41; pp. 42–44, pap.); Chichester is shot (pp. 88–92; pp. 96–101, pap.); and Sam's accident (pp. 119–122; pp. 132–135, pap.).

Additional Selections

In eighteenth-century Japan, a boy runs away to become an apprentice at a puppet theater in Katherine Paterson's *The Master Puppeteer* (Crowell, 1976, $6.95), and in Julia Cunningham's *Come to the Edge* (Pantheon, 1977, $4.95), a boy runs away from an orphanage after suffering brutal treatment. Another exciting story of menace and suspense by a British writer is John Gordon's *The Ghost on the Hill* (Viking, 1977, $6.95). Hestor Burton's *Kate Ryder* (Crowell, 1975, $6.95) is the story of five years in the life of a gallant girl torn between the Parliamentarians and the Royalists in Britain in the seventeenth century. Also suggested are: Barbara Willards' *Harrow and Harvest* (Dutton, 1975, $7.50); William Mayne's *Ravensgill* (Dutton, 1970, $4.95); and Cynthia Harnett's *The Writing on the Hearth* (Viking, 1973, $6.95).

About the Author

Commire, Anne. *Something about the Author.* Detroit: Gale Research Co., 1971. Vol. 1, pp. 99–100.
Doyle, Brian, Ed., *Who's Who of Children's Literature.* New York: Schocken Books, 1968, pp. 105–106.

Alan Garner, *The Owl Service*
Walck, 1968, $6.50

In this, as in several of his other novels for young adults, Alan Garner has intertwined overtones of fantasy and the supernatural with realism and legend. The rugged Welsh setting, the brooding atmosphere, and the conflict involving three young lives separated by background and temperament remind the reader of Emily Bronte's *Wuthering Heights*. Pervading the novel is a Welsh legend from the valley where the story takes place, in which the wizard Gwydion fashions from flowers a bride,

Blodeuwedd, for Lleu Llan Gyffes. However, the girl falls in love with Gronw Pebyr, who slays Lleu. The wizard restores life to Lleu, who kills Gronw by throwing a spear with such force that it passes through a large rock slab that Gronw has used for protection. As punishment, Blodeuwedd is turned into an owl. It is rumored that the legend is fated to repeat itself in different variations from generation to generation. In England, this novel won the Carnegie Medal in 1967. It is read by select youngsters in the junior and senior high school grades, due to its extensive use of English and Welsh expressions and references. For brevity, the incidents in the last 25 pages have been telescoped in time and sequence.

Plot Summary

By her father's will, Alison has been left a large home in a secluded valley in Wales. Her mother, Margaret, has remarried; her new husband is another wealthy Englishman, Clive Bradley, a divorced man whose only child, Roger, is, like Alison, a teen-ager. The four are spending their summer vacation at their new home, with their housekeeper, Nancy, a Welsh woman who has returned to the valley after several years with her son Gwyn, and Huw Hannerhob, the groundsman and a recluse whose mutterings dwell on the past and on Welsh myths that he feels control the fates of all seven of them.

Confined to her bed with a stomachache, Alison hears scratching from the attic. When Gwyn investigates, he finds only some owl droppings and, neatly stacked on the rafters, a whole dinner service of dishes. He brings one plate to Alison, who sees that under the floral design is the shape of an owl, which she traces on paper. When Nancy hears of Gwyn's discovery, she becomes very agitated, races to Alison's room, and demands the plate. Alison gives it to her, but the design has now mysteriously disappeared. Nancy never speaks to Huw, so she directs Gwyn to tell him to board up the entrance to the attic. Before he does, the three young people rescue the dinner set.

Alison works like someone possessed, tracing the designs on paper and cutting them out into little owllike figures. Not only do the patterns on the dishes disappear, so do the cutouts. Other inexplicable events occur. While swimming, Roger uncovers a large stone with a perfect hole through the middle. He photographs it. After developing the pictures, he sees in the hole, silhouetted against the sky, the figure of a warrior with an upraised spear, mounted on either a horse or a motorbike. Mysteriously, a mortared wall begins to crack in the billiard room. Under the falling plaster is a life-size oil painting of a young girl with a background of flowers and bird claws. Within days, the painting vanishes. Roger and Gwyn discover a padlocked room above the stable and, although it appears impossible to enter, sounds come from it as though something was alive inside. The sound of a motorbike is frequently heard passing back and forth on the road by their house.

The youngsters piece together the legend of Blodeuwedd from Huw's mumblings and from a book of Welsh myths. They begin to believe that the malevolent force has been unleashed in the valley.

Gwyn questions Huw about these strange events. The man claims that it was his grandfather who made the dishes and his uncle the painting, and that now once more the power of the legend has been evoked, with Alison becoming the embodiment of Blodeuwedd. He ends by saying that the girl should have traced the flowers rather than the owls, which are a symbol of evil. Gwyn also learns something of his mother's past. Years before she left the valley, Nancy had worked for and fallen in love with Bertram, the cousin of Alison's father and the previous owner of the house. He was killed on the mountain pass near the house when the brakes failed on his motorbike.

Tensions begin to mount. Sensing tragedy, Nancy tells the Bradleys that she and Gwyn must soon leave. Roger, jealous of Gwyn's attachment to Alison, cruelly reminds him that he is a lower-class servant. Smarting under these insults, Gwyn runs away and spends the night wedged in a tree trunk. He is found by Huw, who directs him to some objects hidden around the roots of the tree. There is an ancient flint spearhead and pieces of rubber, brake blocks from a motorbike. Huw tells the boy that he, Huw, is his father and that years ago, as in the recurring legend, his mother, then Huw's wife, had fallen in love with Bertram. Huw's jealousy drove him to tamper with the brakes and cause the fatal accident. He says that through the centuries everyone tried to hide the power of the legend by attempting to encase it in such objects as the dishes and the painting, but it must be set free so that it can do no further harm.

Meanwhile, Roger and Alison break into the room above the stable. They see a dusty motorbike in one corner and Alison's paper owls that, as indicated by markings on the floor, have dragged themselves into the room. In the middle of the room is a huge glass case containing a stuffed owl. Nancy enters with a poker and wildly smashes the case and the owl. The room is filled with feathers and dust, and Alison faints. Her body becomes covered by falling feathers, and clawlike markings appear on her face and legs. Gwyn and Huw enter, but the boy stands apart, unable to withstand the power that has taken possession of the room. Huw again murmurs that it should be flowers not owls, and Roger suddenly realizes how he can help Alison. He tells her she is flowers, not birds, and that the pattern was flowers instead of owls. Over and over he repeats—flowers, flowers. Suddenly the room is filled with petals. The markings disappear and Alison awakens. She has been saved; the strength of the legend has passed.

Thematic Material

Through fact and fantasy, the author connects past and present in a supernatural novel of mounting suspense and terror. The concept of fate and its power over the destiny of others is well explored in this multilayered novel. The reader is also introduced to the rugged Welsh countryside, its people, and its legends. The cultural differences between the wealthy English visitors and the poor townspeople and servants are sharply delineated.

Book Talk Material

An explanation of the title could be used to introduce the book. Some interesting passages are: Gwyn finds the dishes (pp. 3–6); Roger's discovery of Gronw's stone (pp. 7–8); the painting begins to appear (pp. 28–29); the room in the stable (pp. 56–57); Alison compulsively traces the owl patterns (pp. 81–83); and Roger develops the pictures (pp. 100–103).

Additional Selections

In a freak storm, a young boy is transported to a tenth-century Irish monastery in J. S. Andrews' *The Green Hills of Nendrum* (Hawthorn, o.p.). Another Carnegie Award-winning fantasy concerns the gathering of the Ark's passengers and a gentle hero in Rosemary Harris' *The Moon in the Cloud* (Macmillan, 1970, $5.95). Two boys look for a teacher of magic in thirteenth-century England in Robert Newman's *Merlin's Mistake* (Atheneum, o.p.). A boy can read other people's minds in Peter Dickinson's *The Gift* (Little, 1974, $5.95). Other interesting mystery–fantasies are: David Severn's *The Girl in the Grove* (Harper, 1974, $5.95); C. S. Lewis's Narnia books, such as *The Lion, the Witch and the Wardrobe* (Macmillan, 1951, $5.95; pap., Collier, $1.25; condensed in *Introducing Books*, Bowker, 1970); and Susan Cooper's series, including the Newbery Award winner, *The Gray King* (Atheneum, 1975, $6.95).

About the Author

Jones, Cornelia and Olivia R. Way. *British Children's Authors: Interviews at Home.* Chicago: ALA, 1976, pp. 94–100.

Townsend, John Rowe. *A Sense of Story.* Philadelphia and New York: J. B. Lippincott Co., 1971, pp. 108–119.

Scott O'Dell, *The King's Fifth*

Houghton, 1966, $5.95; pap., Dell (Yearling), $1.50 (same pagination); pap., Dell (Laurel Leaf), $1.50

Among many honors, Scott O'Dell has won the Hans Christian Andersen Medal and, in 1961, the Newbery Award for his first novel for juveniles, *Island of the Blue Dolphins* (Houghton, 1960, $4.95; pap., Dell, 95¢; condensed in *Juniorplots*, Bowker, 1967). *The King's Fifth* is a combination of fact and fiction. In search of the seven cities of Cibola early in 1540, Coronado did lead an expedition to what is now Arizona and New Mexico. Some of his men on a separate trip discovered the Grand Canyon, called the Abyss in the story. The novel, a Newbery Honor book, is suitable for junior and early senior high school students.

Plot Summary

The novel is told through a series of flashbacks—entries in a journal by 17-year-old Estaban de Sandoval, a young mapmaker who is part of the ill-fated expedition to Cibola, the legendary cities of gold, during the years 1540-1541. It is now the fall of 1541 and the young man is awaiting trial before the Royal Audiencia in the prison of San Juan de Ula in Vera Cruz, on charges of defrauding his majesty, Charles V, of the king's fifth, the share due the crown of any gold found in New Spain.

Estaban learned the art of mapmaking in Seville before coming to the New World. As official cartographer, he signs on board the ship, *San Pedro*, with an expedition led by Admiral Alarcon, to head northward from Acapulco and bring supplies to Coronado's army. During the voyage, the boy falls under the spell of a dashing, adventurous army officer, Captain Blas de Mendoza, who seems obsessed with a desire for gold. When the Admiral asks for volunteers to accompany Mendoza on a scouting expedition to locate the army, Estaban agrees, along with Mendoza's three musicians, and Guillerno Torres, keeper of the Captain's horses. Torres is first sent ashore with two horses, and then the other five men are lowered into a longboat. As they pull away from the *San Pedro*, the boy wonders about the wisdom of his action.

They are blown off course by a terrible storm and spend days drifting over the sea with little water and food. Estaban notices that Mendoza secretly takes more than his share, but the boy accepts this because he believes that the leader must retain his strength. Lunes, the guitarist, becomes delirious from thirst and exposure, and he jumps overboard. Eventually, they reach land and are found by a scouting party from

Coronado's army. The party is made up of three soldiers, a priest, and a 13-year-old Indian girl, Zia, who is acting as guide and interpreter. They are taken to Avipa, a large Indian village where they find Torres and are soon joined by Coronado and his army.

As they travel northward, they encounter increasingly hostile natives but no gold. A ferocious battle is fought in Hawikuh, in the land of Cibola. Estaban is badly wounded by a young Cibolan warrior, whom Mendoza kills. While Zia is nursing the boy back to health, Mendoza gains permission from Coronado to leave the main force and lead a small expedition farther north. The group represents many motives: Zia loves adventure and the thrill of the unknown; the priest, Father Francisco, wants to convert new souls; Estaban wants to map new territory; and Mendoza, Roa and Zuniga, the other musicians, and Torres are driven solely by greed and lust for gold. They take four horses, eight mules, and Tigre, a powerful greyhound that Mendoza bought from one of the soldiers.

Twelve days north they come to a great chasm which the Indians call the Abyss. They discover a path down, and in the river below collect some gold nuggets. Estaban secretes one larger than a chestnut—he too is beginning to feel obsessed. Mendoza incurs the wrath of the natives by slaughtering the sheep they hold sacred to use the fleece to catch grains of gold settling from the river. Zuniga, trying to collect the last remnants of gold, dies in a fire Mendoza set to aid their escape. The party heads farther north, but one night Torres deserts on horseback, taking all the gold they collected.

Two weeks later the party arrives at Tawhi, or Cloud City, a town inhabited by cliff dwellers. It is a village of mud huts with a small artificial lake. There they find their treasure: through the centuries, as part of a religious ceremony, the natives have covered their chieftain's body with gold dust before he entered the lake. The lake bottom now glistens, thick with the gold. Unknown to Zia and the priest, but with Estaban as an unwilling accomplice, Mendoza and Roa weaken the dike surrounding the lake so that it crumbles, draining the lake and flooding the village. After the mules are loaded with sacks of gold, the party quickly leaves.

Mendoza sends Roa ahead to get reinforcements from Hawikuh, but Estaban wonders if the leader is not merely trying to get rid of Roa to increase his own share of the gold. One night at campfire, Tigre is overly playful. Mendoza hurls a rock at him. The dog tears out Mendoza's throat. The rest of them bury the captain. Father Francisco and Zia beg Estaban to leave the gold behind, but Estaban refuses. Zia realizes that Estaban is enslaved by the same gold sickness as the other Spaniards, and she asks permission to return home by herself. Estaban gives her a horse, although this is forbidden by Spanish law, and she departs.

While crossing a vast desert known as the Inferno, Father Francisco dies of exposure. Now alone, Estaban at last becomes aware of the terrible toll in human lives and honor that the gold represents. He throws the sacks into one of the hot springs where they will never be recovered, and begins his homeward journey.

Through Roa, news precedes him of the gold they found, and now Estaban is in jail facing the charge of withholding the king's share. Despite the urging of Pablo Gamboa, his lawyer, the boy pleads guilty, but more serious charges await him. Torres takes the stand and, to save himself, testifies that he deserted the party only because Estaban often quarreled with Mendoza and threatened his leader's life.

A charge of murder is made against Estaban, and then Zia appears. She tells the truth concerning Mendoza's death, but Estaban is convicted on the first charge and sentenced to three years in prison. The commander of the fortress promises the boy his freedom in exchange for leading another expedition north. But Estaban, sickened by the quest for gold, refuses—he has many maps to draw and, besides, Zia has promised to wait for him.

Thematic Material

The book shows the changes that greed and avarice can produce in people's lives when they are willing to sacrifice their honor and their souls to possess wealth. Estaban's struggle to retain, and later regain, his self-respect and a sense of values is a powerful theme. The story of the expedition alternating with Estaban's trial adds additional depth and suspense to the story. The author brilliantly re-creates the ruthless age of the Conquistadores and the lives of their hapless victims, the Indians of the Southwest.

Book Talk Material

Transparencies of the excellent introductory maps (unfortunately missing in the Laurel Leaf edition) could be used to introduce a group to Estaban's journeys. Some important passages are: Estaban and his lawyer (pp. 36–37; pp. 39–41, pap.); Estaban joins Mendoza's party (pp. 17–19; pp. 20–22, pap.); hardship on the longboat and Lunes' death (pp. 28–32; pp. 30–35, pap.); Estaban meets Zia (pp. 48–51; pp. 48–52, pap.); his fight with a young Cibolan (pp. 89–93; pp. 85–89, pap.); and Mendoza's party leaves Hawikuh (pp. 99–100; pp. 94–95, pap.).

Additional Selections

There is both a recording and sound filmstrip based on this book available from Miller-Brody Productions. Scott O'Dell's *Zia* (Houghton, 1976, $7.95) is about the niece of Karana, the heroine of *Island of the Blue Dolphins* (not the heroine of *The King's Fifth*) and tells about California mission life. Also use the author's *Sing Down the Moon* (Houghton, 1970, $3.95; pap., Dell, $1.25) and *The Black Pearl* (Houghton, 1967, $5.95; pap., Dell, 95¢). Some poems of Ancient Mexico are reprinted in Toni de Gerez' *2-Rabbit, 7-Wind* (Viking, 1971, $4.95). Two other fine novels of the Spanish exploration of the Southwest during the sixteenth century are: Betty Baker's *Walk the World's Rim* (Harper, 1965, $4.95; pap., $1.25; condensed in *Introducing Books*, Bowker, 1970), and Helen Parish's *Este'banico* (Viking, 1974, $5.95). For nonfiction background, use Harold Coy's *The Mexicans* (Little, 1970, $5.95) and Irwin Blacker's *Cortez and the Aztec Conquest* (American Heritage, 1965, $5.95).

About the Author

Fadool, Cynthia R., Ed. *Contemporary Authors*. Detroit: Gale Research Co., 1976. Vol. 61, p. 402.

Fuller, Muriel, Ed. *More Junior Authors*. New York: H. W. Wilson Co., 1963, pp. 161–162.

Hoffman, Miriam and Eva Samuels. *Authors and Illustrators of Children's Books: Writings on Their Lives and Works*. New York: R. R. Bowker Co., 1972, pp. 343–347.

Hollowell, Lillian, Ed. *A Book of Children's Literature*. (3rd Edition). New York: Holt, Rinehart & Winston, 1966, p. 562.

Johnson, Edna et al. *Anthology of Children's Literature*. (4th Edition). Boston: Houghton Mifflin Co., 1970, p. 1252.

Townsend, John Rowe. *A Sense of Story*. Philadelphia and New York: J. B. Lippincott Co., 1971, pp. 154–161.

Ward, Martha E. and Dorothy Marquardt. *Authors of Books for Young People*. New York: Scarecrow Press, Inc., 1964, p. 184.

Who's Who in America (39th Edition). Chicago: Marquis Who's Who, Inc., 1976. Vol. 2, p. 359.

Johanna Reiss, *The Upstairs Room*

Crowell, 1972, $4.50; lge. type ed., G. K. Hall, $7.95; pap., Bantam, 95¢

A few years ago, Johanna Reiss set out to record for her two children her experiences as a Dutch Jew during the German occupation of Holland in World War II. Fortunately the manuscript was published. It is simple, moving, and, the subject matter notwithstanding, a gentle document in which the author has amazingly recaptured the past with the candor and ingenuousness of the young girl she was when these events occurred. In a continuation, *The Journey Back* (Crowell, 1976, $6.95), Mrs. Reiss tells of the first year following peace in Europe and how the deLeeuw family— father and three daughters—try to bring their broken lives together and how the young heroines adjust to a new stepmother and their continued dependence on the Oostervelds. *The Upstairs Room* has received many honors, including an international peace prize, the Buxtehuder Bulle, given by the German people. It is read by youngsters in upper elementary through senior high school grades.

Plot Summary

The story opens in 1938 when the narrator, Annie deLeeuw, then six years old; her father, a prosperous cattle dealer; her·mother and two sisters are living in the town of Winterswijk in Holland close to the German border. Annie's sisters are 21-year-old Rachel, who is about to receive her teaching certificate, and 16-year-old Sini, who is still at school studying farming. News of Hitler's persecution of the Jews and his expansion into East Europe make them all uneasy for the future. Their Uncle Bram and his wife leave for America, but Mrs. deLeeuw, who is frequently ill, cannot be persuaded to leave. After the German invasion, the regulations against Jews, which are posted with other public announcements on a big tree in the marketplace, become more harsh and restricting. Mr. deLeeuw is not allowed to transact business, Rachel loses her teaching job, Annie and Sini are barred from school, and they must wear a Star of David sewed on their clothes to identify themselves as Jews. Their father tries unsuccessfully to get across the Swiss border, while at home the Germans accelerate their roundup of Jews for deportation to concentration camps.

Early in October 1942, the deLeeuws receive a letter stating that they must go to a work camp. Even though Mrs. deLeeuw is seriously ill in the hospital, the father realizes that the rest of the family must go into hiding.

Through a minister, the Reverend Zwaal and a frail old schoolteacher, Miss Kleinhoonte, plans are made to hide Sini and Annie with the Hannink family in Usselo. Rachel and Mr. deLeeuw will find hiding places elsewhere. To get to the Hannink's, Annie has to disguise herself as a boy and ride a public bus. When soldiers enter and she might have to open her suitcase full of girl's clothes for inspection, she has the presence of mind to say that she is taking some clothes to her aunt.

They stay two months at the Hanninks in an upstairs room, but when it appears that the Germans might be preparing to search the house, Mr.

Hannink has the girls moved to the home of a poor farmer and day laborer, Johan Oosterveld. They arrive on New Year's Eve for a stay that is originally to be only two weeks, but that eventually lasts over two years.

There are three in the Oosterveld family—solid and understanding Johan, his wife Dientje, and Opoe, or Granny, Johan's mother. They are plain, humble people and so is their way of living, but Annie and Sini fit in very well and soon grow to love their new hosts. The girls spend their days upstairs in Johan and Dientje's bedroom and at night Annie sleeps in their bed while Sini sleeps on the floor on a mattress.

Fearful that one day the house will be searched by the Germans, Johan constructs a tiny hiding place just big enough for the girls to sit down in behind the bedroom clothes closet. He is proud of his handiwork, and when it is completed he remarks, as he often does about his own actions, "Not bad for a dumb farmer, eh?"

Gradually, bits of news are received from the outside. Mrs. deLeeuw has died in the hospital. Their father is in hiding near Rotterdam with a retired bookkeeper, Mr. Hemmes and his wife, and sister Rachel is with a minister, the Reverend Slomp. Their other relatives, including their grandmother, have been sent to concentration camps. They get news of the war's progress through Dutch programs beamed from England and received on Johan's illegally owned radio.

In such close confinement, tempers sometimes flare, and, therefore, there are disagreements and some arguments. As well, the oppressive monotony often becomes unbearable. The slightest diversion makes for a red-letter day. For example, on Opoe's birthday, the girls are allowed downstairs for the evening meal. Dientje borrows a copy of *War and Peace* from the minister for the girls to read, and on her birthday, Annie is delighted to receive a Monopoly set. These distractions help, as do visits from Miss Kleinhoonte and the Reverend Slomp.

One night Dientje takes Annie on her bicycle to visit with some Jews, including a girl her age named Mimi, who are hiding in a farmer's barn. On another occasion Sini persuades Johan to let Annie and herself spend a day lying in the sun in the wheat field. The girls become so sunburned that they must risk sending for a doctor.

There is a constant fear of searches, and one night comes the inevitable pounding on the door. The girls hide in time, and the German soldiers finally leave, but not before stealing one of Johan's pigs.

News reaches the Oostervelds that there is an informer in town telling the Germans of the whereabouts of hidden Jews. Mimi and her family are exposed and shipped off with their protectors to the camps. Johan is given the assignment of killing the traitor. He does, but the Germans take reprisal by shooting several of the townspeople.

As the war slowly reaches a close, there are other incidents: Rachel, now almost a stranger to them, spends a day with her sisters. For a time the Germans use part of the farmhouse as an office, and only Johan's quick story about a visiting niece saves Annie when she accidentally bumps into one of the soldiers.

Finally, in April 1945, almost two-and-one-half years after the girls arrive at the Oostervelds, the Germans leave and the Canadians enter. All the townspeople turn out to greet their liberators. Many wonder who the two girls are with Johan and his family. He will have some tall stories to tell in the future. "Not bad for a dumb farmer, eh?"

Thematic Material

The Upstairs Room reflects a shameful period in history that is often confined only to history books. It is also a period when many gallant and noble deeds were being performed by simple, unassuming working people like the Oostervelds. The book reveals what war is really about—not massive battles and maneuvers, but the uprooting of individual lives and the ever-present sense of tragedy and waste. Amazingly, this story is told without rancor or bitterness, and the ending is a hopeful one.

Book Talk Material

Some incidents in the book that will arouse interest are: life under the Germans (pp. 11-14; pp. 10-12, pap.); Mr. deLeeuw's try for escape (pp. 17-21, pp. 15-18, pap.); Annie's trip to the Hannink's by bus (pp. 41-44; pp. 35-38, pap.); the girls leave the Hanninks (pp. 54-59; pp. 46-51, pap.); and the search (pp. 148-150; pp. 125-127, pap.). Miller–Brody's recording of *The Upstairs Room* is NAR 3067 (disc, $6.95; cassette, $7.95); with accompanying filmstrip the order number is NSF 3067 and is priced at $32.

Additional Selections

The most popular and perhaps most tragic story of Jews in hiding during World War II is Anne Frank's *Diary of a Young Girl* (Doubleday, 1967, $7.95; pap., Washington Square, $1.50). In *A Pocket Full of Seeds* (Doubleday, 1973, $4.95) by Marilyn Sacks, a Jewish family, the Niemans, living in occupied France, do not realize their danger until it is too late. Yuri Suhl's *Uncle Misha's Partisans* (Four Winds, 1973, $5.95) tells of a group of fighters organized by Misha and dedicated to fighting against their German oppressors. The author's *On the Other Side of the Gate* (Watts, 1975, $5.90) deals with a young couple trapped in a Polish ghetto.

Also recommended are Joseph Zieman's *The Cigarette Sellers of Three Crosses Square* (Lerner, 1975, $6.95); Milton Meltzer's nonfiction *Never to Forget: The Jews of the Holocaust* (Harper, 1976, $6.95); and, for an older audience, the harrowing *I Am Rosemarie* (pap., Scholastic, $1.25) by Marietta Muskin.

Elizabeth Speare, *The Bronze Bow*
Houghton, 1961, $5.95; pap., $1.45 (same pagination)

Elizabeth Speare has a winning record in the field of children's literature. Her *Calico Captive* (Houghton, 1957, $4.95; pap., Dell, $1.25; condensed in *Juniorplots*, Bowker, 1967) was a notable children's book of 1957, and her next two, *The Witch of Blackbird Pond* (Houghton, 1958, $4.95; pap., Dell, $1.25; condensed in *Introducing Books*, Bowker, 1970) and *The Bronze Bow*, each won Newbery Awards, the latter in 1962. *The Bronze Bow* is suited to youngsters in grades seven through ten.

Plot Summary

Daniel bar Jamin is an 18-year-old Galilean who, for the past five years, has lived in hiding in the mountain stronghold of a gang of outlaws led by Rosh. He spent the first years of his life in the village of Ketzeh, a few miles from the city of Capernaum. When Daniel was only eight, his father was crucified by the Romans and his mother, unable to cope with this great loss, died of grief. The boy was later sold into slavery as an apprentice to the cruel blacksmith, Amalek. Unable to stand the harsh treatment from this sadistic master, he escaped, leaving behind his grandmother and pathetically withdrawn sister, Leah. Since then he has lived in hiding with Rosh and his gang, who are dedicated to the harassment and destruction of the Romans and their friends and who plan for the day when all of Israel will rise and rid itself of its hated conquerors.

One day while on a scouting expedition, Daniel sees two young acquaintances from his village hiking up the mountain. They are Joel bar Hezron, the studious son of the town scribe, and his twin sister, Malthrose, nicknamed Thracia. Daniel is overcome with curiosity of news from Ketzeh, and so he questions the pair about his family and the fate of his friend Simon, called Simon the Zealot, who although six years older than Daniel, was also apprenticed to Amalak at the same time as Daniel. Joel and Thracia know little about Daniel's grandmother and sister, but they tell him that Simon now has his own shop and is prospering.

A caravan from Damascus is passing through the valley and while the two intruders hide in the rocks, Rosh, Daniel, and the others raid it and free a slave to join them. He is a black colossus of a man, who seems unable to speak or hear. The gang nicknames him Samson. Joel meets Rosh and immediately wants to join the cause, but Rosh dissuades him, particularly when he learns that Joel and his family are soon moving to Capernaum. A contact there might be very useful.

In time Samson becomes attached to Daniel and, with his mighty strength, operates the bellows at the forge. Having heard through Joel about Daniel, Simon visits the camp and tells Daniel that because Amalek has just died, the boy is now free to visit his family in the village. He does so and is shocked at their poverty and Leah's complete seclusion. With Simon, he visits the synagogue and hears a sermon from a gentle, kindly preacher named Jesus.

Rosh orders Daniel to Capernaum to make contact with Joel, but Joel's father fears that he will lose his son to a gang of reckless extremists, and he orders him out of the house. Leaving town, Daniel becomes forgetful of his own safety and allows his temper and fierce hatred of the Romans to overcome natural caution and common sense—he insults a Roman soldier. He manages to escape, but with a gaping spear wound in his side. He crawls back to Joel's house and Thracia hides him in a basement storage room. Brother and sister secretly minister to Daniel and heal his wound. They read scriptures together and are particularly impressed with the Song of David, which reads:

> —God is my strong refuge . . .
> He trains my hands for war
> So that my arms can bend a bow of bronze.

By the sign of the bronze bow, the three swear dedication to freeing Israel from its oppressors.

Daniel is scarcely back to the mountain retreat when he is once more sent on a mission to Capernaum, this time to secure a rivet to repair Rosh's favorite talisman, a dagger. In a small town near Capernaum, Daniel and Joel see Simon, who has closed his blacksmith shop to become a disciple of Jesus. The boys listen in wonder to Jesus' teachings and watch him perform healing acts that some call miracles.

Daniel's grandmother dies. To take care of Leah, he regretfully leaves Rosh and his friends and accepts Simon's offer to take over his shop at home and become the town blacksmith. But he has lost none of his hate for the Romans. When a young Roman soldier begins bringing work to his shop and one day happens to gaze fondly at Leah, Daniel, ignoring possible consequences, orders him off his property.

Daniel begins to organize some of the young boys in town as a force to work against the Romans. They meet frequently and, whenever possible, Joel travels from Capernaum to join them. They use as their password the Bronze Bow. However, Daniel begins to wonder if violence is the only solution. He begins making more and more journeys to Bathsaida to hear Jesus speak.

Soon Joel is given his own assignment from Rosh. He is to find out the names of the wealthy men of Capernaum who will be attending a large banquet for the Romans so that Rosh and his men can rob their houses while they are away. Joel does so by disguising himself as a fish peddler and picking up information as he travels from kitchen to kitchen. The robbery is a success, but in the following investigation, Joel is arrested and sentenced to deportation.

Rosh reveals his true harshness and severity when he ignores Daniel's pleadings to help rescue Joel. The young boys under Daniel, therefore, decide they must be Joel's rescuers.

Knowing that Joel and the other prisoners will be led by their captors through a mountain gorge, the boys plan to hide in the hills and divert the soldiers by throwing stones while Daniel frees Joel. At the site, the boys find they are hopelessly outnumbered, but the unexpected appearance of Samson and his mammoth rock-throwing ability carry the plan to success. Joel is saved but not without casualties; one of the boys is killed, Samson is mortally wounded, and Daniel is severely injured.

Leah accidentally reveals that during Daniel's frequent absences, she has been having secret conversations with Marcus, the soldier whom Daniel ordered from his property. Daniel flies into a rage and so upbraids his sister that once again she becomes withdrawn. Soon she becomes ill with a fever, and Daniel is afraid she will die. Marcus comes to see Daniel. He says he is not a Roman but a native of Gallia who has been pressed into service. He is soon to be transferred to Corinth, and he begs to see Leah one last time. Daniel threatens to kill him if he sets foot in the house.

When Leah's death seems certain, Daniel thinks of Jesus. The young man sends a message to Simon telling him of Leah's condition. After three days of waiting, Jesus appears at Daniel's house. He enters and gazes at Leah. She opens her eyes and appears well once more. After Jesus leaves, Daniel again sees Marcus waiting. This time he invites him into his home to say farewell to Leah. Perhaps it is only love that has the strength to bend the bow of bronze.

Thematic Material

Two divergent methods of achieving goals are presented and contrasted in this book—the way of Rosh, by force and violence, and the way of Jesus, by acceptance and love. In many of today's causes, these same opposing methods are advocated. Daniel's conversion from one to the other is convincingly handled. The bonds of friendship, family responsibility, and loyalty to a cause are well depicted. Mrs. Speare re-creates the Holy Land of Biblical times with authenticity and color.

Book Talk Material

Some interesting excerpts are: the capture of Samson (pp. 17–20); Daniel's first encounter with Jesus (pp. 45–49); Daniel's temper gets him into trouble (pp. 69–72); he tells his family's tragic story (pp. 80–83); and he waylays a wealthy merchant (pp. 106–110). There is also a Miller–Brody recording of *The Bronze Bow* on NAR 3029 (disc, $6.95; cassette, $7.95).

Additional Selections

For students interested in the history of the Near East and archaeology, see Ronald Harker's *Digging Up the Bible Lands* (Walck, 1973, $8.95) or Marjorie Braymer's life of Heinrich Schliemann, *The Walls of Windy Troy* (pap., Voyager, $1.45). Also use A. L. Sachar's *History of the Jews* (Knopf, 1964, $10; pap., $7.95). Two fine historical novels are Martha Bacon's *In the Company of Clowns* (Little, 1973, $5.95), about an orphan in eighteenth-century Italy and Mollie Hunter's *The Spanish Letters*, in which Jaime, a Scottish guide, helps an English spy in the time of King James. Also use Harry Behn's novel of an ill-fated love set in Bronze Age Denmark, *The Faraway Lurs* (Collins+World, 1963, $4.95; pap., Avon, 60¢; condensed in *Juniorplots*, Bowker, 1967) and Eric Kelly's 1929 Newbery Award winner, *The Trumpeter of Krakow* (Macmillan, 1966, $6.95; pap., 95¢).

About the Author

Commire, Anne. *Something about the Author.* Detroit: Gale Research Co., 1973. Vol. 5, pp. 176–179.

Ethridge, James M. and Barbara Kopala, Eds. *Contemporary Authors.* Detroit: Gale Research Co., 1967. Vol. 1, p. 890.

Hopkins, Lee Bennett. *More Books by More People.* New York: Citation Press, 1974, pp. 330–335.

Ward, Martha E. and Dorothy A. Marquardt. *Authors of Books for Young People.* (2nd Edition). Metuchen, N. J.: Scarecrow Press, Inc., p. 482.

Who's Who in America (35th, 37th, 38th and 39th Editions). Chicago: Marquis Who's Who, Inc., 1968, p. 2063; 1972, p. 2994; 1974, p. 2912; 1976, p. 2968.

5

Understanding Physical and Emotional Problems

Dᴜʀɪɴɢ ᴀᴅᴏʟᴇsᴄᴇɴᴄᴇ, youngsters become more aware not only of their bodies but also of their emotional makeup. It is a period of preoccupation with physical considerations and with a desire to understand their own feelings as well as those of others. Various facets of both these topics are explored in the selections used in this section.

Beverly Butler, *Gift of Gold*
    Dodd, 1972, $4.25; pap., Archway, $1.25

This sequel to an earlier novel by Beverly Butler, *Light a Single Candle* (Dodd, 1962, $5.25; pap., Archway, 75¢; condensed in *Juniorplots*, Bowker, 1967) is the story of Kathy Wheeler, a high school student, and her painful adjustment to blindness caused by glaucoma. Kathy is now beginning her junior year at a girls' school in her hometown, St. Chrysostom College, where she is studying to be a speech therapist. Although she now has a new circle of friends, some of her old acquaintances reappear in this book. In both these books, the author has drawn from her own experiences as a blind person. These novels are popular with girls from the sixth through ninth grades.

Plot Summary

Dr. Jacqueline Paulus has just been appointed chairman of the speech therapy department. Kathy and her close student friend, Amy Rinehardt, wonder how she can ever replace kindly Sister Bernard, who had been an inspiration to all of them. Kathy soon finds out when Dr. Paulus visits her during her first day in clinic with her two young charges, four-year-old

Roddy and five-year-old Craig Fenger. Although the session is something of a shambles, Kathy does not expect the severity of the chairman's devastating appraisal afterward. She questions Kathy's motives for entering speech therapy and suggests that she might be better suited to working in another profession with her own kind—the blind. She also tells Kathy that Mrs. Fenger refuses to have Craig taught by someone who is blind. He is to be replaced, therefore, by five-year-old Lenny Perkins, a mentally retarded boy who has never said a word.

Unhappily Kathy leaves school with her guide dog Trudy. On the way home she is offered a ride by Amy and her boyfriend, Larry Tobin. Also in the car is Larry's friend, Greg Breck, who seems charming to Kathy if just a bit overconfident. They stop at a coffee shop where Kathy meets her former school friend, Joan Norton, who tells her that she is engaged to another old friend, Pete Sheridan. Kathy accepts Joan's invitation to be a bridesmaid.

As the semester progresses, Kathy still seems unable to please the overly critical Dr. Paulus, even though she has made good progress with Roddy and has won the confidence of the frail, waiflike Lenny. She gains some comfort from the mutual dislike the other students feel toward the new department head and from the constant, if somewhat embarrassing, attention from Greg Breck. Most important, Dr. Rosenthal, the young assistant to Kathy's regular opthalmologist, Dr. Kruger, casually remarks during a routine visit that there is hope that part of her sight may be restored. With the joyous thought that she might not remain totally blind, Kathy and her family, her parents and brother Mark, begin counting the days until her next appointment during the Thanksgiving holidays.

Without enthusiasm, Kathy enters into the preparations for Joan's wedding because she realizes that Joan is too immature and headstrong to accept the responsibilities of marriage. The wedding rehearsal is a fiasco, but once again Kathy meets another old friend, Steve Hubert, who has returned home from college to be an usher.

Kathy senses that Greg is becoming overly demanding and possessive, yet she is sorry to refuse his invitation to go to Los Angeles with him for a job interview over Thanksgiving because she must go to her doctor's appointment. At school, Roddy's speech continues to improve and, best of all, Kathy and the Perkins are overjoyed when Lenny utters his first few words. But the triumph is short-lived when he becomes ill and has to leave the program.

In spite of Kathy's progress, Dr. Paulus seems unimpressed, and her stern, unyielding attitude has also demoralized the rest of the students. The girls sign a petition to remove Dr. Paulus. Kathy does not want her signature to be interpreted as a need for special favors, and so she does not sign.

Thanksgiving brings two crushing disappointments. Dr. Kruger tells Kathy that there is actually no change in her eye condition, and later that same day she learns that Lenny Perkins has died. Steve drives her to the funeral home. Afterwards he takes her for a walk in the park where he puts his arms around her and gently kisses her.

Greg accepts the job in Los Angeles, and the rebellion at school subsides when the college authorities take no action against Dr. Paulus and the students learn that Sister Bernard, whom they wanted to return, has suffered a series of strokes and is bedridden. Kathy is called to Dr. Paulus' office, where the chairman admits mistakes as a new administrator and gives Kathy a gift from the Perkins family, a tiny golden apple.

As Kathy thinks of the events of the past semester, including her growing love for Steve, she thinks that in their own way all of these happenings, even her dashed hopes for restored sight, have been gifts of gold because each has helped her to accept herself and become more self-reliant.

Thematic Material

Kathy's growing self-awareness and maturity, although gained through painful experience, is a major theme. Her adjustment to blindness, and the often blundering, sometimes improper adjustments of her friends, are well depicted. Perhaps because of her own experiences, the author has a great ability to make the reader experience the story through Kathy's sightless eyes. Kathy's courage and lack of self-pity, as well as the interesting details of speech therapy, add additional dimensions to the novel.

Book Talk Material

Both *Light a Single Candle* and *Gift of Gold* could be introduced by a description of Kathy's problems. Specific passages of interest are: Kathy's first conversation with Dr. Paulus (pp. 17–23; pp. 15–21, pap.); Kathy's work with Roddy and Lenny (pp. 53–57; pp. 50–53, pap.); and her appointment with Dr. Rosenthal (pp. 97–101; pp. 91–94, pap.).

Additional Selections

Robin befriends a blind girl and encounters mystery and adventure in Phyllis Whitney's *Secret of the Emerald Star* (pap., Tempo, 95¢). A novel about blindness for younger readers is James B. Garfield's *Follow My Leader* (Viking, 1957, $5.95; pap., Scholastic, 95¢). Rose Resnick's inspiring autobiography, *Sun and Shadow* (Atheneum, 1975, $10), is the story of a blind woman who fights continuous discrimination by founding the first recreation facilities and camps for blind children. Some other excellent autobiographies are Harold Krents' *To Race the Wind* (Putnam, 1972, $6.95), the inspiration for the play and movie, *Butterflies Are Free*; Tom Sullivan's *If You Could See What I Hear* (Harper, 1975, $8.95; pap., New Amer. Lib., $1.50); Robert W. Russell's *To Catch an Angel* (Vanguard, 1962, $7.50); and Borghild Dahl's *I Wanted to See* (Macmillan, 1944, $4.95). Dickson Hartwell has written interestingly about guide dogs in *Dogs against Darkness* (Dodd, 1968, o.p.).

About the Author

Commire, Anne. *Something about the Author.* Detroit: Gale Research Co., 1975. Vol. 7, p. 37.

Ethridge, James and Barbara Kopala, Eds. *Contemporary Authors.* Detroit: Gale Research Co., 1962. Vol. 1, p. 142.

Ward, Martha E. and Dorothy A. Marquardt. *Authors of Books for Young People.* New York: Scarecrow Press, Inc., 1964, p..39.

Betsy Byars, *The Summer of the Swans*

Viking, 1970, $4.95; pap., Camelot Books (Avon), 95¢ (same pagination)

The refreshingly candid and unassuming speech by Betsy Byars when receiving the 1970 Newbery Medal for this book (reprinted in *Horn Book*, April 1971) is a reflection of the simplicity and honesty of her writing. This novel is also memorable because, despite the grimness of the situation, her humor and sensitivity help to lighten the subject and add a feeling of tenderness and hope. The book is popular with both upper elementary and junior high school students.

Plot Summary

For 14-year-old Sara Godfrey, this is truly the summer of her discontent. Although she tells her 19-year-old sister, Wanda, that she is neither popular nor pretty—"I'm not anything" (p. 49)—her unhappiness stems from more than growing pains. Sara's life is marred by tragedy. Her 10-year-old brother, Charlie, suffered a severe illness that left him mentally retarded and speechless. Sara's mother died, and her father, once a smiling, attractive person, has retreated into a shell of remoteness and indifference. He now lives several hours away from the small West Virginia town where the children are being raised by Aunt Willie (short for Wilhelmina).

Sara's "nothing" summer consists mainly of visiting her friend, Mary Weicek, watching television, and taking care of Charlie. She has developed a lovely relationship with her brother. Mindful of his needs and protective of him with outsiders, she neither pampers him nor is condescending.

However, she is so incensed that Joe Melby, her schoolmate, has taken Charlie's prized possession, a loud-ticking wristwatch, that even though he returned it, Sara not only refuses to speak to him, but tries to turn others against him.

A minor diversion breaks the monotony of the summer—six swans are sighted on a wooded lake within easy walking distance of Sara's home, and she decides to take Charlie to see them. They feed the swans, and Charlie becomes so enchanted by the birds that Sara actually has to drag him away when it is time to go home.

Charlie is unable to sleep that night because he remembers the swans and wants to see them again. Dressed in pajamas and slippers, he leaves the house and wanders into the woods looking for the lake. He is chased by dogs and becomes hopelessly lost.

In the morning, the family discovers that Charlie is missing. Sara runs to the lake, but Charlie isn't there. A distraught Aunt Willie calls the police, who organize a search party. She also calls Sara's father, who promises to drive down that night if Charlie is not found. Sara thinks he should come immediately, but Willie defends his actions.

Sara decides to search for Charlie in the woods. On the way to pick up Mary, she meets Joe Melby, who volunteers to help. But Sara cannot hide her continued anger and once again accuses him of stealing Charlie's wristwatch.

When Sara tells Mary about meeting Joe, she learns that Joe did not steal the watch. Some boys thought it would be amusing to tease Charlie by hiding his watch. Then they were too embarrassed to return it. Joe learned about the trick, found the watch, and returned it himself. Sara is ashamed of the way she has treated him.

Searching in the woods, Sara and Mary meet Joe. In spite of Sara's anger, he has joined the search team. He has just found a slipper, which Sara recognizes as Charlie's. While they search on, Sara apologizes to Joe.

As they scour the woods, they shout Charlie's name. This awakens Charlie, who has fallen asleep in the woods. There is a joyful reunion, and as the search party returns to town, the swans are seen in the sky. They are leaving the lake and going home.

Joe invites Sara to a party that night. After this dreadful ordeal, could things be getting better?

Thematic Material

One of the most interesting themes developed in the novel is the family's wonderful attitude toward Charlie, an open and complete acceptance based on love, not pity. Other important themes are Sara coping with adolescence; her adjustment to what is really a foster home; the acceptance of personal tragedy and loneliness; and her developing sense of responsibility toward Charlie.

Book Talk Material

The phonograph record that dramatizes the book could be used to introduce it (Newbery Award Record—S-VRD-106). Some incidents in the book that also could be used are: Charlie's first appearance in the novel and the moment when the reader begins to realize his problem (pp. 13-19); getting Charlie to visit the swans (p. 30); the visit (pp. 40-45); and Charlie wanders away (pp. 58-60). Some indications of Sara's problems are given in a monologue with her brother (pp. 31-32) and a conversation with her sister (pp. 47-50). Ted McConis' excellent illustrations also could be used, such as the drawing of Charlie on page 36.

Additional Suggestions

Betsy Byars has written many other fine novels for youngsters. Other novels dealing with the mentally retarded are: Vera and Bill Cleaver's *Me, Too* (Lippincott, 1973, $6.95; pap., New Amer. Lib., $1.25) in which there are two sisters: Lydia, who is bright and interesting, and Lorna, who is thought to be retarded; Caroline Crane's *A Girl Like Tracy* (McKay, 1966, $4.25) about Kathy's sister, who is beautiful, spoiled, and retarded; and Babbis Friis-Baastad's *Don't Take Teddy* (Scribner, 1967, $3.95; pap., Archway, 75¢; condensed in *Introducing Books*, Bowker, 1970). Kin Platt's *Hey Dummy* (Chilton, 1971, $4.95; pap., Dell, 95¢) tells how Neil Comstock meets and tries to protect 12-year-old Alan Harper, a severely brain-damaged child. Pamala Walker's *Twyla* (Prentice-Hall, 1973, $4.95) consists of letters from a retarded girl in love. For younger readers: Matt Christopher's *Long Shot for Paul* (Little, 1966, $4.50; pap., Archway, 75¢), about a boy's efforts to make a basketball player of his mentally retarded brother. In Frank Bonham's delightful *Mystery of the Fat Cat* (Dutton, 1968, $6.95; pap., Dell, $1.25), an incident involves a retarded child.

About the Author

"Betsy Byars," *Horn Book* (September 1971), pp. 359-362.

Commire, Anne. *Something about the Author*. Detroit: Gale Research Co., 1973. Vol. 5, pp. 185-186.

DeMontreville, Doris and Donna Hill, Eds. *Third Book of Junior Authors*. New York: H. W. Wilson Co., 1972, p. 55.

Hopkins, Lee Bennett. *More Books by More People*. New York: Citation Press, 1974, pp. 68-73.

Kinsman, Clare D. and Mary Ann Tennenhouse, Eds. *Contemporary Authors.* Detroit: Gale Research Co., 1973. Vols. 33–36, p. 177.
Ward, Martha E. and Dorothy A. Marquardt. *Authors of Books for Young People.* (2nd Edition, 1971, p. 80; First Supplement, 1967, pp. 45–46). Metuchen, N.J.: Scarecrow Press, Inc.

Mollie Hunter, *The Stronghold*

Harper, 1974, $5.95; lib. bdg., $6.89; pap., Avon, $1.25

Mollie Hunter's novels have won high praise from critics. They also have won awards, among them the Carnegie Medal in Britain (for *The Stronghold* in 1974) and the Child Study Association Annual Award in the United States. Although she often uses her native Scotland as the locale in her novels, *The Stronghold* is unique in its time period—the reign of Julius Caesar (49–44 B.C.)—and setting—the rocky Orkney Islands, directly north of mainland Scotland. The inspiration for the novel came from the author's visit to the ruins of some 500 ancient stone fortresses, or "brochs," which dot the coastline of the Orkneys and northern Scotland. She began to speculate on the genius of the architect who first designed this unique defense against marauding Romans. The novel is intended for junior high school students.

Plot Summary

When Coll was five years old, he was painfully crippled in one leg while trying to escape a Roman slave-gathering raid on his coastal village. His father was killed in the raid and his mother taken captive, but his younger brother, Bran, was saved. As a gesture to placate the gods, Bran was given to the high priest, Domnall, to be reared in the College of the Druids. Since that time, 13 years ago, Coll has been raised by the tribe's leader, Nectan, chief of the People of the Boar, his wife Anu, and two daughters, strong-willed Clodha and younger Fand, Coll's age. Clodha hopes her father will gain permission from his Council of Warriors for her to marry Coll's friend, Niall, who would then be in line to succeed Nectan as chief. Although Coll loves Fand, he is aware that he would not be granted permission to marry because he is a cripple among men whose greatest admiration is for feats of physical strength.

The tribe is divided by serious disagreement between the Druid, Domnall, and Nectan concerning future strategy against the Roman annual slaving expedition. Domnall wishes to continue hand-to-hand combat, but Nectan knows that his tactic is bringing gradual death to his tribe. Instead, Nectan wishes to flee the camp and hide when the Roman galleys are sighted. Coll has secretly been experimenting with models of a stone fortress, which could be a compromise between the two viewpoints. The stronghold would be a massive hollow tower made of the island's sandstone and would consist of eight floors, or galleries. Coll believes it would be impregnable.

A stranger arrives in camp alone on a small boat. He is 25-year-old Taran, a former tribe member who has been a Roman slave for many years but has escaped. Coll openly distrusts this power-hungry man. Taran attempts to kill him, but Coll is saved by 14-year-old Bran, who stole away from the Druids to protect his brother.

Through Bran, Niall and Coll learn that Taran and Domnall are plotting an alliance between the Boars and two neighboring tribes, their ancestral enemies, the Ravens and the Deers. One night the two young men steal away from the village to the holy place, the Druid's stone circle, and witness the consummation of the pact. They know Domnall is acting from genuine motives, but they realize that Taran's ambition is to marry Clodha and become leader of the Boars.

They alert Nectan to the conspiracy, and Coll tells him of his plans for a stronghold. Although the chief proves his strength by killing a wild boar, the tribe later aligns with Taran and Domnall after the Druid threatens to deny access to the afterlife to all who disobey him. As well, to atone for their doubt and to appease the gods, Domnall decrees that Fand shall be their human sacrifice at Beltane, the spring festival.

Everyone, including Nectan and his family, accepts the Druid's edict. But Coll does not; he tries desperately to think of a way to save Fand. Through insinuation, he leads Ogham, one of the Council members, to believe that Coll has slept with Fand, making her unworthy as a sacrifice to the gods. On the day of the festival, Ogham denounces Coll as the seducer and demands that he be the substitute victim. Ogham advances toward Coll with a knife, but Bran steps between them and is killed.

Nectan tells Domnall that Coll, although guilty of lying, has been spared by the gods for a higher purpose. Coll again explains his plan, and even Domnall becomes excited by the boy's ideas. The Druid agrees to delay any punishment until after they have tried the plan.

Feverish work begins under Coll's supervision. Even Taran seems to cooperate. The building is barely completed when the Roman ships are sighted. The women and children flee to safety while the men, anxious and apprehensive, take their places inside the stronghold. The first attack is successfully repulsed, but Domnall is seriously wounded. Before the second attack, it is discovered that the disloyal and bitter Taran has allied himself with the Romans. In a fury, Clodha kills him by driving a spear into his heart. The Romans return and this time are completely wiped out.

Domnall forgives Coll and bestows on him a Druid blessing. Niall and Clodha are to be married, and so, by Nectan's consent, are Coll and Fand. Now Coll must visit other tribes to direct construction of other strongholds.

Thematic Material

The author has combined legend and history to produce an exciting suspenseful novel. The re-creation of the Celtic culture is fascinating in its detail, and the conflict between religious belief and secular allegiance is well portrayed. Essentially, however, this is Coll's story—of courage and sacrifice that prove strength cannot be measured only in physical attributes.

Book Talk Material

An introduction to the period and setting could interest youngsters, or a reading of the foreword, in which the author tells of her visit to the stronghold. Other passages of interest are: Nectan and Domnall quarrel (pp. 9–12; pp. 14–17, pap.); Coll describes his tower (pp. 22–24; pp. 24–26, pap.); the fight between Coll and Taran (pp. 33–37; pp. 32–35, pap.); and Nectan fights the boar (pp. 79–82; pp. 64–66, pap.).

Additional Selections

During the Samurai period, a Japanese boy searches for his father in Katherine Paterson's *The Sight of the Chrysanthemum* (Crowell, 1973, $4.50). Elizabethan England is the setting for a spy story by Ronald Welch, *The Hawk* (Abelard, 1969, $4.95). A power struggle develops among the Aztecs after a mysterious stranger arrives in Eth Clifford's *Burning Star* (Houghton, 1974, $4.95). Other fine historical novels are Jill Paton Walsh's *The Emperor's Winding Sheet* (Farrar, 1974, $6.95); Katherine Paterson's *Of Nightingales that Weep* (Crowell, 1974, $5.95); J. S. Andrews' *Cargo for a King* (Dutton, 1973, $5.95); and Kevin Crossley-Holland's *The Sea Stranger* (Seabury, 1974, $4.95), about the bringing of Christianity to the East Saxons during the seventh century.

About the Author

Commire, Anne. *Something about the Author.* Detroit: Gale Research Co., 1971. Vol. 1, pp. 193–194 (listed under Maureen McIlwraith).

DeMontreville, Doris and Donna Hill, Eds. *Third Book of Junior Authors.* New York: H. W. Wilson Co., 1972, pp. 140–141.

Kinsman, Clare D. and Mary Ann Tennenhouse, Eds. *Contemporary Authors.* Detroit: Gale Research Co., 1972. Vol. 29, p. 402.

Ward, Martha E. and Dorothy A. Marquardt. *Authors of Books for Young People.* (2nd Edition). Metuchen, N.J.: Scarecrow Press, Inc., 1971, p. 255.

E. L. Konigsburg, *(George)*

Atheneum, 1974, $5.95; pap. (same pagination), $1.25

E. L. Konigsburg has produced an impressive list of successes in the field of juvenile literature. Among them are the 1968 Newbery Award winner, *From the Crazy Mixed-Up Files of Mrs. Basil E. Frankweiler* (Atheneum, 1967, $6.95; pap., $1.50), and *Jennifer, Hecate, Macbeth, William McKinley and Me, Elizabeth* (Atheneum, 1967, $5.95; pap., 95¢). (*George*) is enjoyed by readers from grades five through eight.

Plot Summary

Only two people know of the existence of George. Of course, 12-year-old Benjamin Dickinson Carr knows because George lives inside of Ben. The other is Ben's brother Howard, an eight-year-old human tornado, who, before entering grade school, had the distinction of being expelled from practically every kindergarten in Lawton Beach, Florida, where Howard and Ben live with their divorced mother, Charlotte Carr.

George is Ben's alter ego, the Mr. Hyde of Ben. Whereas Ben is outwardly an obedient and docile boy, George is the opposite, sassy and impertinent, who, on occasion, swears. George speaks aloud only to Howard and Ben, but he is continually mouthing off inside Ben and often makes such outrageously impertinent remarks that Ben smiles in spite of himself. A year ago, Ben tried once to tell his mother about George, but it was dismissed as a slight case of imaginary playmate-itis.

Howard may be considered precocious, but Ben is an outright genius. He goes to a special school, Astra, where he is technically in the sixth grade but actually takes advanced courses such as organic chemistry with seniors. It is this course that starts the trouble, because Ben likes chemistry and George loathes it. When the chemistry teacher, Mr. Berkowitz, announces that only seniors will be working together on special after-school research projects, both George and Ben are annoyed. George thinks it is rank discrimination by age, and Ben will miss working with his lab partner, William Hazlitt, a senior. George becomes so furious with Ben when Ben illegally helps William with an experiment, that he begins a talkathon to prevent Ben from paying attention in class.

Over Thanksgiving, while at the beach with the boys, Mrs. Carr meets

UNDERSTANDING PHYSICAL AND EMOTIONAL PROBLEMS · 113

Mr. Berkowitz, who turns out to be a bachelor from New Jersey. He is obviously attracted to Ben's mother, and she in turn is not indifferent. Mr. Berkowitz becomes a fairly frequent house guest.

Quite mysteriously, equipment begins to disappear from the organic chemistry laboratory. Each day brings a new loss—sometimes a major piece like a condenser or electric heater, or on other days perhaps only a few test tubes. William volunteers to make a list of the losses at each desk. The only one that suspiciously has had practically no losses is the one shared by Ben and his new lab partner, Karen. As well, Ben has been known in the past to take home leftover supplies and discarded materials, such as chipped test tubes for his own laboratory. Both the class and Mr. Berkowitz begin to suspect Ben. The teacher confides this to Mrs. Carr, who, without a direct accusation, talks to Ben about it. The boy denies any involvement in the thefts, but George is furious at their (or his) presumed guilt. After this confrontation, the thefts stop as suddenly as they had begun.

During Christmas vacation, Ben and Howard visit their father, his new wife Marilyn, and their young daughter Frederica, in Norfolk, Virginia. While there, George continues to torment Ben about the unjust accusation. One night they begin arguing out loud—Ben in his usual tones, George in a lower, darker key. Marilyn overhears this and, remembering vaguely the symptoms of schizophrenia from her college psychology courses, arranges to have Ben sent back to Lawton Beach to see a psychiatrist, Dr. Herrold. George continues to nag Ben until finally Ben screams at him to shut up. He does.

George is not heard from for several months, although Ben talks about him a great deal to his doctor. Dr. Herrold explains to Mrs. Carr that Ben is really two personalities, the outwardly obedient but lonely Ben and his inner self, the resentful and rebellious George. Particularly because of George's disappearance, the doctor is hopeful of merging the two personalities.

William and his lab partner, Cheryl, are having problems with their research project, and one Saturday, after seeing Cheryl's car in the school parking lot, Ben goes to the lab to see if he can help. Cheryl acts in a strange, remote way as though high on a drug and William is defensive and distant. Ben also notices that the equipment and supplies they are using do not match those required for their research. That night it comes together in his mind—William and Cheryl stole the equipment and are producing LSD!

The following morning before Mrs. Carr is awake, Ben gets Howard and together—Howard at the wheel and Ben taking care of the clutch and brake—they drive to Astra and take the stolen equipment and supplies from the lab before William can do further harm. Suddenly George joins them and forces Ben to realize how great a wrongdoer William really is. Unfortunately, Patrolman Hooper stops the car and takes the two boys and George, who won't stop talking aloud, to the police station. While awaiting Mrs. Carr, George and Ben together hatch a scheme in which Ben will plead guilty of manufacturing LSD, knowing that he will be released in his mother's custody provided he continues treatments with Dr. Herrold. However, to punish William and Cheryl, he will tell Mr. Berkowitz the truth before the end of the school year, so that at least they will fail in organic chemistry.

Everything works according to plan, and within the next few months there are more exciting developments: Charlotte Carr becomes Mrs. Shelden Berkowitz, and Ben, having merged with his alter ego, is released from Dr. Herrold's care. George is gone forever, but secretly Ben wonders what doctors would really find inside him if they ever had to perform surgery!

Thematic Material

As in her other books, Mrs. Konigsburg tells her story with wit and compassion. The combined effects on a sensitive, intelligent boy from a broken home and feelings of isolation and being different are excellently depicted. Ben's dual personality is created so naturally and graphically that the reader begins to realize that each of us has a (George) hidden in the psyche. The process of the cure in which Ben's need for other people exceeds his need for George is developed as an interesting psychological concept.

Book Talk Material

The book could be introduced by a brief discussion of split personalities, imaginary playmates, and other instances of two minds coexisting in a single body. Some interesting passages are: George is introduced (pp. 3–4); Ben's relation to George (pp. 9–10); Howard and kindergarten (pp. 10–16); Ben aids William illegally (pp. 34–38); and the lab thefts (pp. 56–61). As well, the author's illustrations (such as the charming one of Ben on p. 19 and on the cover) could be used.

Additional Suggestions

The transformation, through a wonderful teacher, of an eight-year-old psychotic, unmanageable girl into one who is poised and responsive is the true story in Mary MacCracken's *Lovey, a Very Special Child* (Lippincott, 1976, $7.95). Coping with mental illness is a prominent theme in Robert

Burch's *Simon and the Game of Chance* (Viking, 1970, $4.50). Junior is helped by friends when he gradually loses his hold on reality in Virginia Hamilton's *The Planet of Junior Brown* (Macmillan, 1971, $6.50; pap., 95¢). The effects of divorce on children is a subtheme in Marilyn Sachs' *Veronica Ganz* (Doubleday, 1968, $4.95; pap., Archway, 75¢; condensed in *Introducing Books*, Bowker, 1970) and the main theme in Norma Klein's *Taking Sides* (Pantheon, 1974, $5.99; pap., Avon, 95¢). Gus never shows his emotions in Paula Fox's *The Stone Faced Boy* (Bradbury, 1968, $6.95). For a more mature audience, David W. Elliott's *Listen to the Silence* (Holt, 1969, $5.95; pap., New Amer. Lib., 95¢) is the harrowing story of a 14-year-old orphan in a mental institution.

About the Author

Hoffman, Miriam and Eva Samuels. *Authors and Illustrators of Children's Books: Writings on Their Lives and Works*. New York: R. R. Bowker Co., 1972, pp. 243–246.

Hopkins, Lee Bennett. *More Books by More People*. New York: Citation Press, 1974, pp. 234–239.

Ward, Martha E. and Dorothy A. Marquardt. *Authors of Books for Young People*. (2nd Edition). Metuchen, N. J.: Scarecrow Press, Inc., 1971, p. 290.

Who's Who in America (39th Edition). Chicago: Marquis Who's Who, Inc., 1976. Vol. 1, p. 1763.

Mildred Lee, *The Skating Rink*
Seabury, 1969, $6.50; pap., Dell, 95¢

Mildred Lee grew up in a setting similar to the one in her novel. She was born in the small town of Blocton, Alabama, but, as the daughter of a Baptist preacher, moved frequently from ministry to ministry in a succession of small southern towns in Alabama and Georgia. As a child she enjoyed reading, particularly to her younger brother and sister, and soon began making up stories of her own. She has written many successful young adult titles, beginning with *The Rock and the Willow* (Lothrop, 1963, $4.95; pap., Archway, 75¢), an ALA Notable Book for 1963 and winner of the 1963 Child Study Association award for fiction. *The Skating Rink* has also won several awards, including being named an outstanding book of the year (1969) by the *New York Times* and *Book World*. The novel is recommended to readers in grades six through ten.

Plot Summary

Although it is only early September, Tuck Faraday can hardly wait until March when he will be 16 and can quit school. At last he will be free of the criticism and cold stares of his teachers and, more important, free from the cruel jeers and taunts of Elva Grimes and his other classmates. Tuck's main problem is a severe stutter, which has made him so shy and withdrawn that many people call him "dummy." The boy has vaguely traced his problem to a painful memory that still persists in his nightmares when, at age three, he witnessed his mother's drowning during a flood that inundated the Faraday's modest farm. Even though his father has remarried and moved the family to Wesley, a small farming town in southern Georgia, memories of his mother and her tragic death remain.

Tuck feels equally alienated from his family. His elder twin brothers, Tom and Cletus, are intent on their own concerns, mainly girls, and either ignore him or use him as a butt for their jokes. His younger half-sister, Karen, is the usual pesky preteen-ager, and Tuck is also unable to feel any closeness to his gruff, taciturn father, Myron, who, much like Tuck, has given in to defeat and failure. Ida, Tuck's stepmother, is the only one who attempts kindness and understanding, but Tuck rejects these as signs of pity.

Tuck's fortunes change abruptly when he meets Pete Degley, a stranger in town who is building a roller skating rink next to the Faradays' scraggly peach orchard. Pete is an older man who shows a fatherly interest in the boy. Tuck responds by visiting the construction site frequently and by expressing his feelings and thoughts to Pete in a way he has not been able to do with anyone else.

In a burst of newfound confidence, Tuck even tries to show affection toward Elva during a walk together. But once again he is rebuffed, and she calls him a dummy.

When part of the rink floor is completed, Pete offers to teach Tuck to skate. As a youngster, Degley had dreamed of a roller skating career, but an accident ruined his chances.

Tuck's first attempt on skates is a disaster, and, as usual, Tuck is anxious to admit defeat and give up. Pete, however, will not allow it, and he forces Tuck to continue to try, although, for some reason, he asks the boy not to tell anyone about the lessons.

Tuck begins to make real progress when one day Pete introduces him to his wife, Lily, who has come to join her husband. Tuck was unaware that Pete was married. When he sees how close they are and that she is an excellent skater, he once more feels rejected.

Pete explains that he would like Lily and Tuck to skate as an exhibition team on opening night. Tuck hides his feelings toward Lily, and, as he gets to know her better, he finds out that Lily was once much like himself— a misfit whom Pete sheltered and helped to develop.

Instead of losing something because of Lily, Tuck slowly realizes that his friendship with Pete has gained a new, even deeper dimension. In town there is growing excitement about the opening night of the rink.

During Christmas vacation, Karen follows Tuck into the rink and secretly watches a practice session with Lily. She later tells Tuck what she has seen, but he swears her to secrecy.

Tuck becomes partly aware of many subtle changes within himself—his speech difficulties are lessening and he is beginning to view the people around him with some trust and compassion. He senses, for example, that his father suffers hidden feelings of loneliness and despair much like his own.

Thoughts of opening night suddenly fill Tuck with dread. He is certain he will once more make a fool of himself and bring disgrace to Pete and Lily. But this time he knows that he cannot run away as he has done before.

Practically everyone in town, including Tuck's family, attends the opening. Hidden in the wings, Tuck gets a certain satisfaction in seeing how inept everyone, including his own brother and date, Elva, is on skates. At last Pete announces the main attraction, and everyone gasps when Tuck's name is announced as Lily's partner. Tuck's anxieties and tensions fade as he and Lily skate together. They are a great success, and the crowd screams for more.

Everyone is elated at the evening's success, and, in appreciation, Pete gives Tuck $100. When Tuck gets home, he finds to his surprise that his father has waited up for him. After taking out $10 to buy shoes, the boy gives his father the rest of the money to buy a secondhand stove that his stepmother needs. Tuck sees tears well up in his father's eyes. For the first time in their lives, father and son wish one another a good night before each goes to bed.

Thematic Material

Tuck's difficult and painful adjustments to his handicap and the cruelty of his classmates are realistically portrayed. The growth to emotional maturity that occurs in spite of these difficulties is also well depicted. The importance of having one's own goals in life, as shown by Pete's dream of owning his own rink, is developed as a subplot. The hero-worship aspects of Tuck's relationship with Pete are also handled delicately and effectively.

Book Talk Material

Tuck's first meeting with Pete (pp. 7–8), followed by a few hints on how this chance encounter will change both lives, should create interest. Other suitable passages are: Tuck's unfortunate meeting with Elva (pp. 31–34);

Pete invites Tuck to try skating (pp. 42–47); and the first skate (pp. 51–53). Another suspenseful episode occurs when Karen tells Tuck that she has secretly visited the rink and has seen him skate (pp. 71–74).

Additional Suggestions

Fog, also by Mildred Lee (Seabury, 1972, $6.95; pap., Dell, 95¢), refers to the confusion and aimlessness surrounding 17-year-old Luke and his friends. Two works by the same author with heroines as their central figures are: *The Rock and the Willow* (Lothrop, 1963, $4.40; Archway, 75¢), the story of Enie's growing up in Alabama during the Depression of the 1930s, and *Honor Sands* (Lothrop, 1966, $3.75), a somewhat mellow work about adolescence. *The Sycamore Year* (Lothrop, 1976, $5.50) by Mildred Lee is also recommended. In Reginald Maddock's *The Pit* (Little, 1968, $4.75), the hero, who has a reputation of being a rough kid, is wrongly accused of theft. *Whichaway* by Glendon and Kathryn Swarthout (Random, 1966, $4.99) tells about another "loner," who fights for survival after an accident in which both legs are broken. Other suitable titles with appeal to boys are: Keith Robertson's *In Search of a Sandhill Crane* (Viking, 1973, $5.95) and Finn Havrevold's *Undertow* (Atheneum, 1968, $4.50).

About the Author

Commire, Anne. *Something about the Author.* Detroit: Gale Research Co., 1973. Vol. 6, pp. 142–143.
DeMontreville, Doris and Donna Hill, Eds. *Third Book of Junior Authors.* New York: H. W. Wilson Co., 1972, pp. 174–175.
Ethridge, James M., Ed. *Contemporary Authors.* Detroit: Gale Research Co., 1963. Vols. 9–10, p. 407.

Doris Lund, *Eric*

Lippincott, 1974, $7.95; pap., Dell, $1.75

Doris Lund has courageously written a moving and painfully honest document of her son's lost battle with leukemia. She chronicles four-and-a-half years of hope, despair, occasional joy, heroism, and finally death. The book is both harrowing and inspiring. It is suggested for mature junior and senior high school students.

Plot Summary

In September 1967, Eric Lund, only 17, is preparing to enter his freshman year at the University of Connecticut. His parents, Doris and Sidney Lund, are free-lance writers and artists who live in a suburban

Connecticut community. They have three other children: an older daughter, Meredith, now married and living in Chicago; a younger son, Mark, who is 14; and 10-year-old Lisa.

Eric is a vibrant, bright young man, extremely popular, a fine leader, and excellent all-around athlete. He is already a soccer star and hopes to make the team at college. Two days before Eric is scheduled to leave for school, his mother notices ugly sores on his legs. He is given tests at the local hospital; the diagnosis is leukemia—his life expectancy, six months to two years. However, through drugs the disease may be halted for brief periods known as remissions, but usually there are only a maximum of three of these.

Eric is told that he has anemia and can't enter college until the spring. To effect a period of remission, he is placed on large doses of powerful drugs. After three months of these treatments, Eric begins to suspect the seriousness of his illness. One afternoon his mother tells him the truth; his reply is that he is not frightened and that he will conquer it. His only stipulation is that he be allowed to control his own destiny without interference from the family. This is difficult to grant, particularly for his mother, who has a natural desire to shelter and protect him.

The Lunds scrape together the money for a Christmas vacation in Puerto Rico, and in January, during his first remission, Eric begins taking a few courses at a local college, still being checked frequently at the Sloan-Kettering Clinic in New York City. After another attack, during which stronger drugs are used, he goes into his second remission. His strength returns; he takes a summer job and begins a merciless in-training regimen to regain his muscle tone and robustness.

In the fall of 1968, he enters the university and is promptly made cocaptain of the freshman soccer team. He spends an active, joyous year at college, but in the early summer his condition changes and he is admitted to Memorial Hospital in New York City, for the first time of what will be many times in the future. Eric and his family become familiar with the cancer wards on the eighth floor of the Ewing Building.

There is a third remission, and undaunted by his illness, the boy goes on a cross-country car trip with a buddy, Eddie Kline. In the fall he is back in the hospital, this time for a longer, more painful period. He never loses his courage, and his irreverent humor, cheeriness, and compassion for his fellow patients make him admired and loved by everyone around him. Although the death of several of his friends saddens him, he becomes even more defiant in his will to live.

Eric is released in time to spend Christmas with his family in a vacation home they have bought in Florida, and a fourth remission occurs. Most of the first half of 1970, however, is spent in the hospital trying to stabilize the remission through drug therapy. During the summer he comes home again, but the terrible built-up tensions and anxieties, coupled with Eric's obsessive desire for his own independence and for the noninvolvement of his family, cause some bitter arguments.

After a fall semester at college where he again plays brilliant soccer, there is another onslaught of the disease, and at the end of January 1971, he is again in the hospital. The next weeks are a nightmare of hemorrhaging, high fevers, delirium, and operations. Hundreds of Eric's friends and acquaintances donate blood platelets to keep him alive. When one crisis is passed, another occurs, whether caused by renewed inroads of the disease or complications from the aftereffects of the stepped-up drug treatments. Miraculously Eric pulls through again. He becomes particularly fond of a pretty, young special nurse, Mary Lou, who continues to visit him after leaving the case. His bravery and good spirits continue to amaze the hospital staff, whose activities Eric has learned to satirize gently in a series of cartoon strips he calls "The Adventures of Ewing 8." In the spring, there are two brief remissions during which he again almost pathetically tries to regain his strength. His body, however, has wasted away, and it seems that only his courage and resolution keep Eric alive. After another stay in the hospital, the disease is once again temporarily halted, and he is released. It is the end of October, over four years since the first diagnosis.

The family spends a happy two-and-one-half months together. Mary Lou comes to the house often, and Eric delights in Christmas shopping and revisiting old haunts. The two fly south to spend Christmas together in the sun, but they return in time for Eric's traditional all-night New Year's bash with his friends. On January 3rd, he reenters the hospital for the last time. Again the struggles and crises begin, but this time Eric's mood has changed; he seems more at peace with himself and, in moments of lucidity, speaks of needing a long rest. Days drag on with their all-night exhausting vigils. When death seems near, each member of the family approaches Eric's bedside and whispers parting words of love. In retrospect, Eric's death cannot be considered a defeat but a glowing inspiration for those who live.

Thematic Material

As one of Eric's doctors said, "He taught us all a great deal about how to live and how to die." His supreme courage and vital love of life radiate triumphantly throughout this unforgettable book, as does the loyalty and bravery of his family and friends. The book is also a wonderful tribute to the medical profession. In Eric's words, "Ewing Eight is both a heaven and a hell. The hell is obvious. The heaven is created by the people who work up there."

Book Talk Material

Some of Eric's wonderful, sassy sense of humor is conveyed in the reproductions of his cartoons about Ewing 8 (pp. 260-265; pp. 201-206, pap.; explained on pp. 258-259; pp. 199-200, pap.). Some important passages are: the discovery of Eric's leukemia (pp. 13-15; pp. 9-10, pap.); Eric is told of his condition (pp. 35-37; pp. 25-27, pap.); he goes to college (pp. 70-72; pp. 53-54, pap.); his trip west (pp. 103-109; pp. 78-83, pap.); and he talks about the hospital (pp. 141-143; pp. 109-110, pap.).

Additional Selections

The theme of death has been explored in several biographies for young adults. A young girl's impending death from bone cancer teaches a family how to love in Rose Levit's *Eileen* (Chronicle, 1974, $6.95; pap., Bantam, $1.25). A novelization of the tape-recorded diary of a young woman's 18-month fatal bout with cancer is inspiringly told in Norma Klein's *Sunshine* (Holt, 1974, $7.95; pap., Avon, $1.50). Two books about Brian Piccolo, the Chicago Bear's running back are Jeannie Morris' *Brian Piccolo, A Short Season* (Rand McNally, 1971, $7.95; pap., Dell, $1.50) and Gale Sayers' *I Am Third* (Viking, 1970, $6.95; pap., Dell, $1.25). Also use John Gunther's story of his son's fatal disease, *Death Be Not Proud* (Harper, 1949, $10; pap., 95¢). For younger audiences, use Carol Farley's *The Garden Is Doing Fine* (Atheneum, 1975, $6.95). Other suggestions might include Richard Bach's *Jonathan Livingston Seagull* (Macmillan, 1970, $5.95; pap., Avon, $1.50).

About the Author

Kinsman, Clare D., Ed. *Contemporary Authors.* Detroit: Gale Research Co., 1976. Vol. 17, p. 459.

John Neufeld, *Lisa, Bright and Dark*
S. G. Phillips, 1969, $6.95; pap., Signet, 75¢

The story of *Lisa, Bright and Dark* (original title, *I'll Always Love You, Paul Newman*) is a single, agonizing cry for help from a young girl who is slowly but inexorably sinking into complete madness. What saves this novel from being simply a harrowing and unrelieved account of a descent into insanity is its hopeful ending and the devices used to tell the story. The title refers to the changing and divergent moods that alternate within Lisa Shilling, the 16-year-old heroine. On her good or bright days, she dresses gaily and is her normal, effervescent and friendly self, but on her dark days (and those occur with increased frequency and intensity), Lisa is sullen, malicious, withdrawn, and lost in conversation with imaginary "English voices" that she hears. The book has been popular with both junior and senior high school students for several years. Its dramatization on "Hallmark Hall of Fame" also has added to its popularity.

Plot Summary

Except for an introductory scene in which Lisa tells her parents that she is going crazy and begs for help, the story is narrated by Betsy Goodman, a high school student who lives in an upper-middle-class community on Long Island. Although Betsy is very modest about her own capability, the reader soon realizes that she has a natural warmth and simplicity, not to mention a wild crush on Paul Newman, all of which immediately endear her to the reader. She quickly introduces the other principals in the story— Lisa Shilling, Lisa's unfeeling and stubborn father, her social-climbing mother, and Lisa's school friends, the All-American Girl, M. N. (short for Mary Nell) Fickett, the extremely wealthy and beautiful Elizabeth Frazer, and Brian Morris, Lisa's boyfriend and the eleventh-grade heart-throb.

M. N. is the first to mention Lisa's moodiness. At a party at the Fickett's, Lisa suddenly becomes enraged and orders everyone to stop dancing. Her continued insulting behavior toward Brian eventually leads to their breakup. Even more serious, M. N. and Betsy one day discover Lisa after class crouching under the teacher's desk sticking pins into her wrists and making them bleed. The girls tell Mr. Burstein, their somewhat mealymouthed guidance counselor, who in turn recommends to the Shillings that Lisa be sent away for a rest. She spends six weeks in Florida, but she comes back even more despondent and erratic. The girls become more fearful of the eventual outcome, and they appeal to Mr. Burstein and to Lisa's mother to get help for her, but without success.

It is M. N.'s idea to organize a group consisting of Elizabeth, Betsy, and herself to "group therapy-ize" Lisa by spending all of their free time with her. In spite of their kindness and attention, the bouts of madness increase. M. N. persuades her father, a minister, and Mr. Milne, an understanding English teacher, to visit Mr. Shilling and make him aware of Lisa's plight. In the middle of the conversation, Lisa rushes in and also begs her father for help, but Mr. Shilling is implacable, claiming that all Lisa needs is rest.

In her moments of clarity, Lisa tells the girls about the dreadful abyss into which she is sinking and the hopelessness she feels. But her moments of lucidity are becoming fewer and her bouts of depression more violent and destructive. During an outdoor barbecue, Lisa tries to push Elizabeth into the fire and then brutally attacks all three of the girls when they attempt to subdue her.

A climax occurs when Lisa, in an effort to alert adults to her condition, jumps through a glass wall in the presence of Betsy's father. Lisa is taken to the hospital, but when Mr. Goodman approaches Mrs. Shilling, there is once more a rebuff. This time the girls are forbidden to see Lisa again.

Elizabeth contacts a "friend," Dr. Neil Donovan, a psychiatrist, who is so wildly handsome and charming that Betsy momentarily forsakes Paul Newman. In confidence, Elizabeth tells Betsy that Dr. Donovan had been *her* psychiatrist. At Elizabeth's pleading, her father has agreed to pay for the costs of Lisa's treatment under Dr. Donovan, but first they must get the consent of the Shillings.

This turns out to be less difficult than expected. After her release from the hospital, Lisa once more attempts to take her life, this time with an overdose of barbiturates. She is once more in the hospital and, at last, her parents give in. But is it too late? Dr. Donovan and the girls visit Lisa in the hospital. At first there is no response, only blank stares, but when Dr. Donovan is introduced and Lisa is told that he will help her, she begins to sob. Her cry for help has been heard.

Thematic Material

Lisa, Bright and Dark shows the fine, often indistinct line between mental illness and sanity and that treatment for these disorders is as vital and natural as treatment for physical problems. The novel is remarkable in the sympathy and understanding that the young people show toward Lisa in contrast to the unfeeling, guilt-ridden attitudes of her parents. Betsy Goodman is an engaging heroine with disarming modesty and charm (pp. 14–15; pp. 12–13, pap.). Her presence lends much to the compassion and naturalness of this story.

Book Talk Material

Chapter 1 is a conversation out of context where Lisa tells her family at the dinner table that she is going insane and needs help. A reading of this will certainly arouse interest (pp. 11–13; pp. 9–11, pap.), as will Betsy's retelling of Lisa's first overt signs of insanity (pp. 19–21; pp. 18–20, pap.);

the incident with pins under the teacher's desk (pp. 25–26; pp. 24–26, pap.); and Lisa with amateur psychiatrist M. N. (pp. 75–78; pp. 85–88, pap.).

Additional Suggestions

John Neufeld has written several excellent books for junior readers, including *Edgar Allan* (S. G. Phillips, 1968, $6.95; pap. New Amer. Lib., $1.25; condensed in *Introducing Books*, Bowker, 1970), the story of a trial adoption of a black boy by a minister's family, and *Twink*, (New Amer. Lib., 1971, $1.25), in which care and attention make all the difference to a girl suffering from cerebral palsy. In Susan Wexler's *The Story of Sandy* (New Amer. Lib., 1971, $1.25), foster parents courageously fight for the sanity of their deeply disturbed young boy. Gene Smith's *The Hayburners* (Delacorte Pr., 1974, $5.95; lib. bdg., $5.47; pap., Dell, 75¢) is a horse story in which one of the main characters is an older retired man who lives in a state mental home. Also try Gudrun Alcock's *Run Westy, Run* (Lothrop, 1966, $5.61; pap., Archway, 60¢) and Jeannette Eyerly's *The Girl Inside* (Lippincott, 1968, $5.95; pap., Berkley, 75¢). Two novels of friendship are Honor Arundel's *The Girl in the Opposite Bed* (Nelson, 1971, $3.95), about two boys, and Mary Towne's *The Glass Room* (Farrar, 1971, $5.95; pap., Archway, 75¢).

About the Author

Riley, Carolyn, Ed. *Contemporary Authors*. Detroit: Gale Research Co., 1971. Vols. 25–28, p. 535.

Ward, Martha E. and Dorothy A. Marquardt. *Authors of Books for Young People*. (2nd Edition). Metuchen, N. J.: Scarecrow Press, Inc., 1971, p. 381.

Kin Platt, *The Boy Who Could Make Himself Disappear*
Chilton, 1968, $4.95; pap., Dell, 95¢

The alarming growth in serious mental illnesses among children and the high incidence of teen-age suicides have stimulated several writers of adolescent literature to explore these themes. One of the first, and still one of the best, is this novel, the story of seventh-grader Roger Baxter, who is made to feel so worthless and unnecessary that he tries to withdraw completely, to fade away, to disappear, as the title suggests. In some ways, Roger is the counterpart of John Neufeld's heroine in *Lisa, Bright and Dark* (condensed earlier in this chapter). At the end of the Neufeld book, the reader is convinced of Lisa's eventual recovery, but such is not the case here, where the feeling of hope is much more tenuous. Roger's symbolic tear can be taken as a symbol of possible recovery, or only a lost contact with the outside world. This is an extremely disturbing book that is often painful to read, but nevertheless it has gained and held an enthusiastic audience in junior and senior high school. In 1973, a film version, called *Baxter*, was released, with Scott Jacoby as Roger and Patricia Neal as Miss Clemm.

Plot Summary

Roger is a poor little rich boy. He is an only child whose father is a prominent Hollywood producer, but his detached, self-occupied parents either ignore him completely or nag him until, now, the boy lacks any confidence in himself and feels unwanted. He has had a speech impediment since childhood; his Rs sound like Ws, and he pronounces his own name as "Wa-ja." This is a constant source of humiliation to him. He invents all manner of defensive plays, but mainly he just remains silent.

After 15 years of marriage, the Baxters are divorced, and Roger moves with his mother to Riverside Drive in New York City and is enrolled in the posh East Side Busby School. He is cast adrift in New York without friends and with a mother who acknowledges him only enough to make him feel in the way.

Through flashbacks and daydreams, Roger relives some of the most significant—and usually traumatic—events in his childhood. When he was three, he mistook his father's styptic pencil for candy and severely burned his mouth; his father's reaction—"When are you going to teach this kid not to put everything he sees in his greedy little mouth?" When he was six and went out to lunch with his mother and an old school friend, he had trouble deciding what to eat. His mother then tried to force him to get up alone and stand in line to order his food. Out of fear of embarrassment and ridicule, he sat unable to move. His mother shrilly insisted until the old school friend intervened and hustled them out of the lunchroom. He also remembers the progress he was making with his speech therapist, who once told him that his chief problem was that he was surrounded by mean people. Even his baby-sitter once locked him in his room because he couldn't pronounce her name correctly.

In the New York school, he does everything to avoid attention. In spite of his shyness, Roger defends one student who is unjustly treated by the English teacher, Mr. Rawling, and then fears that he has made an enemy of the teacher. One student, Marion Johnson, daughter of a psychiatrist, tries to befriend him, and he does find solace with the burly but understanding school speech therapist, Miss Roberta Clemm. He begins to make progress with his Rs, but Clemm realizes that his speech problem is only the symptom of a much more serious disturbance.

Many aspects of New York intrigue Roger. He is fascinated by his huge apartment building and the spectacular view from his bedroom window. He is befriended by a wonderful fashion model, Pat Bentley, who lives in the penthouse, and her fiancé, Roger Tunnell, a Frenchman whom Roger secretly worships. There is even a hint of mystery in the building—who is the young girl who spies on him with her telescope from the next wing?

Roger spends some time exploring New York City. One day he sees a young man followed and beaten up by a gang of thugs. The only one who tries to help is a cab driver. Roger is horrified at the crowd's indifference. He also finds out about the girl who spies on him. In December, with snow and ice on the sidewalk, he helps a young crippled girl who has slipped outside the building. Over coffee and doughnuts, she tells him that she is Nemo Neuman and has had 14 operations to restore the use of her legs, crippled in a car accident. Unlike Roger, her problem is that she can't stop talking. Soon he finds out that she owns a black telescope and lives in the next wing. Before leaving him, she gives Roger her long peppermint-stick scarf. He is so pleased that he wears it to bed at night.

After making great progress with Miss Clemm, Roger is so elated that he calls his father long distance one night when his mother is out. His father misunderstands the call and rebuffs him. In anger and disappointment, Roger tears the phone from the wall. The next day he gets into more trouble with the English teacher and, unsure of what he is doing or why, leaves the school and begins to wander. Pat Bentley finds him and, despite her terrible cold, escorts him by taxi around Central Park. When he gets home, he is physically abused by his angry mother, and once more he takes off. After spending the night in a department store, he is found wandering in Central Park by two policemen. He will say nothing but Miss Clemm's name. She is called, and Roger is admitted to Bellevue Hospital. His mother is pleased because now she can go to Nassau for a few days' rest.

When he returns home, Roger is told that Pat Bentley died of pneumonia. This shock, plus his mother's continued cruelty, sends him into complete withdrawal. He barely moves, never speaks, and shows no sign of reaction or recognition. Miss Clemm takes him back to the hospital and visits him frequently, but there is no response. On the fifth day, however, he scrawls Roger Tunnell's name on a piece of paper. The Frenchman comes and speaks to him, and Roger answers. With tears in his eyes, Tunnell gathers the boy in his arms. Roger also cries, and as he is pressed against the man's massive chest, he thinks, "I can feel that. I guess I'm back."

Thematic Material

This is a poignant story, but also a shocking one that, one hopes, will make its readers more aware of the thoughts and feelings of others and perhaps also make them more understanding and tolerant of others' problems. The effects of a home life without love are excellently portrayed. There are interesting literary devices used by the author—for example, a third person narrative interspersed with Roger's inner thoughts—and there is effective use of flashback. Incidental to the story, the author includes many interesting details about speech therapy.

Book Talk Material

Several isolated incidents could be used to introduce Roger's story: Roger tries to write to his father (pp. 1–4; pp. 1–5, pap.); at school in California (pp. 34–39; pp. 39–44, pap.); the styptic pencil episode (pp. 44–46; pp. 50–51, pap.); the lunch incident with his mother (pp. 65–73; pp. 74–82, pap.), and the anger of the English teacher (pp. 104–107; pp. 119–122, pap.).

Additional Suggestions

Kin Platt is a most versatile juvenile writer. He deals with the introspective and sensitive in *Disappear* and with sure-fire mysteries such as *The Blue Man* (pap., Scholastic, 75¢) and Edgar-winning *Sinbad and Me* (pap., Dell, 95¢). In *On the Outside, Looking In* by Joan L. Oppenheimer (pap., Scholastic, 95¢), a disturbed girl gains strength by helping a young man recover from an automobile accident. The problems of a tongue-tied girl are told in Joan Tate's *Tina and David* (Nelson, 1973, $5.25). For young readers, use Michel-Aime Baudouy's *The Boy Who Belonged to No One* (Harcourt, 1967, o. p.) or Paula Fox's *Portrait of Ivan* (Bradbury, 1969, $5.95; pap., Dell, 95¢). For the very mature, try Hannah Grun's *I Never Promised You a Rose Garden* (Holt, 1964, $5.95; pap., New Amer. Lib., $1.25).

About the Author

Kinsman, Clare D., Ed. *Contemporary Authors.* Detroit: Gale Research Co., 1976. Vols. 17–20, pp. 585–586.
Who's Who in America (37th Edition). Chicago: Marquis Who's Who, Inc., 1972. Vol. 2, p. 2510.

6

Becoming Self-Reliant

THE ADOLESCENT must learn to think and behave as an individual and be able to handle new situations with resourcefulness and self-reliance. This requires achieving a degree of self-discipline and independence that often creates conflicts with existing social conditions and moral standards. In other cases, the individual must shoulder responsibilities and face problems that normally would be handled by parents or other groups in authority. These and other aspects of the need to develop self-reliance are dealt with in the books in this section.

Vera and Bill Cleaver, *Where the Lilies Bloom*

Lippincott, 1969, $4.95; pap., New Amer. Lib., $1.25

In their many books, the Cleavers have created such interesting characters as Grover in *Grover* (Lippincott, 1970, $4.50; pap., New Amer. Lib., $1.25) and Ellen Grae in *Ellen Grae* (Lippincott, 1969, $4.75; pap., Dell, 65¢; condensed in *Introducing Books*, Bowker, 1970), but certainly none is more memorable than Mary Call Luther, the enterprising and courageous 14-year-old heroine and narrator of *Where the Lilies Bloom*. This story of a poor family of rural tenant farmers living in the shadows of the Great Smoky Mountains in North Carolina is popular with junior and senior high school students.

Plot Summary

When Roy Luther begins to ail, he makes his daughter, Mary Call, promise that she will bring in neither doctor nor undertaker, and that after his death she will keep the family together without resorting to charity. He also makes her swear never to allow a marriage between her 18-year-old sister, simpleminded Devola, and their crafty landowner, Kiser Pease. The Luther family also includes two younger children, 10-year-old Romey and five-year-old Irma Dean. Their mother died some years before of a fever, and the family now lives in a ramshackle house on the edge of the property owned by Kiser, whom Mary Call describes as "all cheat and sneak." Apart from grubbing out a bare living, the Luthers supplement their livelihood by gathering wild witch-hazel leaves and selling them to Mr. Connell, who owns the local country store some five miles away.

After Roy Luther suffers a massive stroke, the children, headed by Mary Call, try in vain to nurse him back to health. One day while out gathering medicinal herbs, Mary Call and Romey are forced to take shelter from a rainstorm at Kiser Pease's home. Much to their alarm, they find the 32-year-old man delirious with fever from pneumonia. They manage to break the fever by using the old-fashioned technique of dragging him into the bathtub and covering his body with steaming hot onions. During her all-night vigil, Mary Call forces Kiser to sign a paper deeding their house and land to the Luthers.

Realizing that without their father, they need a new source of income, Mary Call begins to read her mother's book on wildcrafting, or gathering wild medicinal plants. She trains herself and the rest of the family and, in the last days of summer, they scour the area and sell their harvest to Mr. Connell for the food and clothing they desperately need.

Roy Luther dies. In accordance with his wishes, Mary Call and Romey drag their father's body by wagon up the side of their mountain, Old Joshua, and bury him. Fearing that news of his death will mean foster homes for the children, Mary Call swears them to secrecy and begins an elaborate plan to convince the neighbors that her father is well and alive. They continue to buy razor blades and such things for him at the store, and when people call, Roy Luther is always out walking or taking a nap. They begin to isolate themselves completely, and when school starts in the fall, they make no friendships for fear that these children will want to visit.

The hardest one to discourage is Kiser Pease, who is now paying serious court to Devola with such welcome gifts as a pig and a cow. Fed up with the delaying tactics, he demands to see Roy to ask for his daughter's hand. Mary Call has run out of excuses, but an automobile accident sends Kiser to the hospital, so there is a reprieve.

Winter brings more trouble. Because of the severe weather, the children are forced to bring all the animals into the house. The living room roof collapses under the weight of the snow. Mary Call clubs to death a starving fox that has invaded their shattered living room in search of food. More disaster strikes when Kiser's sister, Goldie, comes to town to visit her brother in the hospital. She claims that the Luther property is rightfully hers, and she serves notice on the Luthers to vacate in two weeks.

For Mary Call, there is nowhere to turn. Worn out and discouraged, she wonders if life has any meaning but suffering. In.desperation, she visits Kiser in the hospital. After telling of her father's death, she offers to marry him herself to save the family, but Kiser claims he loves only Devola.

Mary Call begins to scout the mountain for a dry cave where the family can live until spring. She returns home one night to find Kiser, out of the hospital, with the family in the kitchen. He has bought the Luther property from his sister, and he offers it to Mary Call as a gift. Once more, he asks permission to marry Devola. Realizing that they really love each other, and that perhaps her father was wrong to oppose the marriage, Mary Call consents.

The marriage takes place and Kiser becomes the children's legal guardian. Slowly spring arrives in the valley, and Mary Call, Romey, and Irma Dean are safe and secure in their own home.

Thematic Material

Mary Call's resourcefulness, courage, and strength are an inspiration to all readers. She exemplifies the pride and independence that can exist amid the most adverse of hardships. The novel also points up the social problem of oppressive poverty in the Appalachian hill country. The authors know and love the Smokies and the people, and they highlight the story with interesting details concerning the plants of the region, including a fascinating introduction to wildcrafting.

Book Talk Material

The paperback edition contains several pages of interesting movie stills taken from the film, made by Robert B. Radnitz from the novel. The hardcover edition has drawings by Jim Spanfeller of the principal characters. Some interesting passages are: Mary Call's promise to her father (pp. 13–15; pp. 15–17, pap.); the hot onion treatment (pp. 27–32; pp. 29–34 pap.); wildcrafting (pp. 54–56; pp. 56–58, pap.); and the burial of Roy Luther (pp. 68–73; pp. 71–76, pap.).

Additional Selections

There are further adventures of Mary Call and her family in the sequel to this novel, *Trial Valley* (Lippincott, 1977, $7.95). In Christine Dickenson's *Getting It All Together* (Scholastic, 1975, 85¢), a 16-year-old girl fights to save her orphaned family from separation. Rosa Rivera, the oldest of seven fatherless children, matures under adverse conditions in Caroline Crane's

Don't Look at Me That Way (Random, 1970, o.p.). A young boy grows up hungry in the Scottish highlands during the Depression in Margaret MacPherson's *The Rough Road* (Harcourt, 1966, $3.95). Siny R. van Iterson's *Pulga* is set in the slums of Bogotá (Morrow, 1971, $6.37). Also use Richard Parker's *Second-Hand Family* (Bobbs-Merrill, 1966, $3.50; pap., Scholastic, 85¢) and Helen Doss' *The Family Nobody Wanted* (pap., Scholastic, 95¢).

About the Author

Ward, Martha E. and Dorothy A. Marquardt. *Authors of Books for Young People.* Metuchen, N.J.: Scarecrow Press, Inc., 1971, pp. 101–102.

Margaret Craven, *I Heard the Owl Call My Name*

> Doubleday, 1973, $4.95; lge. type ed., G. K. Hall, $7.95; pap., Dell, $1.25

In this book, Canadian writer Margaret Craven has sensitively written of a British Columbia Indian tribe vainly trying to retain their values and traditions despite the encroachment of the white man and of a doomed 27-year-old vicar who comes to their village in the early 1960s to minister to their needs. Although written for adults, this novel is enjoyed by both junior and senior high school students.

Plot Summary

The Anglican bishop decides not to tell his young ordinate, Mark Brian, that the doctor has given Brian a maximum of three years to live. Instead, he assigns him to a coastal Indian mission at the end of Kingcome Inlet, roughly opposite the northern tip of Vancouver Island. Caleb, the former canon now in retirement, tells Mark that he should not feel self-pity at being sent to such an isolated post because he will learn much more from the Indians than they from him.

The trip up the coast is on the church's 40-foot launch. Although his church and village are situated at Kingcome Village, Mark will use the launch to visit and hold services in the otherwise inaccessible neighboring Indian settlements, which are also part of his parish. His crew and captain is a young Indian from the village, Jim Wallace, who is about Mark's age. Inside the 20-mile inlet, Mark is impressed with the rugged, unspoiled grandeur of the mountains that dip into the sea and with the lush vegetation and still-plentiful wildlife. They tie up at the government dock and complete the last three-and-one-half miles by speedboat.

On arrival, Mark finds his first task awaiting him. In the vicarage there is the body of an Indian child who drowned 10 days before. The tribe has been waiting for a burial permit from the Mounted Police. After comforting the mother, Mark contacts the Mounties, who fly in the necessary permit, and the service is held. For days afterward the vicarage still contains the sweet, sickening smell of death.

The tribe is at first wary and suspicious of their new vicar, and they wonder if he will be like the only other white man in the village, the elementary school teacher, who alternately despises and ignores them. In the evenings the tribe's elders, including Chief Eddy, T. P. Wallace, their orator, and old Peter, the carver, voice their concerns, as do the matriarchs, Marta Stevens and Mrs. Hudson. The latter now has many great-grandchildren, including the beautiful Keetah, who is betrothed to Gordon, a young man now attending Indian school at the town of Alert Bay. Mark learns that his guide and mentor, Jim Wallace, is also in love with Keetah.

Mark proves to be completely unlike the schoolteacher. He is eager to learn Indian ways and to help them help themselves. He learns to understand and respect their culture and traditions and even tries to master their difficult language. Their myths particularly fascinate him, including the legend that before a man dies he will hear the owl call his name. Although never neglecting his spiritual and humanitarian duties, he participates in many of the activities of the tribe—fishing during the salmon run, joining clamming and hunting expeditions, and attending the sacred potlatches. Gradually he is able to break down their reserve and distrust, and even gains the friendship of his usually taciturn and aloof guide, Jim. The real sign of acceptance, however, does not come until after his first full year with the tribe when the elders offer to help Mark build a new vicarage to replace the present dilapidated one. During the summer, his second with the tribe, the construction is completed, and Mark entertains the bishop and Caleb at a gala dedication ceremony.

The tribe's major concern is that the younger generation, under the growing influences of twentieth-century learning and culture, will lose their Indian heritage and gradually drift into the white man's world, where they are usually unwanted and exploited. Mark realizes that these fears are not unfounded. He notices that when the Indian boys, including Keetah's boyfriend, Gordon, return from school on vacation, they are increasingly disinterested and often scornful of the tribe's customs and way of life. A more tragic aspect of this problem arises when Keetah's sister runs off with a white logger, who has also taken with him the tribe's sacred carved mask. In shame and humiliation, Keetah's family, including her great-grandmother, Mrs. Hudson, leave the village to live in another settlement. The old lady's parting words to Mark are "what has this white man done to our young?" Several months later, during Mark's second Christmas in Kingcome, they return after learning that the girl, deserted by her lover, has died in a Vancouver brothel from an overdose of drugs.

Although not denying the Indians' right to retain their traditions, Mark realizes that their survival depends on a gradual and orderly adoption of the white man's learning. He, therefore, heeds the dying wish of Gordon's mother and arranges for the boy to be sent to a large school in the town of Powell River. Keetah goes to join him, but unable to adjust to her new life, she returns several weeks later now carrying Gordon's child. Jim proposes marriage and is accepted. He says that a child is always welcome and Keetah's baby will now be his.

Spring arrives, and Mark is about to complete his second year in the village when the bishop visits and tells Mark that his work is almost done and that a new vicar will be sent out shortly to replace him. From this conversation and the signs of his rapidly failing health, Mark guesses the truth. He does not encourage the villagers when they suggest petitioning the bishop to have him stay.

After returning from a mission to rescue a logger who was lost, Mark tells his housekeeper, Marta, that in the woods he heard an owl call his name. A few days later, Mark is killed when a mountain slide destroys the launch. As the elders tenderly prepare the body for burial, Jim places a lantern in the church window in tribute to their lost and beloved friend.

Thematic Material

Through his parish work, Mark uncovers the true meaning of humanity and salvation. The novel is filled with the sadness and power of nature and with the tribal beliefs that try to reconcile man's life with these forces. In its simplicity and honesty, the novel is both moving and inspiring. The author has tellingly captured, from the Indians' point of view, their proud heritage and the conflict between two cultures. She also has portrayed with sympathy and compassion the vanishing mores of the tribe.

Book Talk Material

The bishop's conversation with the doctor (pp. 11-12; p. 9, pap.) will introduce the book effectively. Other important passages: the bishop tells Mark about the village (pp. 20-23; pp. 18-20, pap.); Mark's first burial service (pp. 26–31; pp. 23–28, pap.); he watches the salmon run (pp. 47–51; pp. 45–48, pap.); and he attends a potlatch (pp. 72–74; pp. 68–70, pap.).

Additional Selections

At 18, Jordan Phillips discovers he is slowly dying of the same muscular disorder that killed Lou Gehrig in Paige Dixon's *May I Cross Your Golden River?* (Atheneum, 1975, $7.95). A 19-year-old girl discovers she has an incurable form of cancer in Gunnel Beckman's *Admission to the Feast* (Holt, 1972, $4.95). John Donovan's *Wild in the World* (Harper, 1971, $4.79; pap., Avon, $1.25) explores death in rural America. A brother and sister travel through the wilderness in British Columbia in Barbara Corcoran's *A Star to the North* (Nelson, 1970, $3.95). In Jill Paton Walsh's *Goldengrove* (Farrar, 1972, $4.50; pap., Avon, 95¢), a young girl is driven to attempt suicide. The life of Grey Owl is told in Lovat Dickson's *Wilderness Man* (Atheneum, 1973, $10). Also use biographies of Florence Nightingale, Father Damien, and John Muir.

About the Author

Who's Who in America (39th Edition). Chicago: Marquis Who's Who, Inc., 1976. Vol. 1, p. 684.

William Campbell Gault, *The Oval Playground*
Dutton, 1968, $5.95

In the number and quality of his sports stories, William Campbell Gault is in the same league with pros such as Joe Archibald, William E. Butterworth, and John R. Tunis. Although he writes knowingly about many sports, Gault's best stories are about football, like *Quarterback Gamble* (Dutton, 1973, $5.50; pap., 95¢), and various forms of automobile racing, including several, like the one described in this book, on dirt tracks. They are read chiefly by boys in the upper elementary and junior high school grades.

Plot Summary

Some boys specialize in athletics or school-related activities, but Mark Devlin is a grease ball, who, like his late father, has a consuming interest in automobiles and racing. He is finishing his senior year at high school in a small town in southern California and helps supplement the family income and satisfy his interests by working part-time at a garage owned by Al Duncan, his father's boyhood friend. After graduation Mark plans to work full-time at Al's garage until he and his mother, who has a job at the local library, can accumulate enough money so that he can attend college. Al, who is almost a surrogate father to Mark, encourages the boy in his plans and provides many moneymaking opportunities by giving him overtime at the garage.

Al decides that he would like one last fling as a dirt track driver and, although at 42 he is considered old in racing circles, he remembers the great times he had racing with Mark's father. Despite ridicule from many of his peers, he adamantly sticks to his plan. He buys a secondhand, light-blue Rafield and in it Mark and Al install a D–O four engine that they tear down and rebuild after purchasing it in San Diego from an ex-driver, Stan Nowak. Mark patiently explains to his mother that D–O four means an engine with 4 cylinders, 16 valves, and double overhead camshafts.

A new league, the Western Dirt Track Association, has been formed to utilize some of the abandoned or rarely used dirt tracks in the area, and Al plans to enter the Nowak at their Sunday meets. Duncan thinks that with the great car, himself as driver, and two fine mechanics, Mark and his friend, Pete Lopez, as partners, he has an excellent racing combination. However, Mark notices that this ardor cools somewhat when Al puts the car through some practice runs and he sees what tough young competition he will be facing. Al gives Mark a chance at the wheel and, although he has participated previously only in a jalopy at drag races, the young man soon adjusts well to this new form of racing.

At their first meet, Mark is allowed to drive the opener, 10 miles, and, partly because the competition isn't too great, he comes in second, losing to Chris Tyler, a young but very proficient driver. The second race they enter is for 25 miles. Al drives. The competition is much stiffer and includes excellent drivers such as Gus Mayer, Chris Tyler, and the past champion, Tudi Petrini, but, through some luck and skillful maneuvering, Al finishes a respectable fifth, with Petrini, as expected, the winner.

At his graduation, Mark hears his class president, Larry Beam, address the group on how young people should aim to succeed, but not at the expense of their true aspirations and interests. Mark begins to wonder about his own future.

Although he is now working full-time during the week, it is the dirt track racing on Sundays that becomes the focus of his and Al's attention. Each weekend they travel to another track, sometimes as far as Arizona and Nevada. While Mark becomes an increasingly more expert and able driver, Al remains at the same level and begins to show signs of weariness and tension. Mark takes over more of the driving.

Mark and Al learn that Stan Nowak is attending the meets to scout talent. He is looking for a gifted young man whom he can groom to take the place of his championship driver, Ray Gaskin, who is retiring. For the chosen one it will mean the big time, lots of money, and maybe a crack at the Indianapolis 500. From scuttlebutt in the pits, Mark learns that the choice has been narrowed to himself and Chris Tyler.

In an important race, Mark passes Tyler, but still he comes in third, next to Mayer with the winner, as usual, Petrini. The big one, and last of the season, is 100 miles, and because he now realizes his own weaknesses, Al asks Mark to enter. During the first half, the boy drives cautiously, maintaining a sixth position, but later he opens up, passing one by one, including Chris Tyler. In a last-minute burst of speed, Mark finishes first, only a few feet ahead of Petrini. After a round of congratulations, Stan Nowak comes to the pit and offers Mark the position. The young man remembers Larry Beam's graduation address and realizes that an acceptance will mean giving up both his friends and his future education. He turns to Nowak and says politely, "I'm sorry. It's not for me. Thank you just the same."

Thematic Material

This is a slight novel both in length and substance, but it satisfies two prerequisites of this genre: a fast-moving plot and plenty of sports action. The author makes the point that in racing the real competition is not the opponent but yourself and that contributing one's best effort is the true measurement of sportsmanship. Mark's self-reliance and growing ability to make wise decisions affecting his future are also important themes.

Book Talk Material

This book can be effectively introduced by giving a brief plot summary. Al outlines his plan to return to the dirt track and Mark discusses this (pp. 10-12). Some of the racing action occurs in the following passages: Mark's first race (pp. 48-50); Al tries driving (pp. 52-57); Mark is again defeated by Tyler (pp. 83-85); and he turns the tables (pp. 90-94).

Additional Selections

When Steve works at the Amalgamated Motors Corp., he becomes interested in automobile racing in William E. Butterworth's *Team Racer* (Grosset, 1972, $3.95). By the same author, use *Fast Green Car* (Grosset, 1974, $2.50) and *Crazy to Race* (Grosset, 1974, $2.50). When personal tragedy strikes a college freshman, he reconsiders a career in automobile racing in Margaret and George Ogan's *Raceway Charger* (Westminster,

1974, $5.50). Other books by the Ogans are *Donavan's Dusters* (Westminster, 1975, $3.95) and *Desert Road Racer* (Westminster, 1970, $3.95). Under the pseudonym of Patrick O'Connor, Leonard Wibberley has written such "Black Tiger" racing stories as *Black Tiger at Bonneville* (Hale, 1960, $3.72) and *Black Tiger at LeMans* (Washburn, 1958, $4.95; pap., Berkley, 75¢).

About the Author

Commire, Anne. *Something about the Author*. Detroit: Gale Research Co., 1976.
 Vol. 8, pp. 69–70.
Kinsman, Clare D., Ed. *Contemporary Authors*. Detroit: Gale Research Co., 1975.
 Vol. 49, p. 203.
Ward, Martha E. and Dorothy A. Marquardt. *Authors of Books for Young People*.
 (2nd Edition). Metuchen, N.J.: Scarecrow Press, Inc., 1971, p. 195.

Walter Macken, *The Flight of the Doves*
Macmillan, 1968, $5.95; pap., Collier, 95¢

An Irishman by birth, Walter Macken was a distinguished actor and playwright who worked for several years with the famed Abbey Theatre in Dublin. His first book for children, *Island of the Great Yellow Ox* (Macmillan, 1966, $4.95), is a thriller about four young boys who help two villains unearth a giant Druid treasure and then are left to die. *The Flight of the Doves* was published in this country posthumously in 1968 and filmed by Columbia Pictures. It is enjoyed by students from the fifth through eighth grades.

Plot Summary

The novel begins, "Finn made up his mind on an April afternoon." Finn is 12-year-old Finn Dove, and his decision is to run away with his seven-year-old sister, Derval, from the house of "Uncle" Toby, his stepfather. Finn's mother, an O'Flaherty from the western part of Ireland, had come to England to work and later married an Englishman named Dove. They had two children. After his tragic death in an automobile accident, she remarried. Her new husband was Tobias Morgan, the lodger that the Doves had taken in. Two years ago Mrs. Dove also died, leaving Finn and Derval in Toby's hands. Outwardly the man is sociable and polite, but to the children he is a tyrant who administers frequent beatings to Finn and has begun to threaten gentle Derval.

Finn has decided that somehow he and his sister must get to Ireland where kindly Grandma O'Flaherty and his uncles live. Although Toby has deliberately lost contact with this part of the family, Finn remembers his mother taking him to the O'Flaherty's for a happy visit. Unfortunately, he has no specific address beyond the fact that the village is in the western part of Ireland and that, after the boat, he took two trains and a bus. The only lucky aspect of the plan is that the Doves live in the English coastal town from which the boat leaves for Ireland.

One evening after a particularly severe reprimand from Toby, Finn decides they must leave immediately. While Toby is having his after-dinner pint at the Red Dragon, Finn packs their schoolbags and a little food. The only extra items they take are Derval's teddy bear and Finn's geography book, filled with colored pictures of all countries, including Ireland. They have only a few shillings even after Finn sells his air rifle and roller skates to his friend, Joss Bleaker.

By mingling with a large family at the pier, the two children slip by the ticket collector and get aboard the ship. During the night, Finn manages to keep them hidden. In the morning they land in Ireland. Unable to get on the boat train, Finn and Derval wander into town.

In the meantime, Toby has discovered that the children are gone. He only misses them later that day when his employer, a lawyer named Purdom, informs him that one of the children's uncles has died in America and left a goodly amount of money in trust for them. At this point, Toby tells the police that the children are missing and offers £100 reward for their return. He conveniently makes no mention of the trust fund.

Finn and Derval join a group of children in playing soccer, with Derval serving as a goalpost. After the game, the group leader, Poll, and his brothers and sisters take the runaways home for dinner. There they tell their story, and the father, Tom, decides to help them by giving them 10 shillings and taking them to meet Nickser, a jolly lorry driver whose route is through western Ireland. Minutes after the children leave Poll's house, a stranger named Michael arrives and begins to ask questions. He is a detective hot on the trail.

Nickser begins his drive with the children, but almost immediately the police arrive and charge him with transporting stolen goods. The children flee and hide under a bridge. They later learn from Nickser that even the newspapers have their story. Finn cuts Derval's hair and disguises her as a boy, Terry. They set out once more, narrowly missing Michael. As the detective stands over the bridge holding strands of Derval's hair, he wonders if they really should be caught. Perhaps instead they should be helped. So he checks himself off the case and begins a private investigation.

Forced to enter a town to get food, they are spotted by Toby, who has joined the chase. Michael helps them to escape. He questions them and learns about Toby's cruelty. From newspaper accounts and his investigation, Michael has learned that Granny O'Flaherty lives in a town called Carraigmore. He gives Finn a map and directions, but tells them that he cannot break the law by taking them there himself. Instead, he leaves for England to learn more about Toby's real motives for demanding the return of the children.

The children are "adopted" by a young boy, Moses, and his family of gypsies. As part of this large group, Finn and Derval are able to get across the heavily guarded bridge at the Shannon River. Moses' father, Powder, suddenly realizes who these waifs really are and is about to turn them in for the reward, when Moses warns them and they escape once more.

After two more days of wandering, Finn becomes aware that an ugly man with a great scar on his face is following them. His name is Nicko, an American, who is supposedly checking on the disposition of their late uncle's funds. The children are suspicious of him.

On the last part of their journey through a misty bog, they are followed by both the police and Nicko. At last they reach the clearing before their grandmother's house and are scooped up by their waiting uncles, Paddy and Jed, who take them to the safety of their new home.

At the formal hearing, the judge hears testimony from Toby and from the children, but also from Michael, who not only tells about the trust fund but also promises to produce witnesses who will testify as to Toby's cruelty. The court awards custody of the children to their grandmother, and, for the first time, Michael sees Finn smile.

Thematic Material

This is a compelling and affecting story filled with suspense and action. The reader actively sympathizes with the plight of the children and hopes for their success, as well as being touched by the devotion between brother and sister. Throughout the story, Finn displays great courage and heroism. In his writing, the author has vividly and sometimes humorously captured the landscape and inhabitants of rural Ireland.

Book Talk Material

There are a number of excellent incidents in the book, such as: Uncle Toby's treatment of the children (pp. 2–4; same pagination, pap.); Finn and Derval leave Toby (pp. 14–16; pp. 15–17, pap.); they get on the ship (pp. 20–22; pp. 22–24, pap.); Toby and the trust fund (pp. 32–36; pp. 36–39, pap.); and Finn meets Poll and plays soccer (pp. 43–47; pp. 46–51, pap.).

Additional Suggestions

Four runaways try to survive in a condemned building in London in Roy Brown's *Flight of Sparrows* (Macmillan, 1973, $4.95). Its sequel is *The*

White Sparrow (Seabury, 1975, $6.95). In *No Promises in the Wind* (Follett, 1970, $4.95; pap., Tempo, 95¢) by Irene Hunt, 15-year-old Josh leaves home to escape a cruel father. An additional novel about runaways is *Don't Slam the Door When You Go* (Atheneum, 1972, $6.95) by Barbara Corcoran. The ordeal of two boys trapped in a blizzard is excitingly told in Roderic Jeffries' *Trapped* (Harper, 1972, $4.79; pap., $1.25). Two children are marooned on a small harbor island in Bianca Bradbury's *Two on an Island* (Houghton, 1965, $4.95). Other good titles include Gudrun Alcock's *Turn the Next Corner* (Lothrop, 1969, $6.95) and Alberta Armer's *Troublemaker* (Collins+World, 1966, o.p.).

Richard Peck, *The Ghost Belonged to Me*
Viking, 1975, $5.95; pap., Avon, $1.25

In *The Ghost Belonged to Me*, Richard Peck has abandoned the usual contemporary milieu of his novels for a glimpse at an earlier, more gentle period. The time is 1913 and the place, a small midwestern Mississippi River valley town, Bluff City. In its characters and setting, the story is reminiscent of several of Booth Tarkington's novels or those of August Derleth that deal with the amateur boy-detectives Sim Jones and Steve Grendon. The book is suitable for both upper elementary and junior high school youngsters.

Plot Summary

Thirteen-year-old Alexander Armsworth's nemesis is his classmate, Blossom Culp, who appropriately has been nicknamed by Lucille, Alexander's older sister, "Arachnid" because Blossom definitely has a spidery look. She is, in short, a pest, but such a persistent one that Alexander constantly finds her meddling in his affairs. One day, against his better judgment, he allows Blossom to blackmail him into walking her home with the promise of receiving "vital information" from her. It seems that Blossom's mother, who claims to be clairvoyant, has seen a pink halo surrounding the Armsworth's barn, a sure sign that it is haunted by the ghost of a young girl.

Back home, Alexander cautiously explores the barn. He hears a low whining sound and discovers a small dog with a fractured leg. He names the dog Trixie and fashions splints for it. Later that night Alexander sees a candle burning in the barn. He wonders if this might be connected with the suicide, some years back, of Captain Campbell, the original owner of their house, but then decides the whole thing is another one of Blossom's hoaxes.

Over breakfast the Armsworths are joined by their feisty, outspoken Uncle Miles, an 85-year-old Civil War veteran who continually embarrasses the very prim and socially conscious Mrs. Armsworth with his outspoken language. Still a fine carpenter, Uncle Miles is given the job of constructing a latticework pavilion in the front yard. This is to be the site of the Armsworth's social event of the season, Lucille's coming-out party. Although the next few days are taken up with preparing for the gala, Alexander periodically visits the barn where he sees disquieting signs of occupancy, even though Trixie has disappeared as mysteriously as she came.

Up to midpoint the party is properly genteel and seemingly successful, but then disaster strikes. Lucille's beau, Tom Hackett, scion of one of the town's wealthiest families, arrives drunk and drives his car onto the lawn, scattering the guests. His behavior so outrages Mrs. Schumate, a cousin of the Armsworths, who is in charge of the punch bowl, that she in turn tips its contents over the drunken young man. In the next day's newspaper, the incident is tactfully commented on by the young reporter Lowell Seaforth, who states: "A sudden dampness spelled a premature end to one of the season's most select occasions. Mrs. Elvira Schumate poured."

That night Alexander again sees a light in the barn, and, clad only in his nightshirt, he goes out to investigate. There he sees a young girl, who tells him that she is Inez Dumaine. She then mumbles incoherently about an impending accident involving a trolley car, a trestle, and a man with only one arm. She begs Alexander to prevent it. Alexander remembers that one of the townsmen, Amory Timmons, had lost an arm in a streetcar accident and had recently become manic in his obsession for revenge. The boy runs to the local trestle and finds it has been set afire by the half-crazed Timmons. Fortunately, he is able to flag down the trolley car and prevent the tragedy.

Under pressure from prying reporters and inquisitive neighbors, Alexander finally bursts out with the story of his encounter with the ghost of Inez Dumaine. Few will believe him until Uncle Miles sets the record straight with a most remarkable tale.

In the early days of the Civil War, a wealthy New Orleans family, the Dumaines, approached the captain of a Mississippi steamboat, Captain Thibodaux, urging him to take their daughter, Inez, to safety in the North. He agreed, but, because of his recklessness, his ship sank. In spite of his efforts to save her, the girl drowned. Sewn in her clothing, the Captain found hundreds of jewels, the Dumaine family fortune. He carried the body inland to Bluff City and secretly buried the girl along with her crippled dog. With his new wealth, he built a huge home on the same property and changed his name to Campbell. But shortly afterward, unable to contain his guilt and remorse, he hanged himself. Before his death, he told Uncle Miles the macabre story and showed him the burial place alongside what is now the Armsworth's barn. It is obvious to Uncle Miles that Inez is fated to roam the earth as a restless ghost until her body is exhumed and taken to the family vault in New Orleans.

The grisly business of digging begins at the burial site. Amid dozens of reporters and sensation-seekers, the skeleton of the girl and her dog are unearthed, along with a tiny brooch, the only remnant left of the Dumaine fortune.

Uncle Miles and Alexander manage to elude the spectators and catch a train to New Orleans with the boxful of remains. One person they cannot evade is Blossom Culp, who comes along as a stowaway. By one of Blossom's diversionary tactics, they are also able to slip off the train unnoticed and place the remains in the Dumaine tomb. For her help, Blossom is given Inez's brooch.

Gradually things settle back to normal in Bluff City, but there are two beneficial outcomes of the incident—Lucille gives up Tom Hackett in favor of the reporter Lowell Seaforth, and Alexander becomes slightly more tolerant of Blossom.

Thematic Material

This is primarily a tale of the supernatural, complete with eerie effects and macabre details. It also evokes a period of Americana when automobiles were luxury items, trolley cars were a mainstay, and "damn" was a forbidden word. There are wholesome family relationships present, particularly between Alexander and his elderly uncle. The boy's courage and perseverance are also well depicted.

Book Talk Material

To introduce the book, one could use the passage where Blossom tells Alexander that his barn is haunted (pp. 15-17; pp. 16-17, pap.). Other interesting passages are: Alexander finds Trixie (pp. 23-25; pp. 21-22, pap.); Uncle Miles tells a ghost story (pp. 47-51; pp. 36-39, pap.), and Lucille's party (pp. 67-71; pp. 50-53, pap.).

Additional Selections

One could use those authors mentioned in the introduction. Some youngsters foretell a kidnapping and try to prevent it in Catherine Storr's *The Chinese Egg* (McGraw-Hill, 1975, $6.95). A harp and a rumbling mountain figure in Joan Aiken's *The Whispering Mountain* (pap., Dell, $1.50). Also use the same author's collection of suspense and horror stories, *The Green Flash* (Holt, 1973, $5.95; pap., Dell, 95¢). Two boys find a body near an amusement park in Peck's earlier *Dreamland Lake* (Holt, 1973, $5.95; pap., Avon, 95¢). A mystery story set partly in Venezuela, involving a family curse and a portrait of Simón Bolívar, are elements in Madeline L'Engle's *Dragon in the Water* (Farrar, 1976, $7.95). Other tales of the supernatural are Martin Cobalt's *Pool of Swallows* (Nelson, 1974, $5.95); Josephine Poole's *The Visitor* (Harper, 1972, $4.79); and Mabel Allan's *A Chill in the Lane* (Nelson, 1974, $5.95). Further adventures of Blossom Culp are told in Richard Peck's *Ghosts I Have Known* (Viking, 1977, $6.95).

Charles Portis, *True Grit*

Simon & Schuster, 1968, $7.95; pap., New Amer. Lib., $1.25

In this book the author has created two outrageously overdrawn, yet thoroughly believable characters, which readers will remember long after finishing the novel. They are the shrewd, indomitable, 14-year-old heroine, Mattie Ross, and her tarnished Galahad, the one-eyed gunfighter, Marshal Rooster Cogburn. This mismatched pair have only one quality in common—true grit. The novel takes place in the late 1870s, but it is told by Mattie in retrospect some 50 years later. The film version of the novel was so popular that a sequel, *Rooster Cogburn*, was produced. Originally written for adults, *True Grit* is enjoyed by young people in the junior high school grades and up.

Plot Summary

Frank Ross, his wife, and three children, Mattie, younger sister Victoria, and Little Frank, are farming a large stretch on the Arkansas River, some 70 miles east of Fort Smith. Ross takes a newly hired hand, Tom Chaney, and $250 with him to Fort Smith to buy some Texas mustang ponies. After their business is finished, Chaney gets drunk, shoots Ross dead, steals his horses and remaining money, and then flees across the river into the territory called Oklahoma.

Mattie, with Yarnell Poindexter, a friend of the family, goes by train to Fort Smith to bring back the body. There they witness the public hanging of three outlaws. Mattie tells Yarnell that she must stay to rescue her father's horses, and she sends him home with the body. Her real purpose for staying is to find a way to avenge her father's death. From the local sheriff she learns two things: Chaney is believed to have joined a gang of outlaws led by Lucky Ned Pepper, and the meanest, most pitiless federal marshal in the territory is Rooster Cogburn, currently in town to testify at a murder trial.

Mattie's bargaining gets $325 out of the auctioneer, Mr. Stonehill, for the horses, including her father's, which supposedly were under Stonehill's care when stolen. She later visits the courthouse and meets Rooster Cogburn, as rough and tough-looking as his reputation. She accompanies him to his vile-smelling, rat-infested room where he proceeds to get drunk. But they reach a tentative agreement that Rooster will hunt down Chaney for $100.

Back at the boarding house, Mattie meets Sergeant LeBoeuf of the Texas Rangers. He too has been trailing Chaney, who, under the name of Theron Chelmsford, shot a Texas senator. There is a large reward for his capture, and LeBoeuf plans to get it. When he suggests they join forces, Mattie refuses because LeBoeuf wants Chaney taken alive to face trial and Mattie wants him dead.

After Mattie has reached an agreement with Rooster, LeBoeuf outbids her with his offer to share the reward. The following morning the two men leave for the territory, but they are followed by Mattie riding her small horse, Little Blackie, bought from Mr. Stonehill. She is carrying some provisions and her father's revolver. The men try to lose her, but she sticks with them, and they finally let her join them.

The three head for McAlester's store, some 60 miles away, where Ned Pepper's gang was last seen. During the trip, Rooster, often drunk, talks of his former life and the dozens of shootouts in which he was involved—all, until now, on the wrong side of the law. A snowstorm comes up and they stop for shelter in a sand-covered dugout. There they capture two known robbers, Emmett Quincey and a man named Moon. These men obviously know something about Pepper, but when Moon begins to talk Quincey stabs him. Rooster shoots Quincey. Before he dies, Moon tells him that Pepper's gang will stop at the dugout later that evening after a train robbery. Rooster plans an ambush, but in the gunfight five of the gang escape, including Lucky, leaving part of their loot, and two more dead gang members. At McAlester's, the three learn the approximate location of Lucky's hideout.

On the trail again, they stop and Mattie searches for water. At a stream she sees a man watering horses. He looks up, and she is staring into the eyes of Tom Chaney! She tries to shoot him but only wounds him before she is captured and dragged across the stream. The shot arouses the rest of the gang, and when Rooser and LeBoeuf get there they are told that Mattie will be killed unless they leave.

Satisfied that they are gone, Lucky and the rest of the gang push on, leaving Chaney behind to take care of Mattie and act as a lookout. When they have gone a short distance, Rooster charges at them on horseback with revolvers blazing. All four of the gang are killed before the marshal's horse is shot from under him. Meanwhile, LeBoeuf tries to save Mattie, but he is knocked unconscious by a rock thrown by Chaney. Mattie grabs a gun and shoots him. Again she only wounds Chaney, but the backfire from the gun is so powerful that she staggers and falls into a pit of rattlesnakes. Overhead she hears Chaney's voice, then sounds of a struggle. Rooster has come to rescue her. In seconds, Chaney's lifeless body is hurled into the pit. Before she can get out, a rattlesnake bites her hand. Rooster and Mattie set out for Fort Smith and a doctor, leaving LeBoeuf to take Chaney's body back to Texas.

Mattie's arm must be amputated, and she is sent home. Through the years she loses touch with Rooster, until 25 years later, now a successful, unmarried businesswoman, Mattie learns he has joined a Wild West show. She travels to Memphis where the show is playing, but it is too late. Rooster has died a few days before. Mattie brings the body back to her home and has Rooster buried next to her father.

Thematic Material

Portis has written a moving and often uproarious tale that is also a rousing adventure story filled with suspense and action. Mattie's singleminded innocence, along with her courage and resourcefulness, reminds one of the legendary spirit of the Old West and "true grit" responsible for opening up the country. The matter-of-fact writing style matches the tale to perfection.

Book Talk Material

Here are a few of the many wonderful passages that could be used: Mattie witnesses the hanging (pp. 17–20; pp. 20–23, pap.); she bargains with

Stonehill (pp. 29-35; pp. 30-35, pap.); she talks to Rooster for the first time (pp. 55-60; pp. 51-56, pap.); Mattie meets LeBoeuf (pp. 68-72; pp. 62-66, pap.); and she follows the two men until they accept her (pp. 100-107; pp. 90-96, pap.).

Additional Selections

In Patricia Beatty's *By Crumbs! It's Mine* (Morrow, 1976, $6.95), a 13-year-old girl becomes the owner of a hotel in the Arizona territory of the 1880s. A boy searches for his father during the Depression in Edward Fenton's *Duffy's Rocks* (Dutton, 1974, $5.95). In rural Tennessee at the turn of the century, a teen-aged girl copes with the death of father, brother, and dear friend in Diana Glaser's *The Diary of Trilby Frost* (Holiday, 1976, $6.95). *Of Time and Seasons* (Atheneum, 1975, $7.75) by Norma Johnston tells how, during the Civil War, a retiring girl assumes great responsibilities. Also use the sequel, *A Striving after Wind* (Atheneum, 1976, $8.95). Other novels dealing with quests for parents are Harry Mazer's *Dollar Man* (Delacorte Pr., 1974, $5.95; pap., Dell, 95¢) and Jean Montgomery's *Search for the Wild Shore* (Morrow, 1974, $6.95).

Theodore Taylor, *The Cay*
Doubleday, 1969, $5.95; pap., Avon, $1.25

Since *The Cay* appeared in 1969, Theodore Taylor has written a variety of books for young people. Nonfiction works, such as *Air Raid Pearl Harbor* (Crowell, 1971, $4.50) and *Rebellion Town: Williamsburg, 1776* (Crowell, 1973, $5.95) have been interspersed with such fiction as the upper elementary *Teetoncey* stories. A few years ago *The Cay* was adapted for television, starring James Earl Jones as Timothy. It is enjoyed by children in the upper elementary grades and up.

Plot Summary

In February 1942, German U boats attack the Netherlands Antilles. They blow up the oil refinery on Aruba and six small lake tankers in the harbor of Willemstad on Curaçao. For the narrator, 11-year-old Phillip Enright, whose father is an American engineer working in the oil refineries, these attacks set off an amazing chain of events.

Immediately Phillip's mother fears that the attacks will grow and might lead to shelling of civilian areas. She pleads with her husband to book passage on a freighter so that she and Phillip can return to the United States. Reluctantly, Mr. Enright agrees. In early April they sail on a small

Dutch freighter, the *S.S. Hato,* bound for Miami after a stop at Panama. Phillip's father feels confident that the Germans would not waste a torpedo on such an old tub. But he is wrong—two days after leaving Panama, the freighter is sunk.

Phillip and his mother are lowered into a lifeboat, but the boat capsizes and Phillip is knocked unconscious. He awakens some hours later in a life raft with crew member Timothy and the cook's cat, named Stew. Timothy is confident that Phillip's mother has been saved; he is also confident that they will be saved because they have a small supply of water, biscuits, and some matches. He speaks in the colorful speech of the West Indies. Later he tells Phillip that he grew up on St. Thomas in the American Virgin Islands. Timothy protects the boy by building a shelter of his clothing and trying to keep up his spirits. He catches fish for them and rations the water supply. Phillip resents his leadership and remembers his mother's attitude of distrust and scorn toward all blacks as being inferior.

Phillip suffers increasingly from headaches after the blow he received. On the second day, the pain disappears, but Phillip is blind. Timothy tries to reassure him that the blindness is temporary, but Phillip will not be consoled, and he blames Timothy for separating him from his mother.

On the fourth day they sight land. Leaving Phillip on the shore, Timothy explores their new home. He tells Phillip that they are on a small cay—maybe the Devil's Mouth Cay—shaped like a melon. There are sea grapes and palm trees, but, except for small lizards, there is no animal life. Timothy builds a shelter of palm fronds on the highest part of the island and makes a fire pile on the beach to be ignited if they see a plane or ship. Phillip learns that Timothy can neither read nor write when he haltingly asks for assistance in spelling "help" for the message he builds out of large stones on the beach.

With great patience and understanding, Timothy slowly breaks down Phillip's antagonisms and his reluctance to participate in chores. Early in May (Phillip counts the days by dropping a pebble each day into a can), Timothy gets tropical fever. He becomes delirious and rushes into the ocean. Phillip is able to save him from drowning by dragging him back onto the beach, but Timothy never fully regains his strength. As though he senses his own death, he begins to make Phillip as self-sufficient as possible. He teaches him how to fish and to master the skill of climbing palm trees to collect coconuts.

In July a hurricane strikes. As the waves come up the beach to their clearing, Timothy lashes himself and Phillip to a palm tree. The waves crash over their heads and Phillip loses consciousness. When he awakens, the storm has died, but Stew, the cat, is gone and Timothy is unconscious. Phillip unties Timothy and realizes that, in his efforts to protect the boy, Timothy had placed his back to the storm and there is not a place on his legs and back that is uncut. Timothy dies, and Phillip buries him in the sand.

Stew comes back, but Phillip is blind and alone on a forgotten cay. But he has learned his lessons from Timothy well. He rebuilds the shelter, the signal fire, and the stone message. He is able to fish and gather food as Timothy taught him.

Early in August, he hears a plane overhead, but, in spite of his fire and shouting, the plane goes away. But on the morning of August 20, Phillip hears thunderlike explosions and wonders if a sea battle is in progress. He lights a signal fire and throws vines of sea grapes on it to create a dense smoke. About noon a small boat lands on the cay. The sailors are from an American destroyer.

Phillip is reunited with his parents and sent to New York for operations that eventually restore his sight. He often studies nautical maps of the area to see where cays like the Devil's Mouth are located. Someday he knows that he must return to that tiny island where his friend Timothy is buried.

Thematic Material

The author dedicates this book: "To Dr. King's dream which can only come true if the very young know and understand." The book will help to give young people the knowledge and understanding to combat attitudes of racial prejudice and bigotry. Phillip's changes in feeling toward blacks develop logically and convincingly. There is also an interesting contrast in wisdom and strength versus innocence and weakness. The theme of man against nature is also important, with some parts of the book constituting a West Indies survival manual.

Book Talk Material

The Cay is largely episodic; therefore, there are many fine sections suitable for introducing the book: the *Hato* is torpedoed (pp. 28-31; pp. 39-41, pap.); life on the raft and Phillip's prejudice (pp. 35-38; pp. 36-39, pap.); Phillip goes blind (pp. 44-46; pp. 46-48, pap.); constructing the signals on the island (pp. 66-68; 70-72, pap.); and Phillip learns to work (pp. 70-72; pp. 74-76, pap.).

Additional Suggestions

Theodore Taylor has written several fine titles, including *The Children's War* (Doubleday, 1971, $4.95), in which a 12-year-old Alaskan boy helps an American spy operation during World War II, and *Battle in the Arctic Sea* (Crowell, 1976, $6.50), also set during World War II, but the story of the ill-fated voyage of a convoy from Iceland to Russia. How two black boys journeyed from the South to freedom in the pre-Civil War is told in *Steal Away Home* by Jane Kristof (Bobbs-Merrill, 1969, $4.95). The true story of a beginning teacher in a black Philadelphia high school is the theme of Sunny Decker's *An Empty Spoon* (Harper, 1969, $5.95; pap., Harper, 95¢). Marilyn Harris' *The Peppersalt Land* (Four Winds, 1970, $4.88; pap., Scholastic, 95¢) tells about the stormy friendship between a white girl and a black girl. Other recommended titles with racial themes are William E. Barrett's *Lilies of the Field* (Doubleday, 1962, $3.50; pap., Popular Library, 95¢; condensed in *Juniorplots*, Bowker, 1967); Lorenz Graham's many "Town" books, including *Return to South Town* (Crowell, 1976, $6.50); and Mini Brodsky's *The House at 12 Rose Street* (pap., Archway, 95¢).

About the Author

Commire, Anne. *Something about the Author.* Detroit: Gale Research Co., 1973. Vol. 5, pp. 183–185.

Harte, Barbara and Carolyn Riley, Eds., *Contemporary Authors.* Detroit: Gale Research Co., 1969. Vols. 21–22, p. 530.

Who's Who in America (38th Edition). Chicago: Marquis Who's Who, Inc., 1974. Vol. 2, pp. 3044–3045.

Robb White, *Deathwatch*
Doubleday, 1972, $4.95; pap., Dell, 95¢

Robb White first made his mark in young adult literature by drawing on his Navy experience for a series of sea stories, many with a World War II background. Some are: *Up Periscope* (o.p.), *Torpedo Run* (Doubleday, 1962, $3.50), and *The Frogmen* (Doubleday, 1973, $4.95; pap., Dell, 95¢). In *Deathwatch*, he uses his same gifts of taut, gripping storytelling in a tale where two men are pitted against one another in a hostile environment. This is a favorite, particularly with both junior and senior high school boys.

Plot Summary

It was only a desperate need for money to finance his last year at college that convinced 22-year-old Ben that he should go with Mr. Madec, a L.A. corporation lawyer, to act as his desert guide on Madec's hunt for bighorn sheep. Ben had never met a more ruthless, cunning man. In the first three days in the desert he has also shown himself to be a dangerous hunter—a trigger-happy sadist who enjoys killing.

With his high-powered .358 Magnum, Madec accidentally shoots and kills an old prospector, mistaking him at a distance for his real quarry. At first he tries to hide the body from Ben, but when Ben discovers it, Madec tries to bribe the young man into not reporting the incident. He argues that, regardless of how unintentional the killing was, local authorities will be hard on a city man, his name will be in the papers, and the whole incident will cause both embarrassment and inconvenience. Ben will not be dissuaded, and as he makes plans to take the body in the jeep to town 75 miles away, Madec becomes even more insistent and nasty.

Madec takes Ben's rifle and shoots two slugs into the dead man so that it will appear that Ben could have been the murderer. Rather than kill Ben outright before having a chance to work out an alibi, he decides to let nature do the killing. He forces Ben to strip to his shorts and sends him without food or water into the desert.

Ben knows that at most he can last only two days without water. He also knows that it is ridiculous to attempt trekking across the desert to the nearest highway, 45 miles away. On his first night alone, he creeps back to the prospector's body, hoping at least to take his shoes, but Madec has anticipated this and stripped the body. Ben then searches and finds the old man's camp, but once more Madec has outwitted him. It has already been stripped. But, in a deserted area, Ben finds an aluminum slingshot, which he retrieves.

The cat-and-mouse game continues, with Ben forced to remain on an outcropping of rocks or risk complete exposure to Madec and his gun. On the second night, Ben, through an almost superhuman effort, manages to climb the smooth wall of a stone butte, thus at least making it difficult for Madec to pursue him. By this time his body is a raw pulp of wounds and lacerations, his lips have shreds of flesh hanging from them, and his tongue is badly swollen.

Just as an uncontrollable itching, the final symptom of death by dehydration, begins, Ben finds water in a small cave. Through practice with the slingshot, he is able to kill some birds who come there to drink.

The next day rescue seems at hand when a Fish and Game helicopter on a routine patrol lands for a few moments at Madec's camp. Ben tries waving and shouting, but he is not heard over the sound of the propellers.

Madec, now believing that Ben must be dead or close to death, begins making preparation to climb the steep butte by driving pitons into the stone wall. Ben witnesses Madec's work and that night decides on a bold scheme. When he is certain Madec is asleep, he gingerly lowers himself from the butte. Using Madec's footprints to escape detection, he walks in them backward to his enemy's camp. There, close to the jeep, he buries himself completely in the sand, using the hollow slingshot as tubes for breathing and hearing.

The next morning when Ben is sure Madec is again at work on the rock face, he emerges from the sand. He attracts Madec's attention by setting the tent on fire. Ben is able to wound Madec sufficiently by a rain of buckshot from his powerful slingshot; then he takes him captive.

Ben returns to town by jeep with Madec and the body of the old prospector. But there Madec is able to fabricate such an impressive alibi that, with the help of his two crafty lawyers, few people believe Ben's side of the story. Even the slingshot, which he claims he put in the jeep, is not found. Finally, when the slingshot is found where Madec hid it, and an investigating doctor proves that it was Madec's gun and not Ben's that killed the prospector, the case is broken. Madec is placed in custody and Ben is allowed to go free.

Thematic Material

Basically a fine, edge-of-seat thriller, *Deathwatch* is also a study in good versus evil, with good triumphing through fair and aboveboard methods. Ben is portrayed as a young man with human faults, but also as someone who has principles that he will uphold in spite of great adversity. The author describes the desert vividly and the adaptation made by plants and animals to survive in this environment.

Book Talk Material

The significance of the title in context of the story could be used as an introduction, as well as the theme of various forms of manhunts as portrayed on television or in movies and books. Some incidents to use are: Madec finds the prospector (pp. 8-12; pp. 16-19, pap.); Madec sends Ben away (pp. 35-39; pp. 35-41, pap.); and Ben assesses his situation (pp. 38-39, pp. 44-45, pap.).

Additional Suggestions

Two other recommended novels by Robb White are *The Frogman* (Doubleday, 1973, $4.95; pap., Dell, 95¢) and *No Man's Land* (Doubleday, 1969, $4.50), an adventure story about oceanography. In *Split Bamboo* by Leon Phillips (Doubleday, 1966, o.p.), the hero enters China to expose a U.S.-based spy ring and also to save his teen-age son. The true story of a girl who survived 49 days in a Yukon wilderness is told in Helen Klaben's *Hey,*

I'm Alive (McGraw-Hill, 1963, o.p.). A young man is stalked by a gang of killers in Jay Bennett's *Deathman Do Not Follow Me* (Hawthorn, 1968, $5.25; pap., Scholastic, 75¢). A boy's struggle to prevent being broiled alive by scorching heat when he is trapped atop a water pump is the theme of Glendon and Kathryn Swarthout's *Whichaway* (Random, 1966, $4.95). Paul Griffin survives alone in the White Mountains of New Hampshire in Peter Vureck's *The Summer I Was Lost* (Doubleday, 1965, $4.95; condensed in *Introducing Books*, Bowker, 1970). Also use Marian Rumsey's *High Country Adventure* (Manor, 1967, $4.95) and J. Allan Bosworth's *White Water, Still Water* (Doubleday, 1966, $4.95).

About the Author

Commire, Anne. *Something about the Author.* Detroit: Gale Research Co., 1971. Vol. 1, pp. 225–226.

Ethridge, James M. and Barbara Kopala, Eds. *Contemporary Authors*: Detroit: Gale Research Co., 1967. Vols. 1–4, p. 999.

Ward, Martha E. and Dorothy A. Marquardt. *Authors of Books for Young People.* (2nd Edition, 1971, p. 548; First Supplement, 1967, p. 266). Metuchen, N.J.: Scarecrow Press, Inc.

Who's Who in America (39th Edition). Chicago: Marquis Who's Who, Inc., 1976. Vol. 2, p. 3357.

7

Developing Relationships with Both Sexes

PUBERTY BRINGS with it heightened sexuality and an interest in exploring various aspects of this subject. Because society's values concerning sexual behavior and family relationships change rapidly and are often in conflict, sexual maturity in the social sense is often difficult to achieve. Each title in this section provides a different set of experiences that reveal facets of this problem.

Benedict and Nancy Freedman, *Mrs. Mike*
Coward, 1947, $7.95; pap., Berkley, $1.75

For over 30 years, the Freedman's novel biography of gallant Kathy Flannigan, the Mrs. Mike of the title, has been entertaining both adult and adolescent audiences. It is particularly enjoyed by girls in grades seven and up.

Plot Summary

Sixteen-year-old Katherine Mary O'Fallon, petite and as charming as any Irish colleen could be, is sent by her mother from Boston to recover from a pleurisy attack in the cold, dry climate of Uncle John's ranch north of Calgary. It is March of the severe winter of 1907, and the train trip alone from Montreal to Calgary takes 18 days. She is met by her Uncle John Kennedy, who recognizes her by a prearranged signal, a blue bow in her long auburn hair. Kathy gets a foreshadowing of the life ahead when she and her uncle go to a hotel to visit a widow, Mrs. Neilson, who is leaving the north country. Her husband lost his way to his barn in a blizzard and froze to death, although he was only a few yards from his home.

At her uncle's ranch, Kathy, who is one of the few white women in the

153

area, is naturally very popular and soon adjusts to this rough-and-tumble existence. She helps Johnny Flaherty, the cook, who is a Boer War veteran like her uncle, but who is also a fine toper. On one of his drunks, he is brought home by Sergeant Mike Flannigan of the Northwest Mounted. Mike is what every girl would expect in a Mountie—tall and handsome, with black, wavy hair. Kathy is immediately attracted to the man even though he is 11 years her senior. By his charming, teasing way and his attraction to Kathy, it is apparent that he feels the same attraction.

The courtship is a speedy one. On October 20, they are married and leave almost immediately on a two-month trip by train and dogsled to Hudson's Hope, 700 miles north of Edmonton on Great Slave Lake where Mike is to be stationed. The air becomes so cold that Kathy's right lung collapses, and Mike constructs a chest brace for her.

At Hudson's Hope, Kathy learns that Mike must be much more than a conventional Mountie; he is expected to be a priest, doctor, and even dentist, as well as a peace officer. It is a small village of slightly over 100 people. Kathy soon meets the inhabitants, becomes acquainted with their ways, and, in time, learns the rudiments of their Beaver language. At first she is overly anxious to teach the Indians hygiene and health care and to change such behavior as the belief that women are chattels who must be treated as animals, completely subservient to their men. Mike understands her feelings, but as one who knows thoroughly the Indians and their culture, and also the Mountie's role in the community, he tries to cool her crusading ardor.

Kathy meets the white proprietor of the Hudson's Bay Post, Jim Henderson, an embittered man who left his wife and came north after the death of his beloved son, Tommy. He has taken into his house a Klooch, an Indian woman who has given him a son, another Tommy, on whom he again showers attention and love.

During the summer Kathy redecorates their cabin and plants a small garden. A special happiness comes to the couple when Kathy realizes she is pregnant. However, before the summer is over, a catastrophe occurs. A forest fire gets out of hand and sweeps through the town. Some of the fortunate townspeople, including Kathy, take refuge by wading in the river. Only by staying under icy water until her lungs are about to explode is she able to escape the suffocating smoke and blistering heat. When it is over, 37 bodies—about one-third of the village—are collected. A few of those had taken refuge in a well. One of the charred bodies is that of a child—Tommy Henderson.

Before the Flannigans can rebuild their home, Mike is transferred south to a larger village, Grouard, on Lesser Slave Lake, about six weeks traveling time. While still on the trail, Kathy feels her first labor pains. Mike sends to Grouard for a reliable Cree midwife, Mrs. Carpentier, who arrives in time to deliver their firstborn, Mary Aroon.

Mrs. Carpentier, whom Kathy calls Rachel, is only one of the many new friends the Flannigans soon have in Grouard. There is Mike's helper, Constable Ned Cameron, the canny McTavish brothers, the sisters and Bishop Grouard from the Mission, and, most of all, Constance Beauclaire and her family. Constance's story is a tragic one. As a girl Kathy's age, her entire family died of smallpox on the trip from France to Canada. She married and came north, but of the nine children she has borne, only four have survived the disease and hardships of life in the wilderness.

At Mike's suggestion, Kathy brings home a live-in maid from the Mission School, a spirited and genial 15-year-old Indian girl, Mamanowatum, or Oh-Be-Joyful. The girl is in love with a proud and laconic canoe maker, Jonathan Forquet, but Kathy tries to convince Oh-Be-Joyful that she is too young for marriage.

Jonathan has a deadly enemy named Cardinal, a villainous thief who has stolen furs from trap lines, including Johnny's. Shortly after Cardinal's arrest by Sergeant Mike for robbery, he is found stabbed to death in his cell with Jonathan's knife in his throat. Jonathan will not deny or affirm his guilt, so reluctantly Mike arrests him. Eventually a deranged townswoman, Mrs. Marlin, admits using a knife Jonathan had given her to stab Cardinal, the man who, unknown to anyone, had savagely raped her some months before. Jonathan is freed, and he and Oh-Be-Joyful leave the town to begin their own lives together.

A second baby, Ralph, is born to Mike and Kathy. But before he is scarcely a few months old, diphtheria breaks out in town. Mike tries to isolate his family and begins living in his office, but without vaccine it is impossible to protect anyone. Kathy witnesses the painful death of both her children. With no more reason for remaining home, she goes to the village to nurse the sick and has to beat off starving sled dogs, who are fighting over the bodies of the dead and dying. The sights sicken her, but she continues to help.

Eventually the plague passes, but Kathy finds that something else has gone: the closeness and tenderness in her marriage. She decides she must get back to Boston for a visit, but as she leaves, the townspeople, including Mike and inwardly herself, wonder if she will ever return. But she does. Her love for Mike, plus her hatred of the pettiness and artificiality of Boston society convince her that she must remain in the North.

After World War I, another plague, the flu, hits Grouard. Constance is stricken, but before she dies she asks Kathy to adopt her orphaned grandchildren, Georges and Connie. Shortly after, Jonathan Forquet comes to Mike's home with a baby in his arms. Oh-Be-Joyful has also died of the flu, and he wants the Flannigans to raise Kathy, their only child. Mrs. Mike again has a family.

Thematic Material

In *Mrs. Mike*, the reader watches a love begin, grow to maturity, and then through hardship and tragedy, become tempered and stronger. However, this is more than a heartwarming and romantic love story. It gives a realistic, often brutally graphic picture of pioneer life in the North, which will sometimes make the reader wince with the pain of the situation. The novel also effectively describes the spartan beauty of the North country as well as the interesting and austere life of its inhabitants.

Book Talk Material

Because *Mrs. Mike* is largely episodic, there are many fine passages for use in book talks: Kathy meets Mrs. Neilson (pp. 9–14; pp. 9–13, pap.); Mike helps Kathy ride and cook (pp. 40–44; pp. 37–40, pap.); Mike's proposal after a dance (pp. 60–63; pp. 55–58, pap.); dinner on the trail and Kathy loses control (pp. 70–82; pp. 71–74, pap.); and Kathy meets some Indians (pp. 92–95; pp. 83–86, pap.).

Additional Selections

A Michigan farm family in mid-1950s and a settlement for escaped slaves figure in Elizabeth Howard's *North Winds Blow Free* (Morrow, 1949, $6.50). Rose Wilder Lane's *Let the Hurricane Roar* (Watts, 1966, $7.95) is a pioneer story about a young couple, Caroline and Charles, who live in a dugout in Dakota. The story of Anne Hobbs' life in 1927 when she was a schoolteacher in a one-room school in Alaska is told in her *Tisha* (St. Martin, 1976, $8.95). Also recommended is Mary Medearis' *Big Doc's Girl* (Lippincott, 1950, $6.50); Helen Miller's *Julie* (Doubleday, 1966, o.p.); and Mary Pearce's adult novel, *Apple Tree Lean Down* (St. Martins, 1976, $10).

About the Author

Who's Who in America (39th Edition). Chicago: Marquis Who's Who, Inc., 1976. Vol. 1, p. 1065.

Ann Head, *Mr. and Mrs. Bo Jo Jones*
Putnam, 1967, $7.95; pap., New Amer. Lib., 95¢

The term "sleeper" is usually applied in film circles to a modest, often unpretentious movie that has achieved an unexpected success at the box office. In the field of young adult literature, there are also many examples of "sleepers." Perhaps the classic is Maureen Daly's *Seventeenth Summer* (Dodd, 1942, $5.50; pap., Archway, 75¢), which, although now showing signs of age, has continued to remain popular through the years. Another is *Mr. and Mrs. Bo Jo Jones.* Since its first publication, this story of two star-crossed lovers, forced into a marriage for which they are woefully unprepared, has become a lasting favorite of readers, particularly girls, in the junior and senior high school grades.

Plot Summary

July Greher is 16 and a junior at Tilby High School in a small town close to Savannah, Georgia. Her family, upper middle class and well established, consists of her father, one of the town's bankers, and her mother—both kind and understanding parents—a younger sister, 14-year-old Grace, and brother, Gregory, nicknamed Gory, who is 12. July's boyfriend of the past few months is 17-year-old Bo Jo (short for Boswell Johnston) Jones, a senior and the school's star halfback, who hopes to earn a sports scholarship to college. Both are naive, carefree teen-agers until one night, after a party, they lose their sexual innocence by making love on a deserted beach. Both are equally stunned and mortified by their actions. They try to pretend that nothing has happened, but when July misses her monthly period and begins suffering spasms of nausea, she is filled with mounting dread and shame. Still not completely sure if she is pregnant, July confides in no one, not even her best friend, Mary Ann Simmons. She is about to tell Bo Jo, but because he has just received news granting his scholarship, the two, in company with four friends, instead celebrate at a Savannah night club where they are entertained by a talented amateur singer, Louella Consuela.

One day July skips school, buys a cheap wedding ring, and visits a doctor in a neighboring town, who confirms her worst fear. The next day she tells Bo Jo, and they decide to sneak across the state line, lie about their ages, and elope. Using a picnic as an excuse for an outing, Bo Jo picks July up the following Saturday in his father's truck, and in a sordid, undignified ceremony, using the same dime-store ring, they are pronounced man and wife by a justice of the peace more interested in his $10 fee than in their happiness. On the way back Bo Jo phones his parents, whom July has yet to meet. They are furious at the news and order him never to return to their home. At the Grehers, July has to entertain her parents' guests for the evening, including a handsome, outgoing Stanford sophomore, Horace Clark. After the gathering, she tells her shocked parents of her marriage. The despondent newlyweds spend the night in a hotel, thanks to Mr. Greher's gift of $20.

The next few days are spent trying to pacify the in-laws. July meets Bo Jo's parents, a working-class couple with pretensions of gentility who openly show their bitterness and disappointment at what they see as "the fall" of their only son. To mollify the Grehers, another "legitimate" marriage ceremony is performed, which the Joneses refuse to attend but at which July's wealthy Grandmother Greher, usually stern and forbidding, shows unusual kindness and understanding toward the couple.

Mr. Greher secures a job for Bo Jo at his bank, and after two agonizing weeks at the Joneses, the two move to a small but comfortable apartment over the garage of the Greher's friend, Hatty Barnes.

The days become lonely and despairing for July. She knows nothing about housekeeping; their former school friends, including Mary Ann, sensing the real reason for the marriage, are either uncomprehending or distant; and both pairs of in-laws, culturally and socially miles apart, are incompatible. These tensions, plus the knowledge that neither really wanted or was prepared for marriage, produces frequent, bitter quarrels during the first months together.

July finds a little consolation in two diversions: she carries on a secret correspondence with Horace Clark. In these letters she shares her interests in music and reading with the young man, but never tells him of her marriage. She also spends days with the young singer, Louella Consuela, whom she accidentally meets one day in a supermarket. Lou, also a lonely and confused teen-age bride, is married to Nick, an older man who is frequently absent from their home. When Lou becomes pregnant, she is so appalled at the idea of having a child that she has an abortion while her husband is away. July, although shocked at her friend's actions, helps nurse her back to health.

Later in the summer, Lou leaves Nick to try a singing career in New York City, and July, when she hears that Horace plans to visit her, guiltily breaks off their correspondence. However, after weathering the first stormy months together, Bo Jo and July begin to adjust to each other's differences and, for the first time, find some happiness in their marriage.

During the seventh month of her pregnancy, July begins hemorrhaging and is rushed to the hospital, where she gives birth to a boy. After only two days, their son, Jonathan, dies.

After July's recovery, the in-laws begin planning for the future: their children's lives can revert to where they were seven months before. Without the burden of a family, a divorce can be obtained; Bo Jo will attend college as planned; and July will attend a finishing school in New England. Uncertain of how the other feels, the couple silently consent, but when they return to their little apartment, filled with both bitter and pleasant memories, they realize that, through all of their misfortune, they have grown to love one another and that they must not part.

Thematic Material

The plight of two average young people facing the too familiar problem of a forced marriage is told without self-pity or moralizing. The author realistically conveys the confusion and dislocation when two teen-agers are suddenly made to assume adult roles without warning or preparation. Their growing maturity and sense of responsibility to each other is also well portrayed. The problem of reconciling in-laws while retaining stability in a marriage is one faced by many newlyweds.

Book Talk Material

A description of the problems facing Bo Jo and July will make a good introduction. Some specific passages are: the basic situation (pp. 7–9; pp. 7–8, pap.); July and Bo Jo plan to elope (pp. 33–35; pp. 26–27, pap.); their wedding (pp. 47–49; pp. 36–37, pap.); Mr. and Mrs. Greher's reaction (pp. 61–64; pp. 46–49, pap.); and the apartment and the couple's first quarrel (pp. 113–115; pp. 85–86, pap.).

Additional Selections

A young man becomes involved with a troubled young girl in Gunnel Beckman's *A Room of His Own* (Viking, 1974, $5.95). In Patricia Windsor's *Diving for Roses* (Harper, 1976, $5.95), a 17-year-old pregnant girl is living with an erratic mother in an isolated country house. In the novelization by Patricia Dizenzo of the National Film Board of Canada's *Phoebe* (McGraw-Hill, 1970, $5.95; pap., Bantam, 95¢), a 16-year-old girl tries to hide her pregnancy. A 17-year-old divorced mother begins her life anew in Phyllis Anderson Wood's *Song of the Shaggy Canary* (Westminster, 1974, $4.95; pap., New Amer. Lib., 95¢). Other titles to use include Hila Colman's *Bride at Eighteen* (Morrow, 1966, $5.21); Zoa

Sherburne's *Too Bad about the Haines Girl* (Morrow, 1967, $6.50; pap. $2.25); Richard Peck's *Don't Look and It Won't Hurt* (Holt, 1972, $5.95; pap., Avon, 95¢); and Blossom Elfman's *The Girls of Huntington House* (Houghton, 1972, $5.95; pap., Bantam, $1.25).

Katie Letcher Lyle, *I Will Go Barefoot All Summer for You*
Lippincott, 1974, $5.50; lge. type ed., G. K. Hall, $7.95; pap., Dell, $1.25

Katie Letcher Lyle has had a career as an English teacher and professional folk singer. This, her first novel, was followed by another success, *Fair Day and Another Step Begun* (Lippincott, 1974, $4.95; pap., Dell, 95¢). Its use of flashbacks and dream sequences makes *Barefoot* as complex and multilayered a novel as its heroine, lonely and directionless Jessie Preston. However, it is a rewarding reading experience, particularly for girls in the junior high school grades.

Plot Summary

For the past two years, Jessie has been living with distant relatives, Charlie and Rose Wilson and their 13-year-old daughter Frances, in Borden, the little town in southern Virginia where Jessie was born and raised. Her mother died in childbirth, and Jessie's first 11 years were spent with her Aunt Dorothy, her mother's older sister.

Through painful memories, Jessie often tries to reconstruct her childhood. Aunt Dorothy referred to her father as "common." But practically everything Jessie loved—Mrs. Miller who taught her how to make vinegar taffy; stray kittens; her friend Teresita, whose father was a night watchman—were all considered common by Aunt Dorothy. Jessie always knew that Aunt Dorothy tolerated, not loved, her. When her aunt died of a heart attack, Jessie remembers a frail old lady, whom Rose Wilson called Willa, at the graveside. The woman said she was Jessie's grandmother. Later Jessie tried to find her, but she had disappeared.

Since then Jessie has tried to adjust to life at the Wilsons, and although she knows her foster parents love her, it is not the same as their love for their own daughter. Both girls are in early adolescence.

At the beginning of the summer, Rose announces that Toby Bright, Frances' 14-year-old cousin (not related to Jessie) is coming from Baltimore to spend two days. Although Frances claims he is the ugliest boy alive and is interested only in bugs, Jessie notices that she begins primping and trying out new shades of lipstick. When Toby arrives, Jessie sees that

Frances was correct. He is cross-eyed, wears thick glasses, and is severely pockmarked.

She and Toby bicycle into the countryside, and soon Jessie is fascinated by this gentle, quiet boy who knows a great deal about nature. They wander through a meadow and discover a field sparrow's nest, which Toby gives to her. He tells her that going barefoot as she is, is really neat. When Jessie falls, Toby helps her to her feet and gently kisses her. Fearing that her awkwardness will cause her further embarrassment, Jessie avoids Toby for the rest of his stay, but in her room she fantasizes about the boy's tenderness and affection for her.

When Toby leaves, Jessie thinks she must perform some act to prove her love. She decides that she will go barefoot all summer for him. Her crusade is conducted successfully for two months, but it comes to a halt when Rose insists that she wear shoes into a restaurant.

Now obsessed with Toby's memory, Jessie decides she must visit him in Baltimore. She steals out of the house one night, with her entire fortune of $8.88, and boards a night bus.

At a stopover in Washington, D.C., Jessie decides to visit the Smithsonian, which Toby had told her about. She strikes up a conversation with the cab driver, Bob Brunelli, who has left his wife in Memphis to come to Washington and sort himself out. Bob is intrigued with this sad little girl, and he finds in her some of the loneliness and rebellion he feels. They spend an enchanting few hours together at the museum, and afterward he volunteers to drive her to Baltimore, where Jessie claims she is to visit her grandmother. When they stop at a restaurant, Bob hears a news report that the police are looking for Jessie. She begs him to take her back to Washington, but Bob convinces her that she must go home.

Bob takes Jessie home, after giving her a copy of a book of philosophical essays, and tenderly bids her good-bye.

Summer comes to an end. Jessie is delighted to receive a letter from Bob stating that he is going back to his wife and asking her to visit them in Memphis over Christmas. One day Jessie locates Willa in town. The old lady tells her that Jessie's parents, Virginia and Willa's son William, were childhood sweethearts, but even after Virginia became pregnant with Jessie, Dorothy would not give permission for her younger sister to marry. William had then left Borden, never to return. Thinking of her parents' unfulfilled love, Jessie wanders away, now more confident of her past and her future.

Thematic Material

This is the story of a girl searching to discover her roots while still trying to cope with the emotional and physical growing pains of adolescence. Through Bob, Jessie learns the fleeting nature of love and beauty, but also that pain and unhappiness are fleeting too. The novel also shows that one can often find unexpected understanding and kindness from strangers.

Book Talk Material

Some passages for use in a book talk are: Jessie meets Toby (pp. 25–27; pp. 24–27, pap.); Jessie gets kissed (pp. 35–37; same pagination, pap.); she dreams of Toby (pp. 72–75; pp. 82–84, pap.); Jessie's crusade is lost (pp. 83–87; pp. 95–99, pap.); and the trip to Washington (pp. 100–104; pp. 116–121, pap.).

Additional Selections

Kathy, an insecure 13-year-old, copes with adolescence in Jean Van Leeuwen's *I Was a 98 Pound Duckling* (Dial, 1972, $5.95; pap., Dell, 95¢). The heroine of Elizabeth Winthrop's *Walking Away* (Harper, 1973, $4.95; pap., Dell, 95¢) finds that past and present don't mix in this novel of change and incompatibility. The fear and anxiety behind a delinquent's tough exterior is dealt with in Hall Ellson's *Tomboy* (pap., Bantam, $1.25). "Boy" Sword seeks his identity during the Depression in Borden Deal's *The Least One* (Doubleday, 1967, o.p.). Additional titles are: Zoa Sherburne's *Stranger in the House* (Morrow, 1963, $6.50); Ethel Gordon's *Where Does the Summer Go?* (pap., Pocket Bks., 75¢); and the Cleavers' *I'd Rather Be a Turnip* (Lippincott, 1971, $4.50; pap., New Amer. Lib., $1.25).

About the Author

Commire, Anne. *Something about the Author.* Detroit: Gale Research Co., 1976. Vol. 8, pp. 121–122.

Kinsman, Clare D., Ed. *Contemporary Authors.* Detroit: Gale Research Co., 1975. Vol. 49, p. 346.

Robert McKay, *Dave's Song*

Hawthorn, 1969, $4.95; pap., Bantam, 95¢

Like Mason Campbell in *Dave's Song* and in his previously published novel for young adults, *Red Canary* (Hawthorn, 1968, $4.95; pap., Scholastic, 85¢), Robert McKay learned about birds while serving a sentence for robbery in the Ohio penitentiary. Like Dave, he has trained a pet starling to speak. *Dave's Song* is the story of two high school seniors,

Dave Burdick and Kate Adams, and the gradual unfolding of their love. The novel is told alternately from their two points of view. It is well liked, particularly by girls in grades seven through twelve.

Plot Summary

In the flat farmlands of Ohio, it should be difficult to be claustrophobic, but that describes perfectly Kate Adams' state of mind. She feels hemmed in, almost incased, in her hometown of Tylerton. Without any real interests or ambition, she occasionally dreams of independence after graduation by moving to Columbus to attend a business school. Most of these feelings of restlessness she doesn't understand herself nor does she show them outwardly. At home she is still the gentle, dependable daughter, and at school she remains an attractive, well-liked, and conscientious student.

Dave Burdick is vastly different; extremely handsome but remote, unattached, stubborn, a loner who is nevertheless willing to fight for causes in which he believes. Occasionally a remark will reveal a sensitive, idealistic side, but this is usually hidden under a layer of aloofness and isolation. His father, Judson, who is as fiercely independent as his son, and his mother operate a chicken farm 10 miles out of town. This is not a standard "meat and egg" operation but one dedicated to maintaining and perpetuating fine breeds of poultry. One day, to prove that such farms still exist, Dave brings in to Mr. Weber's biology class some of these birds—a Buff Orpington, Buff Cochin, and Light Brahma. Everyone, including Kate, is impressed. Dave's interest in nature extends beyond the farmyard to all living things. At 12, he cared for an orphan starling, nicknamed Jack, and taught him to speak. Jack, now free, has never left the property and still returns to perch on Dave's shoulder and try once again to find bugs in his ears. As the years have gone on, Dave's interest has deepened to the point where he now reads such authors as Konrad Lorenz and Robert Ardrey.

Things pick up slightly for Kate when Mal Reed, a rich boy whose father owns the local department store, invites Kate to come with him in his new Mustang to a rock concert in Columbus. She enjoys herself and is flattered that the boy "with everything" has chosen her. Mr. Adams piques Kate's interest one day when he returns from buying eggs at Burdick's farm and announces that Dave kept playing "some fool song" on his tape deck. Kate is curious to know what song could possibly be a favorite of Dave Burdick's, and she phones to ask. He tries to play it over the telephone, but the sound is muffled. Within a few minutes, Dave's old pickup truck is at the door. He takes Kate to the farm where she hears for the first time Leonard Cohen's haunting "Suzanne," sung by Noel Harrison. Kate is moved to tears. At once this tender unforgettable ballad becomes Dave's song. Before Kate leaves the farm, Dave kisses her passionately. Kate fights back, and they return to town in silence. A few days later she relents somewhat and consents to go with Dave that weekend for an evening at Miller's, the local bar and dance hall.

The date is a disaster. A new rock group is playing and Kate asks to dance. Dave tells her that he doesn't know how, but she insists. Dave makes a fool of himself and is aped unmercifully by a local tough, Jiggs Banion, who claims to be doing a new dance, the chicken noodle. Jiggs is joined by two friends who continue to insult Dave until a fight is provoked. The odds are too great for Dave. Before the fight is over, he has several cuts and bruises and a black eye. Again there is silence on the drive home.

Meanwhile, Mal Reed's assault on Kate's affections continues. Even though she suspects that Mal is basically shallow and dull, Kate consents to go steady with him. She refuses Dave the next time he calls for a date.

A stranger, who introduces himself as Mason Campbell, calls at the Burdick farm to buy some purebred breeding fowl. Dave believes that the stranger knows little about prices of poultry, and he overcharges him. Later Dave feels guilty about his action and wants to return the money, particularly after his father tells him that he knows and respects Mason Campbell. Dave soon learns why. He drives the 60 miles to Campbell's home and finds that the man operates a wild bird farm. In its gigantic enclosure, Dave sees pheasant, hummingbirds, peacocks, and even bald eagles. This so impresses Dave that back home he decides to do his college scholarship paper on the biological phenomenon, imprinting, and the conflict between nature and nurture, using Campbell's findings and Dave's experiences training Jack as data.

Dave persuades Mr. Weber to take his biology class to Mason Campbell's for a field trip. Arrangements are complete when suddenly the school board, under the chairmanship of Mal Reed's father, cancels the trip. The class learns that it is because Mason has a criminal record, having served a sentence some years before as a bank robber. Dave checks and finds it is true, but he is horrified at the injustice of the board's decision. Single-handedly, he wages a struggle to have the trip reinstated, and after Dave reminds Mr. Reed that he himself might have some shady deals in his past that could bear forgetting, he succeeds. The trip is a great success, and Kate begins to admire Dave's courage and single-mindedness.

One day close to Thanksgiving, Kate and Mal stop by Burdick's farm to buy some eggs. Mrs. Burdick shows them the thimble-sized Button Quail chicks that Dave is raising in the living room. When Dave enters, Mal offers to buy some of them for a Christmas window display in his father's store. Dave refuses. Mal increases the price and an argument ensues, but Dave is adamant. When Dave and Kate's eyes meet, she again feels attracted to this proud individual who will always remain unbossed, his own person.

That evening as Kate is pensively playing with her food at the dinner table, she hears music in the distance and goes to the front door. Dave's old truck is parked on the street and he is standing there smiling, his hair covered with blowing snow and his tape recorder blaring out the song "Suzanne." Kate rushes into his arms.

Thematic Material

In describing the growth of Dave and Kate's relationship until it flowers, the author has captured something of the agony and ecstasy of adolescence. Each protagonist is realistically portrayed with both faults and virtues, although Dave, the strong, silent type, tends to dominate the story. The shifting point of view adds an unusual dimension. In spite of references to past rock heroes and such events as the Vietnam War, today's youngsters will find the story fresh and appealing, one with which they can easily identify. The reader also will learn something about biology in general and poultry raising in particular from this novel.

Book Talk Material

One might begin by playing Dave's song. A number of artists have recorded "Suzanne," including Noel Harrison and Judy Collins. Some key passages are: Dave is introduced (pp. 12-17; pp. 8-13, pap.); their first kiss (pp. 30-33; pp. 23-26, pap.); the starling, Jack (pp. 43-49; pp. 34-39, pap.); and the disastrous date at Miller's (pp. 66-73; pp. 53-59, pap.).

Additional Suggestions

Another excellent love story by Robert McKay is *The Troublemaker* (Nelson, 1971, $5.95; pap., Dell, 95¢), about Jesse Wade who is born for trouble and the girl to whom he brings an injured bird. In Joan L. Oppenheimer's *The Nobody Road* (pap., Scholastic, 95¢), a teen-age boy finds difficulty in communicating with others and in planning his future. John Craig's *Zach* (Coward, 1972, $6.95), retitled *Who Wants to Be Alone?* (pap., Scholastic, $1.25), is about three kids on the road trying to escape the past and searching for a secure future. *Me, Cassie* (Dial, 1968, $5.95; pap.,

Dell, 95¢) by Anita Feagles describes the hectic life of Cassie Spencer until she becomes engaged to an intellectual boyfriend. Joan Tate's *Tina and David* (Nelson, 1973, $5.25) is a love story involving Tina and her boyfriend, who can only communicate with her by notes. Two other novels, particularly for girls, are Ruth Wolff's *Linsey, Herself* (pap., Scholastic, 75¢) and Margaret P. Strachan's *What Is to Be* (Washburn, 1966, o.p.).

K. M. Peyton, *The Beethoven Medal*

> Crowell, 1972, $4.50; pap., Scholastic (retitled *If I Ever Marry*), $1.25

K. M. Peyton is a distinguished English author of children's fiction whose third novel in her Flambards trilogy, *Flambards in Summer* (Collins+World, 1970, $4.91), was awarded the 1969 Carnegie Medal. *The Beethoven Medal* is her second novel about the brilliant, fractious, and totally ingenuous Patrick Pennington. In the first, *Pennington's Last Term* (Crowell, 1971, $6.95), he encounters problems (many referred to in this novel) during his last year in secondary school. All three books in the Flambards trilogy are suited to junior high school readers.

Plot Summary

Ruth Hollis, almost 17, is infatuated with the noncommittal, but very handsome, young man, some two years her senior, who delivers bread and pastries to her house in a van. It is summer vacation, and apart from frequent visits from her brother, Ted, whose marriage to Barbara is somewhat shaky, she is alone with her middle-class parents on the outskirts of the seaside town of Northend, some 50 miles by rail from London. Ruth has recently broken with her overly polite, stodgy boyfriend, Gordon Hargreaves, and at present her only real love, outside her family, is her pet pony, Flax, now recovering from a jumping accident at the McNair farm.

One day Ruth hitches a ride in the bakery van into town and learns from the sullen, seemingly disinterested boy that his name is Pat and that during the school year he is a student at a university in London. The town gossip, Mrs. Pareter, reports to Mrs. Hollis that Ruth should not be seeing Pat because he was on parole and had to report regularly to a probation officer in town. To Ruth, this only adds more mystery and intrigue, and she is delighted when Pat quite unexpectedly invites her to spend a Sunday with him in London, where he has to go on some "business."

The business turns out to be a concert to hear a performance of

Rachmaninov's Second Piano Concerto. At the hall, they bump into a beautiful young acquaintance of Pat's, Clarissa Cargill-Smith. Although Pat greets her casually, Ruth senses that their relationship was once something more.

Slowly Pat gives details about himself. He is studying the piano under Professor Hampton in London and is spending the summer in Northend, his hometown, but is living with parents of an old school friend, Mr. and Mrs. Bates, because he is estranged from his own family. Every spare moment is spent practicing in the village hall. In a few weeks, he is to play a small joint recital with Clarissa, who is indeed an ex-girl friend and a fellow music student who plays the violin. A week following the recital he is scheduled to make his concert debut playing Rachmaninov at Northend with a visiting German orchestra under the leadership of the distinguished conductor, Otto Bachhaus.

Because of his jobs (he also plays piano in a pub) and heavy practice schedule, Ruth sees Pat infrequently, particularly after he gives up the bakery job to devote more time to the piano. However, the bond between them grows, and Ruth realizes that she is seriously in love with this strange young man, who, although often silent and moody, has a great capacity for understanding and affection. One day when they are swimming, she notices a medallion around his neck. Afraid he will tell her it is a gift from Clarissa, she doesn't ask how he got it.

After the successful joint recital in London, where Ruth was a nervous page turner, Pat tells her that he served a three-month sentence for breaking the jaw of another music student during a quarrel.

Back in Northend, they decide to celebrate the recital. Pat "borrows" the bakery van and, with their friends Maxwell and Rita, they take an illegal swim in a closed swimming pool and then go to a disco. While there, the police arrive and accuse Pat of stealing the van. He resists arrest and knocks down a police officer who has caused him trouble in the past. With his concert less than a week away, Pat is sent to Brixton prison until his trial.

In desperation, Ruth visits Pat's teacher in London. Professor Hampton assures her that he will get Pat released in time for the morning rehearsal and evening performance.

On the day of the concert, Ruth goes to the hall and finds Pat at work. By special appeal from Hampton, Pat was released for the day, but he must return before midnight. The concert is a great success, and even Mr. and Mrs. Hollis are impressed. Before Pat goes back to prison, the two young people tenderly speak of the great love they feel for one another.

At the hearing, Pat is allowed out on bail to await trial in two weeks, but his lawyer is sure that striking an officer will bring at least a nine-month term. During one of their few remaining moments together, Ruth tells Pat that she will always love him. He places his medallion, a good-luck Beethoven medal, around her neck. The thought that she will be waiting for him is all the good luck he needs.

Thematic Material

This story of young love between an innocent and trusting girl and a dedicated, militant young artist is touching and convincing. The picture of contemporary English life is interesting, but, above all, the reader will be intrigued by the complexities of Pat's character.

Book Talk Material

Some of the interesting passages are: Ruth rides with Pat in the van (pp. 10–13; pp. 11–15, pap.); the two on the train to London (pp. 23–26; pp. 25–29, pap.); Maxwell talks about Pat (pp. 43–45; pp. 48–50, pap.); and at the disco (pp. 110–113; pp. 120–124, pap.).

Additional Selections

An off-beat English boy gains recognition after refinishing two large statues in Richard Parker's *The Quarter Boy* (Nelson, 1976, $5.95). In Robert McKay's *Bordy* (Nelson, 1977, $6.95), a troubled high school graduate tries to determine life's values while employed by an elderly lady. The various levels of responsibilities involved in the friendship of three interesting heroines are explored in Robin F. Brancato's *Something Left to Lose* (Knopf, 1976, $6.95). A girl is reunited with her husband in Joan Tate's *Sam and Me* (Coward, 1969, $4.95). Also use Jay Bennett's *Masks, A Love Story* (Watts, 1971, $4.95); Isabelle Holland's *Amanda's Choice* (Lippincott, 1970, $4.50); and Mildred Lawrence's *Inside the Gate* (Harcourt, 1968, $5.95).

About the Author

DeMontreville, Doris and Donna Hill, Eds. *Third Book of Junior Authors.* New York: H. W. Wilson Co., 1972, pp. 224–226.

Jones, Cornelia and Olivia R. Way. *British Children's Authors: Interviews at Home.* Chicago: American Library Association, 1976, pp. 127–136.

Townsend, John Rowe. *A Sense of Story: Essays on Contemporary Writers for Children.* Philadelphia and New York: J. B. Lippincott Co., 1971, pp. 172–181.

Ward, Martha E. and Dorothy A. Marquardt. *Authors of Books for Young People.* (2nd Edition). Metuchen, N.J.: Scarecrow Press, Inc., 1971, p. 408.

Sandra Scoppetone, *Trying Hard to Hear You*

Harper, 1974, $5.95; lib. bdg., $5.79; pap., Bantam, $1.25

One of the hitherto taboo subjects that began to receive some attention in juvenile literature during the 1960s and 1970s was homosexuality. Of the teen-age novels dealing with this topic, one of the best is this touching and often humorous novel by Sandra Scoppetone. It is intended for mature junior and senior high school students.

Plot Summary

For 16-year-old Camille Crawford, also known as Cam, the summer of 1973 was one in which she learned more about both life and death than she either expected or wanted. She decides to write down the story before the details become hazy or lost. Cam's father is dead and she lives with her mother, a psychoanalyst who commutes part-time to New York City, and her 14-year-old sister, Rachel, in Peconic, a small town on the north fork of Long Island. Cam's best friend and platonic companion is handsome Jeff Grathwohl, her next-door neighbor, who is slightly older, saddled with truly horrible parents, and interested in books and research. There are five other members of the group Cam hangs out with—six if you count Tina Heacock, but she is more out than in. The two other boys are Walt Feinberg, a brain but so outspoken that not many people like him, and Sam Ahler, a talented, creative boy but somewhat preoccupied with himself. The girls are Janet Clark, the fat mother confessor of the group, Mary El Merensky, true blue and secretly in love with Sam, and zany, unpredictable Penny Lademan.

The really exciting event of the summer is the projected August production of *Anything Goes* with an all-youth cast. Since most of the gang participated in last year's *South Pacific,* they attend this year's tryouts late in June. One of the few adults connected with the show is the director, Susan Stimpson. She has as an assistant, a local boy, 19-year-old Phil Chrystie, who has just returned from his first year in college. Cam remembers this quiet, attractive young man from last summer's production, and the crush she had then is immediately rekindled.

As a result of the auditions, Cam, Jeff, and Penny get roles and the rest of the gang become part of the production staff. The two leads go to Eben Clay, an egocentric show-off and to Maura Harris, a loner, caused partly because her boyfriend, Hank Allen, is Black.

The summer seems to be progressing very well. Cam's summer job at the A & P, though dull, gives her money and a sense of independence; pesky sister, Rachel is more or less being kept in line; rehearsals are fun; Mrs.

Crawford is becoming interested in a Wall Street broker, Ray Fowler, of whom Cam thoroughly approves; and, best of all, Phil has asked Cam to a movie.

For Cam the date is divine, except Phil seems to ask an inordinate number of questions about her friend Jeff. Back home it is a different story. In the absence of Cam and Mrs. Crawford, who is away for the weekend with Ray, Rachel has had her own friends in and the place is a mess. Jeff comes from next door and he and Phil help clean up, and the two boys spend the next day together unsuccessfully trying to mend an antique spinning wheel that was broken in the general fracas.

Cam notices that Jeff and Phil frequently leave rehearsals and don't attend the usual postmortems with the gang. The group become suspicious and think that they must be visiting new girl friends. An attempt one night to gain information by following them ends in frustration when the gang loses their track.

Cam is delighted when Phil declines an invitation to attend the big Fourth of July party at Eben Clay's and instead agrees to come to her family's outdoor barbecue. However, immediately after dinner, he asks if the two might be excused to go to Clay's. When there, Phil leaves Cam and joins Jeff. Shortly afterward, amid shouts of "faggots" and "queers," a fight breaks out among the boys. Jeff and Phil have been seen kissing in a clump of trees. Neither denies it; in fact, under pressure Jeff admits that Phil and he love each other. Eben becomes livid and orders the two "goddamn fairies" off his property. Amid jeers and derisive remarks, they leave. Cam is thunderstruck.

This begins a period of alienation and persecution for the two boys. Not only is there name calling and direct insults from both girls and boys, but even during rehearsals, much to Stimpson's mystification, suddenly limp wrists and lisps become common. Because she thinks Jeff has stolen Phil from her, Cam guiltily joins in the ostracism and even rebuffs Jeff when he tries to talk to her about his homosexuality.

One night, the lead, Maura, arrives at rehearsal drunk because Hank Allen has been unable to withstand the social pressure caused by dating a white girl and has broken off their relationship. Cam, Phil, and some of the gang manage to avoid Stimpson and get Maura home, but when they return they find that Eben and some of his friends, who are equally manic about having homosexuals in their midst, have taken Jeff to a deserted beach to "teach that fag a lesson."

The lesson is tar and feathering. When Cam and her group arrive, they see a large circle of teen-agers with Eben in the center hovering over Jeff, who is lying in the sand spread-eagled and gagged and tied down by his ankles and wrists. Phil is also seized. As Cam watches helplessly and the tar and feathers are brought out, Hank Allen and his friends join the crowd. Hank questions Eben's motives and soon realizes that he is witnessing a persecution similar to that experienced by his own race for centuries and not unlike the kind that caused his breakup with Maura. He frees the two boys.

The night before the opening, real tragedy strikes. Phil and Penny Lademan are killed in a car crash. Phil, trying to prove his manhood, has accepted Penny's proposition to go all the way with him, and to fortify themselves they consumed a quart of tequila before Phil's car struck a tree. Cam has to break the news to Jeff who, shaken and weeping, blames the gang for Phil's death. He states that he will not appear in the show, but he later changes his mind when he realizes that much of the present situation had been caused by similar vindictive and irresponsible behavior.

Despite the tragedy that surrounds it, the show is a success, and summer ends. School starts, and Cam begins dating a new boy. From his first year in college, Jeff writes that he has met a new friend, Richard. He will bring him home at Thanksgiving. Cam look forward to meeting him.

Thematic Material

In this story, ignorance and prejudice produce so much interference that the youngsters can't communicate even when they try to "hear" one another. The point is made that it is the presence of love between two people that is important in life, not who they are. Although specifically a plea for understanding and compassion for young homosexuals, the novel is more an appeal to accept and assimilate the many differences that are found in society whether racial, religious, or sexual. In spite of the gravity of the story, there are many amusing passages and some touching scenes between Cam and Jeff and Cam and her mother.

Book Talk Material

It might be difficult to introduce this book without bordering on the lurid or sensational. Some interesting passages that convey the general flavor of the story are: Cam introduces Jeff (pp. 8-11; pp. 7-9, pap.); the gang (pp. 18-25; pp. 15-21, pap.); Cam's crush on Phil (pp. 42-44; pp. 35-36, pap.); the Crawford's weekend guest (pp. 47-52; pp. 39-43, pap.); the A & P (pp. 72-74, pp. 60-61, pap.); and Jeff admits he loves Phil (pp. 181-186; pp. 148-151, pap.).

Additional Selections

A 14-year-old boy develops a close friendship that ends in a single homosexual experience in Isabell Holland's *The Man without a Face* (Lippincott, 1972, $5.95; pap., Bantam, 95¢), and a boy is falsely accused of homosexuality in Lynn Hall's remarkable *Sticks and Stones* (Follett, 1972, $4.98; pap., Dell, 95¢). *The Other Side of the Street* (Brockhampton Pr., o.p.) by Pamela Brown is an English story of a girl who does well on a television quiz show. Also use Lynn Hall's *The Siege of Silent Henry* (Follett, 1972, $4.95); Barbara Rinkoff's *Name: Johnny Pierce* (Seabury, 1969, $5.95); and two collections of short stories about outsiders, Jean McCord's *Bitter Is the Hawk's Path* (Atheneum, 1971, $4.50) and, for an older group L. M. Schulman's *The Loners* (Macmillan, 1970, 95¢).

About the Author

Commire, Anne. *Something about the Author*. Detroit: Gale Research Co., 1976. Vol. 9, pp. 162–163.

John Rowe Townsend, *The Summer People*
Lippincott, 1972, $5.95; pap., Dell, $1.25

John Rowe Townsend is not only one of the foremost English writers of young adult books, he is also the author of two excellent books about children's literature: *Written for Children* (Lippincott, 1974, $10.95) and *A Sense of Story* (Lippincott, 1971, $6.95), which is subtitled *Essays on Contemporary Writers for Children*. *The Summer People* is read chiefly by girls in the junior and early senior high school grades.

Plot Summary

It is 1972, and the narrator, an Englishman named Philip Martin, is writing a letter to two young people in America—Stephen and Carolyn—on the eve of their wedding. He feels compelled to tell them, in a manuscript that accompanies the letter, about some important events that occurred during his summer holiday in August of 1939, on the eve of his seventeenth birthday and of the outbreak of World War II.

The same three families have been coming for years to spend August vacations together in their adjoining bungalows at the summer resort and coastal fishing village of Linley Bottom (since renamed Smuggler's Cove to attract tourists). The families are: Mr. and Mrs. Martin, Paula, age 18, Philip, and a younger sister, Alison, who is seven; the widowed Mrs. Pilling (her husband had been a partner in Mr. Martin's clothing factory), Sylvia, who is Philip's age, and 15-year-old Brian; and Bernard, or Bernie, Fox, his wife, and two children, Rodney, 18, and 15-year-old Brenda.

This year promises to be different because the youngsters are outgrowing childish activities of the past and are becoming restless, particularly with the possibility of war growing more certain every day.

All three families are promoting a match between Philip Martin and Sylvia Pilling. This is an embarrassment for the two of them because, although they are extremely fond of one another, their feelings are similar to that of a close brother and sister.

On his first morning in Linley, Philip sets out to reexplore his old haunts. He walks along the cliff path where there are three stone cottages precariously perched on a promontory so eroded by the elements that the townspeople know it will only be weeks before all three crumble into the sea. Two are deserted, but the third still contains the furnishings of the owners, the Partingtons, who are summer people. Repeated efforts to contact them to move their belongings have failed.

Filled with curiosity, Philip enters the cottage and, to his amazement, finds someone there, a young girl about his age but extremely thin and frail. With mock gallantry, and feigning extremely formal, upper-class conversation, they laughingly introduce each other. Her name is Ann Tarrant, and later she tells Philip that her mother works in the town's tourist hotel, The Imperial. Mrs. Tarrant, who is separated from her husband, has taken the job so that her daughter could have plenty of sunshine and fresh air. Ann has just been released from a sanatorium where she was recovering from an attack of pleurisy. Philip is strangely attracted to this sad, defenseless girl, who has been coming frequently to the deserted Partington house to be with her daydreams. He promises to come back the next day.

On the way home he meets Sylvia, who has also come from an assignation. On a brief visit to Linley earlier in the summer, she had met and become attracted to a handsome, 18-year-old boatkeeper, Harold Erikson. Both Sylvia and Philip know that neither of their new friends would gain the approval of their very middle-middle-class parents, and so Sylvia devises an ingenious subterfuge. Each day the two of them will leave the family compound arm in arm and when they reach town, they will go their own ways.

For the first two weeks everything goes well. Sylvia meets with her Harold and Philip, his Ann. Philip takes Ann on picnics and sailboating and one weekend when both Mr. and Mrs. Martin and Ann's mother are away, they spend a tender but innocent night together in the Partington house. However, the strain of continual deception and the knowledge that their days together are numbered cause both couples to have quarrels, although they soon are reconciled. Sylvia learns that her time with Harold will be shortened because he is to be inducted into the navy before the end of the month.

Although Sylvia and Philip try to avert suspicion by occasionally spending time with the gang or on family outings, both fear discovery. It comes gradually. First Rodney and Brenda Fox see Sylvia and Harold together, and when confronted with this knowledge, Philip tells them the truth, but they promise secrecy. However, one day Paula, Philip's sister, follows him to the Partington house and finds him with Ann. Back at home she tells the whole story. For Sylvia, the forced breakup with Harold comes easily because she has had another fight with him, during which he struck her. But for Philip it is different. He feels a genuine love, albeit tinged with pity, for his pathetic waiflike girl friend. They are able to spend one more innocent night together without being discovered. The following morning a part of the cottage falls into the sea.

War is now only a matter of days away, and Mr. Martin, who must, therefore, tend to the future of his business, cuts short the family vacation. Philip and Ann say good-bye and promise to write.

The manuscript ends, and the letter to Stephen and Carolyn continues. Philip briefly tells how all three families generally prospered after the war and how Ann had become a librarian and moved to Australia where she married. She had only one child, Carolyn, before her death in an automobile accident. Philip eventually married Sylvia. It is their son who is the Stephen of the letter. Perhaps the strange fate that brought these two together will lay to rest the unhappy events of that summer years ago.

Thematic Material

The author has captured the bittersweet, fleeting nature of first love. He also creates an atmosphere of the period and the feeling that we are experiencing the end of an era. This is symbolized by the changes that the oncoming war will bring, the artificiality of rigid social classes, the coming adulthood of the protagonists, and even the land erosion that ultimately destroys the youngsters' hideaway. His handling of family relationships is honestly but delicately done.

Book Talk Material

The hard-cover edition gives as a frontispiece a map of Linley Bottom. Some passages of importance are: exploring the Partington house (pp. 27–31; pp. 25–29, pap.); Sylvia hatches her scheme (pp. 40–45; pp. 38–43, pap.); a near-accident while boating (pp. 88–92; pp. 87–90, pap.); and Brenda tells Philip she knows his secret (pp. 133–135; pp. 131–133, pap.).

Additional Suggestions

Nine episodes in a girl's life in pre-World War II Yorkshire are described in Jane Gardam's *A Few Fair Days* (Macmillan, 1972, $4.95). Paula has difficulty getting over an infatuation in M. B. Goffstein's *The Underside of the Leaf* (Farrar, 1972, $4.50; pap., Dell, 95¢). A brother and sister develop a close, almost frightening relationship in Elizabeth Winthrop's *A Little Demonstration of Affection* (Harper, 1975, $5.95; pap., Dell, $1.25). Jane's unhappy memories of growing up during World War II in England with her brother are recalled in Penelope Lively's *Going Back* (Dutton, 1975, $6.95). One could also use Doris Smith's *Kick a Stone Home* (Crowell, 1974, $6.95); Sidney Offit's *Only a Girl Like You* (Coward, 1972, $5.95); and Townsend's *Good Night, Prof. Dear* (Lippincott, 1971, $4.95; pap., Dell, 1977).

About the Author

Commire, Anne. *Something about the Author.* Detroit: Gale Research Co., 1973. Vol. 4, pp. 206–208.

Kinsman, Clare D. and Mary Ann Tennenhouse, Eds. *Contemporary Authors.* Detroit: Gale Research Co., 1973. Vol. 37, p. 503.

Who's Who in America (37th Edition). Chicago: Marquis Who's Who, Inc., 1972. Vol. 2, p. 3195.

Patricia Windsor, *The Summer Before*

Harper, 1973, $4.95; lib. bdg., $5.79; pap., Dell, $1.25

This tender story of young love and adjustment to death was Patricia Windsor's first book for young adults. It is divided into three parts: "The Winter After," in which the heroine, Alexandra describes the events that follow the emotional breakdown she suffers after the death of her dear friend Bradley; "The Summer Before," which details the events leading to Bradley's death; and a continuation of the first part, "A Spring that feels like Autumn." For continuity, this plot summary is given as a continuous narrative. The novel is popular with mature readers of junior and senior high school ages.

Plot Summary

Alexandra Appleton, a high school student growing up in a typical American town, Ravanna River, is know by a number of nicknames: her parents call her Sandy; her school chums, Alex; and to her very special friend, Bradley, she is Apple. Alexandra has grown up with the constant companionship of Bradley, and now their warm friendship has developed into a pure and still innocent love. Bradley is Alexandra's ideal—he is extremely intelligent, individualistic, and, above all, a warm and compassionate person. To Alexandra, Bradley is someone special, but to her parents—a distant, preoccupied father and a nagging, overly protective mother—the boy is simply different and somewhat odd. They wish that their daughter would expand her circle of friends and see less of Bradley.

At school's close, the two young people go swimming in the nude, as they have on other occasions, in a local creek and afterward lie naked in the sun. This time someone sees them and reports the incident to both sets of parents. The reaction is swift and severe. They are forbidden to see one another, and plans are hastily made to send Alexandra away to summer camp. Bradley is so incensed at this injustice and the thought of an enforced separation that he decides to strike out on his own for the summer. Alexandra begs him to take her with him, and one night they guiltily leave their homes and hitch a ride to the home of an understanding elderly couple, friends of Bradley's family, whom he knows as Aunt Ev and Uncle Tim. After reassuring their parents of their safety and well-being, the two leave once more, this time to join a commune known as Deliverance.

Life at the commune is much tougher and more arduous than expected, particularly for Alexandra, whose sheltered middle-class life has ill-prepared her for both the chores and the people she encounters there. The leader, John Baker, has established rigid and firm rules. The men and women sleep in separate buildings, drugs are not allowed, and, because the commune is very poor, there is no electricity or hot water. Everyone is assigned specific chores—Alexandra helps in the kitchen and Bradley becomes a handyman and painter. As the days pass, Alexandra gets to know several of the residents: her roommate, Joan, who often sneaks out at night to join her husband, Flint; their year-old-baby, Jimmy; and the pathetic older girl, Mary, who stays down the hall with her eight-year-old son, Jesse. Mary has a severe foot infection, which remains untreated because the commune lacks the funds to call a doctor.

Alexandra rarely sees Bradley, and her loneliness and sadness grow, until one night after discovering Mary lying in a pool of blood, she tells Bradley that she must leave. He persuades another inhabitant, Link Elliott, to drive them away, but on the slippery highway the car crashes down an embankment. Badly injured, Alexandra crawls out of the car seconds before it explodes into flames.

Although her body slowly mends, the magnitude of her loss at Bradley's death causes a complete emotional breakdown. After weeks at a mental hospital, she is sent home under the watchful care of her parents and a capable but remote psychiatrist, Dr. Kovalik. During the autumn and early winter, her only companion is Jazz, short for Jasmine Paine, a wealthy, somewhat mixed-up young girl who visits Alexandra after school and on weekends. But Jazz, whom Alexandra calls her crazy-sitter, is attracted more by the girl's case history than an honest desire to help. One day Alexandra suffers another traumatic experience when, because of Jazz's insensitivity and selfishness, she becomes lost in the woods and is later found and brought home by Owen Anderson, caretaker of an estate.

Although her inner fears and persistent guilt concerning Bradley's death continue, Alexandra gradually makes tentative steps to reach outside her shattered emotions. Fearfully she returns to school and is impressed at the unspoken understanding of her teachers and friends.

One day she begins for the first time to talk to Dr. Kovalik about Bradley and his importance in her life. That night she searches through her belongings for the newspaper clipping of the car accident. She reads it through and then tears it into bits. Now she knows that she has successfully made the journey back and can face life again.

Thematic Material

This novel poignantly depicts the intensity and beauty of first love and the tragic consequences when death separates the two lovers. It is also the harrowing account of a young girl's struggle to regain her sanity and rid herself of guilt and anxiety. The contrast between life in a small town and that in a commune is interestingly handled as is the creation of many memorable characters, in particular, the two protagonists.

Book Talk Material

The book could be presented by naming and briefly describing the three sections of the novel or by introducing the two main characters. Some important passages are: Alexandra runs away (pp. 144–147; pp. 113–116, pap.); life on the commune (pp. 186–188; pp. 145–147, pap.); and she talks with Dr. Kovalik (pp. 15–18; pp. 17–20, pap.).

Additional Selections

Andrea Boroff Eagan's nonfiction *Why Am I So Miserable if These Are the Best Years of My Life: A Survival Guide for the Young Woman* (Nelson, 1976, $6.95) is an excellent title. A young couple explores friendship and the purpose of life in Ursula K. LeGuin's *Very Far Away from Anywhere Else* (Atheneum, 1976, $5.95). In Eleanor Cameron's *To the Green Mountain* (Dutton, 1975, $6.95), a 13-year-old girl spends her last summer in a small Ohio town before moving to Vermont. A girl confronts her own death in Gunnel Beckman's *Admission to the Feast* (Holt, 1972,

$4.95; pap., Dell, 75¢). Judy, who has a learning disability and her overweight boyfriend fight the heartlessness of their peers in Louise Albert's *But I'm Ready to Go* (Bradbury, 1976, $6.95). Other novels particularly for girls are Elizabeth Christman's *A Nice Italian Girl* (Dodd, 1976, $4.19) and Peggy Woodford's *Please Don't Go* (Dutton, 1973, $6.50; pap., Avon, 95¢).

8

Developing a Wholesome Self-Image

THE ADOLESCENT often has difficulty in accepting his or her worth and in developing the ability to evaluate objectively his own actions, emotions, and physical attributes. Lack of a sense of identity, under-estimation of abilities and merits, or—sometimes the opposite—inflated egos are problems often faced during this period. In this chapter, the books show adolescents in situations where a truthful self-image has developed out of necessity.

Judy Blume, *Then Again, Maybe I Won't*
> Bradbury, 1971, $6.95; pap., Dell (Yearling), $1.25; Dell (Laurel Leaf), 95¢

Since her first two books in 1970—*Iggie's House* (Bradbury, $5.95; pap., Dell, 95¢) and *Are You There God, It's Me Margaret* (Bradbury, $5.95; pap., Dell, 95¢)—Judy Blume's popularity has grown immensely. She deals neither with momentous events nor weighty themes, but she writes instead honestly and sympathetically about the everyday concerns involving popularity, physical appearance, and sexual motivation that absorb youngsters in the upper elementary grades through the first year of junior high school. One evidence of her wide appeal is that paperback reprints of her works are often published in two editions. For example, *Then Again, Maybe I Won't* is available from Dell in the large format of Yearling Books, as well as in the more adult-looking Laurel Leaf Library. The paperback pagination in *Book Talk Material* is taken from the latter.

Plot Summary

Until his thirteenth year, Tony Miglione is having a normal, fairly uneventful childhood, growing up with his family in a two-family house in Jersey City. His father is an electrician for a construction company, and

179

his mother sells ladies' underwear in Ohrbach's department store. The housekeeping is done by Grandma, Mrs. Miglione's mother, an excellent cook and deeply religious woman, who has lost the power of speech because of a cancer operation that removed her larynx. The other tenants in the building are brother Ralph, a beginning teacher, and his wife, Angie, who is about to finish college. The family members rarely speak of the oldest son, Vinnie, who was killed in Vietnam. Tony has a paper route, likes to shoot baskets with Frankie Bollino and his other friends, and is looking forward to his coming first year in junior high school.

After Ralph announces that Angie is pregnant, the various generations of the family wonder how they will cope with this new financial burden. Father begins spending more time in his basement workshop. Instead of going to work, he begins, without explanation, commuting each day to New York City carrying a strange metal box. Tony can think of three possible explanations: he must have become a secret agent; he has cancer, which requires treatment in the city; or perhaps he is in trouble with the Jersey "mob." Tony becomes so worried that his nervous stomach begins to give him severe pains.

After two weeks of this mysterious behavior, Mr. Miglione "confesses." Their economic worries are over because he has invented a new type of electronic cartridge that will be manufactured by the plant that he will manage in Queens. The family will move during the summer to a large house on an acre lot in the upper-middle-class suburb of Rosemont, Long Island, and Ralph and Angie will take an apartment in Queens, where Ralph will continue to teach. Neither Tony nor Grandma is happy with the move, but both try to hide their feelings.

Life in Rosemont soon becomes a display of "keeping up with the Joneses," or in this case the Hoober's, a snooty family of some wealth next door. Mr. Miglione buys a fancy hardtop and trades in the family pickup for a second car when the neighbors point out that it is "declassé" to own a truck. Mrs. Miglione decides they need a live-in housekeeper. She chooses Maxine, an efficient, but iron-willed, tyrant who soon banishes Grandma from the kitchen. The old lady retreats, proud and unbowing, to her bedroom and newly acquired color television, refusing to join the family even at meals. Tony is sickened by all this, and his stomach pains recur with frightening intensity.

At summer's end, the neighborhood children return from camp. Tony meets the Hoober kids—16-year-old Lisa, to whom, in his first awakening to sex, he is violently attracted, and Joel, a boy Tony's age. Joel outwardly impresses everyone with his manners, but Tony soon finds that he is really a spoiled and indulged brat, who, to Tony's horror, shoplifts for kicks.

At school Tony makes new friends, Marty Endo and Scott Gold, and through the efforts of their neighborhood priest joins the basketball team of the church youth group. He repulses the advances of Kathryn Thomas—Corky—who has a crush on him, but he is still attracted to Lisa, whom he views regularly, but with great guilt, from his bedroom window when she undresses at night. His sexual awareness increases, and he worries about wet dreams and seemingly uncontrollable erections. At Christmas, after suggesting an interest in birdwatching, he receives a pair of binoculars. Actually, he uses them only to view Lisa more closely, and he begins to feel totally depraved.

In February, Frankie Bollino visits him, and, under Joel's expert guidance, the three of them get drunk—and violently ill. More guilt.

Tony spends 10 days in the hospital. While there he talks to Dr. Fogel, a psychiatrist. Friends visit him, including Lisa, and Corky sends him a touching love note, which Tony decides to keep. He recovers and resumes normal activities. Some of his faith in justice is restored when Joel is caught shoplifting and banished to a military school. Tony decides to change some of his ways and be less critical of others. He might even stop using his binoculars—then again, maybe he won't.

Thematic Material

The novel deals honestly, and without moralizing, with a boy's struggle to develop a workable system of values. Tony is a fascinating character—believable, warmhearted, and vulnerable. He tries to retain his idealism and puritan ethics, while reconciling them to his growing sexuality and social needs. The painful adjustments, particularly of children and old people, that "upward mobility" causes in society are well portrayed, as are some of the seamier aspects of middle-class life in suburbia.

Book Talk Material

Judy Blume's books are usually not difficult to sell to an audience. A very brief plot introduction generally is all that is necessary. Some interesting episodes are: the strange behavior of Mr. Miglioni (pp. 11–15; pp. 14–17, pap.); the truck incident (pp. 33–34; pp. 30–31, pap.); Tony witnesses Joel's shoplifting (pp. 51–52; pp. 43–44, pap.); and the housekeeper arrives (pp. 63–66; pp. 52–55, pap.).

Additional Selections

Everything goes wrong during Wakefield's Christmas vacation in June Shore's *What's the Matter with Wakefield* (Abingdon, 1974, $4.95). Joshua straightens himself out through the help of a friendly family in *Lands End* by Mary Stolz (Harper, 1973, $5.95; pap., $1.50). Jason's bumbling behavior is pitted against his father's efficiency in Susan Terris' *The Drowning Boy* (Doubleday, 1972, $4.50). In Harry Mazer's *Guy Lenny* (Delacorte Pr., 1971, $4.95), a young boy faces a serious family crisis. In the following books, all the boys face problems: Emily Neville's *It's Like This, Cat* (Harper, 1963, $4.95; pap., $1.50; condensed in *Juniorplots*, Bowker, 1967); Maia Wojciechowska's *The Hollywood Kid* (Harper, 1966, $3.50); and *Midway* (Coward, 1968, o.p.) by Anne Barrett. Other novels by Judy Blume could be used, except *Forever* (pap., Pocket Books, $1.75), which is too mature.

About the Author

Commire, Anne. *Something about the Author.* Detroit: Gale Research Co., 1971. Vol. 2, pp. 31–32.
Kinsman, Clare P. and Mary Ann Tennenhouse, Eds., *Contemporary Authors.* Detroit: Gale Research Co., 1972. Vol. 29, p. 66.
Who's Who in America (39th Edition). Chicago: Marquis Who's Who, Inc., 1976. Vol. 1, p. 311.

Hester Burton, *In Spite of All Terror*
Collins+World, 1969, $5.71; pap., Dell, 95¢

Hester Burton is the distinguished English writer of many fine historical novels. *In Time of Trial* (Collins+World, 1964, $5.71; pap., Dell, $1.25), set in early nineteenth-century England, deals with the struggle for freedom of speech as seen through the eyes of 17-year-old Margaret Pargeter, daughter of an idealistic bookseller. It won the Carnegie Medal in 1963. Another, *Castors Away!* (pap., Dell, $1.50) has as its climax the Battle of Trafalgar. *In Spite of All Terror* is more contemporary. It deals with the first year of World War II—September 1939–1940—and its effects on a London school girl, 15-year-old Liz Hawton. The title comes from a speech by Winston Churchill in 1940 in which he asks for "Victory at all costs, victory in spite of all terror." Its audience will be mainly girls, grades 6–8.

Plot Summary

Unlike everyone around her, Liz Hawton sees the oncoming war as a salvation because it will mean that she and her entire school will be evacuated from London to the English countryside. This uprooting will enable her to escape her dismal, oppressive existence with her Aunt Ag and Uncle Herb Trimble and their family. Liz's mother died when she was young, and her father, a vibrant idealist whom she adored, was killed in an automobile accident three years ago. Since then, she has been supported by the dwindling income from her father's insurance. There is scarcely a moment in the day when Aunt Ag doesn't criticize Liz's "uppity" ways because she attends a grammar school on scholarship, or remind her that she is practically a charity case. Liz will miss her wonderful cockney Gran and her pathetic cousin Rose, the eldest of the Trimble children, who, although Liz's age, is working as a store clerk. Nevertheless, it is with a sense of relief that she leaves with her school chums and new form mistress, Miss Garnett, for the tiny village of Chiddingford in Oxfordshire.

Because they were expecting a boy, the Brereton family is at first reluctant to accept Liz as their billet. Mr. Brereton is an erudite, somewhat stuffy Oxford don, and Mrs. Brereton is a brisk, seemingly dispassionate person who, more than the rest, resents Liz's presence. Mr. Brereton's parents, who have also left London and become part of the household, are more approachable. They are Brigadier General Sir Rollo Brereton, nicknamed Grumph, a direct, but amiable gentleman with an amazing facial scar gained during World War I at Gallipoli, and his wife, Lady Brereton, affectionately called Goose, who is dignified but understanding and also a touch scatterbrained. There are three Brereton boys: Miles, who is a little younger than Liz and inclined to be pesky; 17-year-old Ben, a charming loner who immediately befriends Liz but who is, unfortunately, away a great deal of the time at boarding school; and Simon, 19 years old, the gentle, aesthetic brother.

It takes time for Liz to settle into the Brereton household. She is sensitive and high-spirited and, therefore, resents her initial rejection. There is also the "class thing." Her table manners are unpolished and, although she has learned to speak "posh" English as well as her native cockney, her speech still seems inferior to that of the highly educated Breretons.

Overnight the effects of the war are felt, even in this quiet, isolated English hamlet. Ben tries to enlist but is turned down because of his age. Out of a sense of honor and duty, not inclination, Simon volunteers and is inducted into the army. Sadly each day, the General marks the series of Allied defeats on his map of Western Europe. But for Liz, there are also happy moments—at New Year's, for instance, when Ben is on Christmas holiday and Simon is on leave before being sent to France, the three go ice skating on the river.

In the early spring of 1940, the defenses of Western Europe suddenly crumble, and the Germans overrun France. The authorities press all privately owned boats into service should a withdrawal of troops from France be necessary, and the General turns over his 30-foot Thames cabin cruiser, the *Lottie II.*

When the evacuation appears imminent, the General, although ailing, suddenly leaves for London, and, at the same time, Ben is reported missing from school. Liz, realizing their plans, hitches a ride to London and finds them both aboard the *Lottie II* ready to take off for the French coast with a convoy of small boats. She stays with them on the journey down the Thames, but at Grumph's insistence, she goes ashore at Ramsgate. Liz remains there helping soldiers as they disembark from troopships, anxiously awaiting news of the *Lottie II.*

In the meantime, Ben and the General, now at Dunkirk, begin ferrying soldiers from the shore to the large ships. Under constant enemy bombardment and surrounded by confusion and disorder, the *Lottie II* has made seven successful trips when one of the large ships is hit and explodes. The General is killed by a piece of flying timber. Ben continues the rescue operation, hoping blindly that one of the soldiers he saves will be his brother Simon. On the tenth journey, the *Lottie II* is accidentally rammed by another ship and sinks.

At Ramsgate, Liz hears the dreadful news of Grumph's death and the sinking of the *Lottie II.* There is no news, however, of Ben. Exhausted and in shock, she returns to London to visit with Gram before making the dreaded journey back to the Breretons with her sad news. On her return, however, she finds that all the news has preceded her via Ben, who was picked up at sea and, except for a few burns, is safe and well. Lady Brereton takes the news of her husband's death with great courage, but the family still has heard nothing of Simon, and their anxiety increases.

In the summer Ben, now 18, joins the air force. While he is home on leave, Liz receives news that her cousin Rose has become pregnant by a married man and has been thrown out of the house by Aunt Ag. A distraught Liz, accompanied by Ben, leaves for London and, during a massive air raid, races from one shelter to another in the neighborhood looking for Rose. They are successful and bring her back to Chiddingford where Mrs. Brereton very generously offers her a home. Liz is touched beyond words.

Toward the end of the year, the family receives the joyous news that Simon is alive, although a prisoner of war. Ben is sent to Canada for special training, and as 1940 ends, the family settles in, resigned to a long and painful siege, but confident of victory in spite of the war and all its terrors.

Thematic Material

The author authentically re-creates such important historical events as the evacuation at Dunkirk and the Battle of Britain. She also presents an interesting picture of the social structure of prewar Britain and its emphasis on class differences. The book also shows how in time of national crisis these differences are forgotten, and everyone pitches in to help one another. There is an effective contrast between the hectic depersonalized life in London and the quiet pastoral existence in rural England. Each of the characters is well drawn. Readers will particularly like the lively heroine, Liz, and identify with her struggle for acceptance in her new life.

Book Talk Material

A brief discussion of the exciting historical events that serve as a background to the novel will help introduce it. Some effective passages are: life at the Trimbles (pp. 17-21); Liz leaves Aunt Ag (pp. 24-25); Lady Brereton chooses Liz (pp. 44-47), but Mrs. Brereton tries to get rid of her (pp. 53-54); Liz meets Ben (pp. 75-79) and they go skating (pp. 88-90); Liz goes to the *Lottie II* (pp. 103-106). The fine illustrations by Victor G. Ambrus also could be used.

Additional Suggestions

Another fictional account of the evacuation at Dunkirk is given in John R. Tunis' exciting *Silence over Dunkerque* (Morrow, 1962, $5.81; condensed in *Juniorplots*, Bowker, 1967). In Nina Bawden's *Carrie's War* (Lippincott, 1973, $5.95), Carrie and Nick are evacuated to a Welsh mining town during World War II. A young boy's awakening to the meaning of World War II is told in Susan Cooper's *Dawn of Fear* (Harcourt, 1970, $5.95). Other recommended books about this war are James Forman's *Ceremony of Innocence* (Hawthorn, 1970, $6.95) and *The Traitors* (Farrar, 1968, $3.95), and Erik Haugaard's *The Little Fishes* (Houghton, 1967, $4.95; condensed in *Introducing Books*, Bowker, 1970). Red Reeder gives an interesting account of the war in his two-volume *Story of the Second World War* (Hawthorn, 1969-1970, $5.95 per volume).

About the Author

Commire, Anne. *Something about the Author*. Detroit: Gale Research Co., 1975. Vol. 7, pp. 35-36.

DeMontreville, Doris and Donna Hill, Eds. *Third Book of Junior Authors.* New York: H. W. Wilson Co., 1972, pp. 54-55.

Doyle, Brian. *Who's Who of Children's Literature.* New York: Schocken Books, 1968, pp. 45-46.

Ethridge, James M., Ed. *Contemporary Authors.* Detroit: Gale Research Co., 1964. Vol. 9, p. 64.

John Donovan, *I'll Get There, It Better Be Worth the Trip*

Harper, 1969, $4.95; pap., Dell, 95¢

The trip mentioned in the title is the journey from childhood through adolescence. A steamship company once advertised, "Getting there is half the fun." This certainly does not apply to this transitional stage of development as experienced by the narrator and hero of the story, Davy Ross. With this book, his first novel, John Donovan immediately established himself as an important American writer for young adults. *Trip* is enjoyed by junior high school students.

Plot Summary

Since his parents' divorce when he was five, Davy has been living with his grandmother in a quiet coastal town not far from Boston. Although growing up with a much older person with a somewhat severe New England temperament is not always easy, Davy and Grandmother develop a close and loving relationship. To help lessen the boy's loneliness and isolation, the old lady gives him a black dachshund, Fred, for his eighth birthday. Fred and Davy are now inseparable.

When Davy is 13, his quiet and sheltered life comes abruptly to an end. Grandmother dies of a heart attack. After the funeral, the assembled relatives including Davy's mother, Helen, who works in an ad agency in New York City, and his Aunt Louise and Uncle Bert, who live locally, begin discussing Davy's future. Although he doesn't hear most of the conversation, Davy realizes the situation and he and Fred take frequent long walks on deserted beaches or to Grandmother's grave. Only Fred is able to share and help Davy's loneliness and grief.

It is decided, after much arguing, that Davy will stay with Aunt Louise until his mother can remodel her apartment to add another bedroom; then Davy will move to New York City with her. At first his mother refuses to accept Fred too, but she relents when Davy says he won't go without his dog.

On the day after Christmas, Davy and Fred arrive at the refurbished apartment in the Chelsea area and find that Helen has decorated the bedroom in a style suited to a much younger boy. This is typical of the amount of insight Helen has regarding her son. Basically, she is a self-indulgent, immature woman whose behavior alternates between exaggerated shows of affection, combined with other superficial gestures of love for the boy, and bouts of extreme self-pity when she bemoans her life of sacrificing, first for her husband and now for her son. In addition, Mrs. Ross has what could be most charitably called a drinking problem. It is during these spells with the bottle that she becomes most self-righteous. Another fly—or in this case, dog—in the ointment is Fred, hyperactive, noisy, and, in times of great excitement, not completely housebroken.

It has been arranged that Davy will spend Saturdays with his artist-designer father, David, and his second wife, Stephanie. Although Davy is somewhat intimidated by his father, he likes Stephanie, who is genuine and understanding in her attitude toward the boy. On their first outing together, they visit Central Park and the Museum of Natural History, where Davy is particularly impressed with a friendly looking stuffed coyote.

Davy is enrolled in an all-boy private Episcopal school in the Village, and his first encounter in class is with the boy who sits in front of him—the hostile, outspoken class jock, Douglas Altschuler. Davy later learns that part of Altschuler's animosity toward him stems from the fact that the desk assigned to Davy formerly belonged to Altschuler's best friend for many years, Larry Wilkins, who is dying of a blood disease. At school, Davy befriends eight-year-old Frankie Menlo, who soon becomes Davy's hero-worshiping mascot.

Slowly Altschuler and Davy become friends. They live close by, and on their walks home Doug introduces Davy to the many wonders he shared with Larry in Greenwich Village, including a terrific candy store operated by kindly Mrs. Greene. After Larry's death, Altschuler, also a product of a broken home, becomes more desirous of Davy's companionship, and Davy realizes that Altschuler, in spite of his outward ways, is like himself, vulnerable and lacking a sense of belonging.

One afternoon while alone in Davy's apartment, the two boys are roughhousing with Fred on the living room carpet. Spontaneously they kiss, and then, embarrassed by their action, they part. But the following weekend, when Doug stays over at Davy's, they engage in an overt sexual act, which both confuses and alarms Davy.

A few days later, after school, the boys become tipsy on whiskey at Davy's home and, their arms around each other, fall asleep on the rug. Helen finds them and becomes hysterical at the implications of this incident. She sends for David, who quietly takes Davy away from the apartment for a man-to-man talk. By the time they return, tragedy has struck. While being walked by Helen, Fred has escaped and is killed by a passing car. Davy is broken with grief and begins to believe that, because his friendship with Altschuler caused his absence when Fred should have been walked by him, he and his behavior with Altschuler caused his pet's death.

For weeks, Davy avoids Altschuler, but one day in the showers at school, Altschuler tries to congratulate Davy on a sensational baseball victory by patting him on the shoulders. Davy strikes out wildly, and they fight bitterly.

Davy feels remorse and shame for the action, and when Altschuler phones to say he too is sorry, he decides to resume their friendship, but on a different non-guilt-producing basis. The two go to the Museum of Natural History together and Davy shows Altschuler his beloved coyote.

Thematic Material

The rites of passage through the beginnings of adolescence are excellently portrayed, as is a realistic picture of a far-from-ideal home situation. The sexual exploration of the two boys trying to determine the limits of their own sexuality is told with tact and delicacy. Other important themes are teen-age friendships and Davy's attachment to his dog.

Book Talk Material

Some important passages are: Davy and his Grandmother (pp. 10-13; pp. 12-14, pap.); the new apartment (pp. 40-42; pp. 34-36, pap.); at the Museum (pp. 62-66; pp. 54-56, pap); and Davy meets Altschuler (pp. 70-74; pp. 59-63, pap.).

Additional Selections

Brian Moody, saddled with an alcoholic mother and bossy older sister, finds friendship with some black classmates in Emily Cheney Neville's *Garden of Broken Glass* (Delacorte Pr., 1975, $5.95). Family problems and the search for identity and self-reliance are the subjects of the eight stories in Norma Fox Mazer's *"Dear Bill Remember Me" and Other Stories* (Delacorte Pr., 1976, $6.95). Greg meets his real father in Arthur Roth's *The Secret Lover of Elmtree* (Four Winds, 1976, $6.95). Kevin's older brother is hooked on drugs in Maia Wojciechowska's *Turned Out* (Harper, 1968, $4.95; pap., Dell, 95¢). Other recommendations include Kin Platt's *Headman* (Morrow, 1975, $5.95); John Donovan's *Remove Protective Coating a Little at a Time* (Harper, 1973, $3.95; pap., Dell, 95¢); and Jerome Brooks' *Uncle Mike's Boy* (Harper, 1973, $4.95).

About the Author

Ethridge, James M. and Barbara Kopala, Eds. *Contemporary Authors.* Detroit: Gale Research Co., 1967. Vols. 1-4, pp. 259-260.

C. H. Frick, *The Comeback Guy*

Harcourt, 1961, $5.50; pap., $1.45 (same pagination)

C. H. Frick's novels, like this one, usually combine suspenseful sports action with solid statements concerning adolescent behavior and responsibility. Junior high school boys and some fifth and sixth graders enjoy his books.

Plot Summary

At the beginning of his senior year at East High School, 17-year-old Jeff Stanley, who has significantly chosen his own nickname, King, is in the school auditorium to participate, under Mr. Gray's supervision, in the tryouts for this year's cheerleading team. It seems impossible in Jeff's eyes that he and his girl friend, Tracy Summers, won't be reappointed. Jeff has held the only male position on the team for the past two years, and during that time he feels that he has become indispensable. His arrogance and conceit have grown so great that he has some admirers but, with the exception of Tracy, few friends. When one of the candidates, Philip Newton, accidentally jostles him onstage, Jeff creates a scene and maliciously calls the boy Banana Nose. The judges—eight students and seven teachers—overhear these callous remarks. There are 65 students trying out for the five positions, and the balloting is long and tedious. Finally, Tracy and three other girls are elected, but Jeff is stunned into disbelief when Philip is chosen over him. Tracy tries gently to tell him that his defeat was caused by his inflated ego and constant bragging. Defiantly, Jeff accuses her of being disloyal and bitterly breaks off their relationship. Back home, his overly solicitous and protective mother comforts him and refuses to believe that his actions could in any way be responsible for his failure to make the team.

The following day, Jeff asks Mr. Gray what went wrong, and the teacher suggests that the boy visit the guidance counselor, Mr. Fitch. When he does, the counselor tells him in a straightforward manner that his recent behavior, including the stage flareup, alienated the judges. On the positive side, Mr. Fitch advises Jeff to assess his attitudes and values, to try to mold himself into someone that not only his fellow students, but also Jeff, can grow to like and respect.

That night in his room the boy does some earnest soul-searching and realizes he must change his ways. He also decides that he will try to regain the regard of his former friends by endeavoring to make the school team in the only sport at which he feels somewhat proficient—pole vaulting.

He secretly begins training to build up his arm and chest muscles, and to further this aim and secure enough money so that he won't have to take his father's charity to buy a pole, he takes a job on Saturdays loading beer trucks. His mother is horrified, but Mr. Stanley, who admires the boy's spunk, pacifies her.

After four Saturdays, Jeff has accumulated enough to buy the equipment. He and his father construct, in the woods, a pit complete with sawdust, two movable standards, and an old fishing rod that will serve as the crossbar.

Now estranged from the few friends he shared with Tracy, Jeff becomes something of a loner at school, his only friend being a new boy in class named "Magoo" McLaughlin. Jeff confides in Magoo his plans to try out for the team in the spring and shows him his secret practice pit.

One of the presents Jeff receives at Christmas from his parents is a case in which to carry his pole. Mr. Stanley is so proud of his son's accomplishments that he has printed on the case his own school nickname, Stanley the Manley. Although Jeff is touched by the gesture, he tells Magoo that he dreads the day when he will have to take the case to school and face the taunts of his classmates.

That day arrives late in February when the first track tryouts are held in the school gym. As predicted, the case causes more accusations of boasting and an inflated ego, but Magoo saves the day by explaining to the boys the origin of the nickname.

Jeff makes the team and is overjoyed to pin five blue ribbons on his bedroom walls from the first five competitions that he enters. However, his teammates are amazed at his modesty and sportsmanship—it is almost like meeting a new and different Jeff Stanley.

Magoo, a natural folk singer, persuades Jeff to join him and his girl friend, Adele, in preparing a skit for Senior Talent Assembly. Through a series of unintentional errors, their presentation becomes the riotous hit of the show.

Jeff begins preparing for the big sectional track meet, which, to the victor, will mean entry into the state finals. On the day of the competition, Jeff notices that the grandstands are full and that Tracy and the other cheerleaders are busy whipping up the crowd's excitement.

On the first of his three trips in the final competition, Jeff becomes distracted by the cheerleaders' song and knocks down the crossbar. On the second, faulty hand placement brings the same result. He clears the bar easily on the third, but a gust of wind dislodges it and Jeff is disqualified. However, his gracious acceptance of defeat leads to a reconciliation with Tracy, along with the school's other athletes.

At the annual awards assembly, Jeff, along with the other athletes, receive their letter-sweaters, and Tracy is named the most popular girl in the school. Jeff is dumbfounded when, at the end of the ceremony, he receives the award for the best-liked male student. The "comeback guy" has made it all the way.

Thematic Material

In addition to lessons on good sportsmanship and the nature of lasting values, this novel shows that often from humbling experiences can come greater understanding and awareness of one's self. Jeff's changes in attitude and behavior are convincingly portrayed, as are the many interesting details on the sport of pole vaulting.

Book Talk Material

A brief description of Jeff's character and his disappointment at losing the tryouts will attract prospective readers. Some passages of interest are: his fight with Tracy (pp. 24-28); his meeting with the guidance counselor (pp. 56-63); Jeff tells his parents about his brewery job (pp. 84-89); and the "Stanley the Manley" incident at school (pp. 143-147).

Additional Selections

A series of losses are suffered by a basketball team after Bud Cane becomes one of *The Unbeatable Five* (Dodd, 1974, $4.95) by William R. Cox. By the same author, try *Rookie in the Back Court* (Dodd, 1970, $4.50) and *Trouble at Second Base* (Dodd, 1966, $4.50). Joshua tries to prove his worth as a goalie in Mike Neigoff's *Terror on the Ice* (Whitman, 1974, $4.50) for a younger audience. A high school track star worries about his future in Doris Smith's *Up and Over* (Morrow, 1976, $6.95). For students interested in this sport use the nonfiction *Inside Track* by Jim Bush (Regnery, 1974, $5.95) and W. Harold O'Connor's *How to Star in Track and Field* (Four Winds, 1961, $2.95). A girl joins a football team in R. R. Knudson's *Zanballer* (Delacorte Pr., 1972, $5.95; pap., Dell, 95¢). There is also a sequel, *Zanbanger* (Harper, 1977, $6.95).

About The Author

Commire, Anne. *Something about the Author*. Detroit: Gale Research Co., 1974. Vol. 6, pp. 119–120.

Ethridge, James M. and Barbara Kopala, Eds. *Contemporary Authors*. Detroit: Gale Research Co., 1967. Vol. 4, p. 488.

Bette Greene, *Summer of My German Soldier*
Dial, 1973, $4.95; pap., Bantam, $1.25

Bette Greene's first juvenile, *Summer of My German Soldier*, was followed the next year by a work for a slightly younger audience, the Newbery Medal Honor Book, *Philip Hall Likes Me I Reckon Maybe* (Dial, 1974, $5.95; lib. bdg., $5.47; pap., Dell, $1.25), another story set in rural Arkansas, but in a lighter, more humorous vein. *Summer* is read and enjoyed by students from sixth grade through senior high school.

Plot Summary

The story takes place in the small town of Jenkinsville, Arkansas, during the early 1940s. One summer afternoon, many of the local townspeople, including the narrator, Patty Bergen, the 12-year-old daughter of the owner of the local department store, gather at the train station because the first shipment of German prisoners of war is scheduled to arrive for the new camp that has been built just out of town. Patty is surprised to find that they look like ordinary American boys, not the ferocious murderers she expected. She rushes home to tell Ruth, the Bergen's black maid, and her younger sister, six-year-old Sharon.

Patty is a scrawny, nervous, unhappy young girl. Her parents ignore her or nag at her. In their eyes, she can do no right. Her father has a terrible temper and often beats her. She has no real friends except Ruth, who understands and tries to protect Patty. Her isolation is due partly to the fact that she is Jewish and feels excluded from many activities, such as those at the Baptist summer camp where practically all the children in her grade are now attending. She escapes her loneliness by often retreating into a world of make-believe. Her wild imagination and preposterous lies, however, often get her into trouble. Her only respite comes when the family drives off to Memphis to visit her Grandpa and Grandma Fried, both of whom Patty adores. But this is a fairly long trip and, with gasoline rationing in effect, those visits have become infrequent.

One day a group of German prisoners are marched into Bergen's Department Store to do some shopping. Patty is intrigued with the spokesman of the group, a handsome, young, dark-haired prisoner who speaks flawless English. She waits on him and falls under the spell of this jaunty, intelligent man, who introduces himself as Anton Reiker from Gottinger, the son of a university professor and an English-born mother. She sells him pencils and paper and is amazed when he also buys a cheap piece of ladies' jewelry with pieces of glass in it to simulate diamonds.

Patty's encounter with Anton and a visit to Grandma are the only two events that have added diversion to the hot and seemingly endless summer. The rest of her days are spent talking with Ruth or cleaning up her private hideaway, unused servants' quarters that consist of a bedroom, kitchen, and bath over the garage.

One day she is playing a game of Hit the Hubcap with slightly retarded Freddie Dowd. The game involves throwing tiny stones at the hubcaps of passing cars. One stone is deflected and shatters a motorist's windshield. He complains to Mr. Bergen, who that evening beats her with his fists and belt and forbids her ever to see Freddie again.

Later that week, Patty is watching the sunset over the railway yards from her kitchen window when she notices the furtive movement of a man along the railway embankment. It is Anton—he has escaped. She rushes to him and brings him back to the safety of her hideaway. Patty gives him food and some of her father's clothes and, whenever possible, she steals away and has long talks with him. Anton has escaped by bribing one of the guards with the "diamond" pin he bought at Bergen's. He tells Patty about himself and how he hated Hitler, but he had either to capitulate or be exterminated. This warm and honest man also takes an interest in Patty and draws her out. For the first time, she feels like a person of some worth and value.

Charlene Madlee, reporter of the *Memphis Commercial Appeal* comes to Jenkinsville to investigate Reiker's escape, and she uses Patty as her guide. Patty hears the prison camp officials refer to Anton as a fine and worthy man, and she now feels free from guilt.

Freddie Dowd wanders aimlessly into the Bergen yard one day, and Mr. Bergen, thinking this is defiance of his authority, begins to beat Patty mercilessly. Alerted by her screams, Anton leaves the safety of the garage to protect her just as the beating stops. He returns to his hiding place, but not before Ruth has seen him.

Ruth agrees to help Patty feed and shelter Anton, but she makes Patty realize that he will soon have to leave. Patty decides that she will run away with Anton, and on the night he is to leave she packs her bag and steals out to the hiding place. Anton very gently dissuades her from leaving with him, but before they part he asks her never to forget him and gives her his only prize possession, his great-grandfather's gold ring.

A few weeks later Patty carelessly shows the ring to a clerk in her father's store, claiming it was a gift from a tramp wanting food. Her father, thinking that Patty has been involved with a child molester, calls in the sheriff, but the investigation is soon dropped.

In the fall, Patty starts back to school and life resumes its regular pattern when one day two FBI men come by to question Patty about the ring. They produce a shirt that she had given Anton. It has bullet holes in it and is stained with blood. Anton has been shot and killed in New York City while resisting arrest. Stunned, Patty blurts out the truth, but she avoids incriminating Ruth. However, the servant is fired by Mr. Bergen when she tries to defend Patty's actions.

The girl is arraigned in court on a charge of delinquency and sentenced to four to six months in a state reformatory. While there Patty is visited only by Ruth, and she forlornly wonders what the future will bring. She decides to live one day at a time and hopes that somehow things will get better.

Thematic Material

Patty's painful search for strength and a feeling of worthiness is well portrayed, as is the theme that one should evaluate humans as individuals, not as a group. Also well depicted are the townspeople's bigotry and hypocrisy that stem from their ignorance and narrow-mindedness. These are brought into sharp contrast by the truth and honesty of the "losers" in the novel, Patty, Ruth, and Anton.

Book Talk Material

Miller–Brody has recorded excerpts from *Summer* on YA 401 (disc, $6.95; cassette, $7.95). A brief introduction to the historic period might be necessary. Some interesting passages are: the prisoners arrive by train (pp. 3–7; pp. 1–4, pap.); Patty's first encounter with Anton (pp. 40–46; pp. 32–38, pap.); Hit the Hubcap and its consequences (pp. 63–69; pp. 53–59, pap.); and Patty helps Anton escape (pp. 80–82; pp. 69–70, pap.).

Additional Selections

When one reads the conversations that Patty has with Ruth, one thinks immediately of the similarly unhappy heroine of Carson McCullers' poignant *The Member of the Wedding* (Houghton, 1946, $5.95; several pap. editions including Bantam, $1.25). The central character in Honor Arundel's *The Blanket Word* (Nelson, 1973, $5.95) is also looking for family ties. *Mollie Make-Believe* (Harper, 1974, $4.95) by Alice Bach tells about a girl who must learn to face reality. A rebellious 13-year-old girl narrowly escapes reform school in Robert Burch's *Queenie Peavy* (Viking, 1966, $5.95). Her gentler male counterpart is in Burch's *D. J.'s Worst Enemy* (Viking, 1965, $5.95; condensed in *Introducing Books*, Bowker, 1970). Also use Jean Little's novel of a young girl's growing awareness of her Jewishness, *Kate* (Harper, 1971, $4.95; pap., $1.25), and Paula Fox's *Blowfish Live in the Sea* (Bradbury, 1970, $6.95).

About the Author

Commire, Anne. *Something about the Author*. Detroit: Gale Research Co., 1976.
Vol. 8, p. 73.
Kinsman, Clare D., Ed. *Contemporary Authors*. Detroit: Gale Research Co., 1975.
Vol. 53, p. 247.

Virginia Hamilton, *M. C. Higgins, the Great*
Macmillan, 1974, $6.95; pap., Dell, $1.25

In her acceptance speech for the 1975 Newbery Award (*Horn Book*, August 1974), Virginia Hamilton states that no book gave her greater pleasure and pain in writing than *M. C. Higgins, the Great*. Many young readers will also find that the book, like the land it describes, slowly and sometimes grudgingly gives up its wealth. The rewards, however, far outweigh the efforts. This novel also won the Boston Globe–Horn Book Award and the National Book Award. It was written for young readers in the upper elementary and junior high school grades.

Plot Summary

Mayo Cornelius Higgins is the 13-year-old great-grandson of an escaped slave named Sarah, who fled from the South with her baby and settled on the slope of what later became known as Sarah's Mountain, in a mining area close to the Ohio River. There are many reasons why M.C. could be called "the Great": he is considered one of the best swimmers in the area; he comes from a wonderful family; he has a mother, Banina, whose voice matches the sweetness of her temperament; and when he sits atop the 40-foot pole his father gave him, he feels like an emperor surveying his dominions. Inwardly, he also feels great because to him his thoughts are more great and daring than those of others, and he is willing to take risks that would confound anyone else.

By economic standards, the Higgins family would be considered poor. Jones, M.C.'s father, works in the mine only when a regular hand is absent, and Banina does cleaning jobs in town. There are three other children, all younger than M.C., two boys, Lennie Pool and Harper, and a girl, Macie Pearl. Their modest cottage is built on an overlapping on the mountainside, but, thanks to Jones' ingenuity, they at least have hot and cold running water. What is most troubling to M.C. is that a huge spoil heap left by the mining company above them on the mountain seems to be moving gradually glacierlike down the mountain and will soon engulf their house and property. Despite M.C.'s warnings, Jones refuses to admit to the danger because he knows it means eventual loss of his family's property.

Apart from his family, M.C. has only one friend, Ben Killburn, who belongs to a large clan of social outcasts that live together in an enclave on Kill's Mound. They are known as the "witchy people." Not only are the Killburns supposed to have supernatural powers to heal wounds and drive out devils, but their physical appearance is abnormal and grotesque. Each has six fingers and toes, pale yellowish skin, and red hair. In spite of his parents' warnings, M.C. still meets Ben away from home, but he has never had the courage to cross the swinging rope bridge that leads to Kill's Mound.

At one of their meetings, Ben tells M.C. that there is a man in town who is recording folk songs and because he has been told of Banina's lovely voice, he will soon be calling on the Higgins. M.C. begins dreaming that his mother will become a big recording star and take them away from the danger of the mountain. He rushes up the trail to await the coming of the "dude," and sees a stranger on the path, a young girl who runs away when she sees him.

At home, he climbs up his 40-foot pole and engages in his pastime of viewing the countryside. Here past and present meld, and he often imagines that Sarah is down below working her silent way through the underbrush to freedom. The pole was part of an array of junk that his father has dragged up the mountain to their yard. Jones gave it to M.C. as a prize for swimming, and the boy attached a bicycle seat and two tricycle wheels and pedals to it before erecting it in the front yard.

M.C. sees the man with the tape recorder in the distance and runs to meet him. His name is James K. Lewis. On their way to the Higgins home, they pass the spoil heap. Lewis reaffirms M.C.'s deepest fears about the impending landslide. Because Banina is not yet home from work, Lewis leaves, promising to come back that evening.

The family assembles and dinner is prepared. Through speech and action, M.C. reveals how much he loves each of his parents but how differently he feels toward them. With his father he has a surface, physical relationship that at times is competitive, but with his mother, there is a deeper emotional bond of felt, but often unspoken, understanding and love.

After dinner, M.C. tries to explain to his mother the importance of her getting a record contract and of their leaving the mountain. She gently explains that Jones' roots are here and that, at her insistence, years ago he had removed the external signs of the family graveyard in front of their house. However, it had been his intention to use the 40-foot pole as a suitable memorial for all his ancestors.

Ben reports that the girl M.C. saw on the trail is camping in the valley. M.C. investigates and, even though he finds her attractive, she is so defiant and unfriendly that he returns home.

Lewis returns and tape-records Banina, but there is no mention of a contract. Early the next morning before Banina must go to work, M.C. goes swimming with her in the cirque, a small lake in a deep hollow. They notice that the girl with whom M.C. has had two unfortunate encounters is camped on the bank. After Banina leaves, M.C. rouses the girl. She is older than M.C., taciturn, enigmatic, and totally enthralling to the boy. M.C. displays his swimming prowess by negotiating a dangerous underwater tunnel. At her insistence, he takes her through it. She almost drowns and later confesses that she cannot swim. Some girl!

M.C. takes her home for lunch and there she tells Jones something about herself. Her name is Lurhetta Outlaw. With her mother's permission, during her summer vacation she leaves home to explore the countryside.

After lunch M.C. takes her to see his rabbit traps, and on the trail they meet Ben. Lurhetta is fascinated by him and consents to go to Kill's Mound. M.C., not wishing to be branded a coward, tags along. The commune is far from the witchy place that M.C. expected. The Killburns are a closely knit, industrious group who are friendly to their guests even though they have been ostrasized by suspicion and prejudice from the community.

M.C. invites Lurhetta to dinner, but she doesn't appear. Lewis does drop by, however, to give the Higgins a cassette of Banina's voice. Before leaving, he tells M.C. that his mother is too pure, too natural ever to withstand the rigors of the commercial music field. The next morning M.C. finds Lurhetta's camp deserted, but she has left him her knife. Dejectedly M.C. returns home. Suddenly he has one of his great notions. He will not sit passively by and see his family's home destroyed. He starts to dig up the earth and, by using all the junk in their yard, creates a wall to shield them against the oncoming spoil pile. Some of the family begin to help. At M.C.'s insistence, Ben is, for the first time, allowed on the Higgins property also to help. Quite unexpectedly, Jones crawls under the house and drags out Sarah's gravestone. That will surely make M.C.'s wall strong.

Thematic Material

M. C. Higgins is not a conventional novel of plot, but instead is one of feelings, sensations, and emotions that transcend time and space. The novel is a reaffirmation of life, a hymn to those who help us survive, a tribute to the human spirit that never passively accepts fate. There are many other themes in the complex novel, such as conflicts of the past and the present and between illusion and reality. The novel also portrays many family relations and tells how physical differences in people can make them objects of fear and suspicion. It is also the story of a boy's maturation.

Book Talk Material

A description of the central character, his family, and his amazing 40-foot pole might be used to interest readers. Individual passages are rather difficult to isolate; however, one could use: M.C. finds Lurhetta on the trail (pp. 18–20; pp. 22–24, pap.); atop the 40-foot pole (pp. 25–28; pp. 29–31, pap.); meeting with the dude (pp. 38–40; pp. 39–41, pap.); and M.C. remembers a past birthday (pp. 84–87; pp. 77–79, pap.).

Additional Selections

A boy from another planet creates a stir when he arrives in southern Appalachia in Alexander Key's *The Forgotten Door* (Westminster, 1965, $4.75; pap., Scholastic, 95¢). There is a lively combination of realism, history, and fantasy that ranges from England to New Guinea in Penelope Lively's *The House in Norham Gardens* (Dutton, 1974, $5.95). In the historical novel set in upstate New York, Walter D. Edmond's *Bert Green's Barn* (Little, 1975, $6.95), Tom's dream is to help his destitute mother by purchasing a barn. For young readers, there are three novels on the problems of growing up black in poverty: Louisa A. Shotwell's *Roosevelt Grady* (Collins+World, 1963, $4.95; pap., Scholastic, 95¢; condensed in *Juniorplots*, Bowker, 1967); her *Adam Bookout* (Viking, 1967, $3.95); and Betty K. Erwin's *Behind the Magic Line* (Little, 1969, $4.95).

About the Author

Commire, Anne. *Something about the Author.* Detroit: Gale Research Co., 1973. Vol. 4, pp. 97–99.

Hoffman, Miriam and Eva Samuels. *Authors and Illustrators of Children's Books.* New York: R. R. Bowker Co., 1972. Vol. 2, pp. 186–192.

Hopkins, Lee Bennett. *More Books by More People*. New York: Citation Press, 1974, pp. 199–207.
Ward, Martha E. and Dorothy A. Marquardt. *Authors of Books for Young People*. (2nd Edition). Metuchen, N.J.: Scarecrow Press, Inc., 1971, p. 223.
Who's Who in America (39th Edition). Chicago: Marquis Who's Who, Inc., 1976. Vol. 1, p. 1308.

John Ney, *Ox: The Story of a Kid at the Top*
Little, 1970, $4.95; pap., Bantam, $1.25

To say that Ox Olmstead's family is rich is to understate the case. They are so shamefully, outrageously rich that by comparison practically everyone else is poor. Their 100-plus-room house in Palm Beach is so large that guests aren't missed until several days after they leave. To say that Ox, whose real name is Franklin, is big for his age would also understate the case. By nature he has a large body, but he is so lonely and unhappy that he constantly overeats. The chief cause of his unhappiness is his parents, whose main pleasure is drunken parties. They ignore Ox so much that for days his only contact with either parent may be to help Charles, the chauffeur, carry one of them off to bed after an all-night bash. Ox also cries a lot when someone is kind to him. In the first book in this series about Ox, the boy is 12 years old and should be in the sixth grade; he is only in the fourth. This book is enjoyed by upper elementary school readers and up. The rest of the series, described below, is for a slightly older group.

Plot Summary

Mrs. Hollins, Ox's fourth grade teacher, assigns a composition on Cows and How They Work. When Ox mentions the assignment to his father, Mr. Olmstead takes his son by helicopter to a friend's ranch so he can see a cow. The ranch turns out to have only beef cattle so Ox doesn't see his cow, but their visit is an excuse for a great party for his father. Ox is forgotten and eats by himself in the kitchen.

Then the whole party decides to fly to the ranch of another friend, Harry Ming, who lives in Pebble Beach, California. Ox and his composition have become the excuse for a transcontinental spree. In California, Ox meets Harry's son, Vinnie. They visit old, and also wealthy, Mrs. Appleton, who talks about her patrician childhood. It becomes obvious to Ox that there is a difference between money and class.

Now the group is off to Acalpulco, still in search of cows. Ox meets two American hippies, who need money to get back to America. Ox convinces them that begging is the answer, but their first "touch," an American, is so outraged that he calls the police and all three are whisked off to jail. With the help of some outrageous lying, Ox frees his friends and gets a contribution of $500 from the outraged American for the hippies' "medical expenses."

After a brief stay in Mexico City, the group, which now includes a young starlet named Clive whom Ox likes, presses on to Houston, Texas, and there real trouble begins. Mr. Olmstead's former wife hears he is in town and has him arrested for nonpayment of alimony. Ox meets an old school friend, Dale Tyler, who now calls himself Baxter. He has been hired by a movie company to play the role of a famous television personality in childhood. Ox is invited to appear in the movie, but he decides to stick by his father. The alimony mess is cleared up, and they fly home. The trip took one week and Ox never saw a cow. When he returns to school and Mrs. Hollins warmly welcomes him back, he has a good cry.

In *Ox Goes North* (Harper, 1973, $4.95; pap., Bantam, $1.25), Ox, now 15 and in the eighth grade, is sent to Camp Downing in Vermont. He becomes friendly with his two cabinmates and spends the summer trying to free one of them from domination by grandparents.

Ox is 17—and huge—in *Ox under Pressure* (Lippincott, 1976, $6.95). He accompanies his father to Long Island to recover two million dollars misplaced by a family friend. Ox is attracted to Archella Marlborough, a fascinating but neurotic young girl who lives on the estate of a hostile old lady, Lizzie Revere. The growth of their relationship and its final ending form the basis of the book.

Thematic Material

Ox is truly an original character—inventive, astute, pathetic—but, in his own way, he conveys the attitudes and differences between the rich and poor, and in so doing makes a satiric commentary on American mores and morals. Much of the book is funny, but the way in which the social life and family relationships of the wealthy are depicted makes "life at the top" seem less appealing.

Book Talk Material

A discussion of the meaning of the title, who Ox is, and what life at the top involves could be used to introduce the book. Specific passages of interest include: life in the fourth grade (pp. 5-11; pp. 2-8, pap.); Ox helps some Indians (pp. 17-24; pp. 13-20, pap.); and Ox and the hippies (pp. 64-75; pp. 55-64, pap.).

Additional Suggestions

The problems of two young men growing up are explored in Carolyn Balducci's *Is There a Life after Graduation, Henry Birnbaum?* (Houghton, 1971, $5.95; pap., Dell, 75¢). Unlike Ox, the hero of Dorothy Hamilton's novel *Jason* (pap., Herald Press, $2.50) is able to work out his problems with the help of his family and friends. Two dropouts, Jim and Rachel, meet at a party and change each other's life in Phyllis A. Wood's *I've Missed a Sunset or Three* (pap., New Amer. Lib., 95¢). Also use Bob and Jan Young's *Where's Tomorrow?* (Abelard-Schuman, 1968, $5.95). For the younger group, there is Margaret Hodges' story of a young boy's first year at boarding school, *The Making of Joshua Cobb* (Farrar, 1971, $4.50) and Jane Langston's account of a girl moving to a new school, *The Boyhood of Grace Jones* (Harper, 1972, $4.95).

Mary Stolz, *In a Mirror*

Harper, 1953, o.p.; pap., Dell, $1.25 (same pagination)

Mary Stolz is one of the most prolific, versatile, and successful writers of juvenile fiction. During the 1950s, she gained initial fame with novels for and about teen-age girls, such as *The Sea Gulls Wake Me* (Harper, 1951, $5.79), *Organdy Cupcakes* (Harper, 1951, $5.79; condensed in *Juniorplots*, Bowker, 1967), and *In a Mirror*. In the 1960s, her work expanded to include books for the upper elementary grades, such as the Barkam Street series, and several delightful picture books. Her most recent works, however, again concentrate on junior and senior high school audiences. *In a Mirror* also could be enjoyed by better readers in the upper elementary grades.

Plot Summary

The summer before her junior year at an exclusive New England girls' college, Bessie Muller begins a journal in which she candidly recalls important events in her past and accurately records the present. She is an only child, daughter of a successful mystery story writer and a patient, somewhat distracted mother. They live harmoniously in a spacious home on the Long Island Sound. Although Bessie calls her parents "portly," she honestly refers to herself as "fat." Diets come and go, but her overindulgence in food remains. She is an English major, an avid reader, and bent on a career in writing. These interests are encouraged at home, and through the attention of her former high school English teacher, Miss Berstein, a story written when she was 16 won third prize in a contest.

Her best friend and college roommate is Til Carey, who has been spending the summer with the Mullers while her mother is in England tending to Mrs. Carey's ailing sister. In many ways, Til is Bessie's opposite. She is a dance major, lithe, beautiful, and never without a succession of boyfriends. Her current and most serious is Johnny Todd, who attends the boys' college close to their own. Bessie is secretly also attracted to Johnny and hopes that Til will not behave as callously toward him as she has to so many former admirers. Bessie thinks that Til's attitude toward men stems from the cold, insensitive treatment of both her parents during childhood. Although Til often nags Bessie when they are alone about her weight, she is fiercely protective of her friend. Last year at college, Til stole Carol Fuller's boyfriend because Carol had called Bessie "Fatso."

The two girls return to college in the fall, where Bessie is still dateless and fat. She begins her new classes, which include a poetry seminar conducted by a first-year teacher, handsome and reserved Mr. Dunn. Bessie and Donald Dunn clash immediately because ultraprogressive Bessie finds his ideas about poetry old-fashioned. However, when she interviews him at home for an article in the school paper, her attitude changes. She meets his wife and two children and finds a home filled with warmth and love. Soon Bessie visits them often to babysit. Partly through their influence, she gains greater self-awareness and begins to stick to a diet.

After Thanksgiving, Bessie brings a kitten back for Dunn's son, five-year-old Josh. Til and she deliver it, and Til also develops an instant affection for the family. Soon Til is visiting them regularly, with or without Bessie, and Bessie becomes concerned when she thinks Til has fallen in love with Dunn.

The two girls begin work on a ballet. Til, who now refers to Mr. Dunn as Donald, grows distant and edgy. She stops seeing Johnny, and Bessie becomes alarmed.

Before spring vacation, the ballet is performed with great success. Til is particularly elated because Donald Dunn attends all three performances. Mistaking this as a sign of romantic love, she visits him in his office and confesses her love for him. He says, "I love you too, Til, and so do Audrey and Josh." Thinking he has misunderstood her, Til kisses him—at that moment Carol Fuller enters the office.

Afraid she will cause more trouble, Til hastily leaves to join her mother in Europe. She writes Bessie that she is too hurt and ashamed to return, but will continue her studies abroad.

By the end of her junior year, Bessie is dating and leading a more active social life. Hardly "thin," she has become more presentable. However, she misses Til very much. While most people look back on their college years with fondness, Bessie knows her memories will be tinged with sadness.

Thematic Material

Although part of the novel deals with a girl's efforts to control a weight problem, it is Bessie's growing self-awareness and assurance that become the major theme. The friendship of the girls is touching and believable, as is the pain and anguish of Til's unrequited infatuation.

Book Talk Material

A description of the two girls and their problems will serve as a fine introduction. Because the story is told in a journal format, it is difficult to isolate specific passages. However, try: Bessie and Til meet (pp. 46–49); Bessie's first class with Mr. Dunn (pp. 65–68); and Bessie at the Dunn's (pp. 103–105).

Additional Selections

Maggie tries to look glamorous and attractive in Betty Cavanna's *Stars in Her Eyes* (Morrow, 1958, $6.37). Robin's constant bragging, and not her fatness, cause rejection in Rowena Boylan's *Better Than the Rest* (Follett, 1970, o.p.). An overweight tenth grader, Carol, is growing up in the Bronx in the witty *Will There Ever Be a Prince* (St. Martins, o.p.) by Sondra Rosenberg. A girl tries taking pills to lose weight in Isabelle Holland's *Heads You Win, Tails I Lose* (Lippincott, 1973, $5.95). Other novels that deal with obesity are Constance Greene's *A Girl Called Al* (Viking, 1969, $4.95; pap., 95¢); Zoa Sherburne's *Girl in the Mirror* (Morrow, 1966, $6.50); and M. E. Kerr's *Dinky Hocker Shoots Smack!* (Harper, 1972, $4.95; pap., Dell, 95¢).

About the Author

Fuller, Muriel, Ed. *More Junior Authors*. New York: H. W. Wilson Co., 1963, pp. 195–196.

Hopkins, Lee Bennett. *More Books by More People*. New York: Citation Press, 1974, pp. 343–350.

Harte, Barbara and Carolyn Riley, Eds. *Contemporary Authors*. Detroit: Gale Research Co., 1969. Vol. 5, pp. 1104–1105.

Who's Who in America (37th Edition). Chicago: Marquis Who's Who, Inc., 1972. Vol. 2, p. 3063.

9

Developing a Respect for Nature and Living Things

Besides the need to get along with people, the adolescent must learn about other forms of life and develop a respect for the wonders of nature. In this section are books dealing with domestic animals and pets, wild animals, conservation, the great outdoors, and even an exciting tribute to the marvels of the human body.

James Aldridge, *A Sporting Proposition*
    Little, 1973, $6.95; pap., Dell, $1.25

Many variations on the theme of determining ownership through a difficult decision occur in literature. In this novel, two young people each claim possession of a Welsh pony. The solution is both unusual and fascinating. The story is told by the same young narrator, Kit Quayle, that the author used in his previous work, *My Brother Tom* (Little, 1967, $5.95). The book is suitable for readers in both junior and senior high schools.

Plot Summary

The time is the 1930s and the setting is the bush town of St. Helen, on the border between New South Wales and Victoria in southern Australia. Thirteen-year-old Scott Pirie is the only son of poor Scottish immigrants, who live on a very unproductive farm about five miles from town. Being isolated from children his own age and living in circumstances of oppressive deprivation, Scotty has grown up to be an independent but mischievous boy. For his first school years, Scott rode into town with Beebe Dancy on the Dancy's mare, but when Beebe is killed in an accident and the mare shot, the boy is without transportation. Mr. Pirie is able to buy, for only three pounds, a wild Welsh pony from Ellison Eyre, owner of a vast and very prosperous sheep and cattle station called Riverside.

Scott very carefully breaks in the rebellious, self-willed pony, which he names Taff, and the two become inseparable. Because he is able to get away fast on Taff, Scott's pranks become more daring. He makes enemies in town, although everyone knows that basically he is an honest, never devious boy. Then one night Taff breaks out of his enclosure and disappears. Scott is disconsolate and often leaves home for days searching for his pony.

Meanwhile, at the Riverside estate, the owner's 13-year-old daughter, Josie Eyre, asks her father's permission to choose a Welsh pony from their large herd to be trained to pull the beautiful small carriage she has received as a present. When she was 11, Josie suffered a crippling attack of polio, which has left her confined to a wheelchair. She is self-conscious about her condition and is rarely seen in town; she has a private tutor.

Josie chooses a pony that matches her own personality—independent and somewhat stubborn. The stockman, Blue Waters, trains the pony, called Bo, to take the bit and shaft of the carriage, and he converts the wild pony into a real buggy horse. Josie becomes so confident of her pet's abilities that she decides to enter one of the horse and buggy competitions at the local agricultural fair.

Scotty, with Kit Quayle and his brother Tom, attends the races. He sees Bo, whom he recognizes as his own Taff, and when the Eyres will not let him reclaim his pony, he becomes hysterical and has to be subdued. Although Scott is convinced that Taff had somehow rejoined the herd of horses at Riverside after his escape, he cannot point out any distinctive markings as proof of ownership. Therefore, the people in St. Helen are dubious about the truth of his claims.

One night the paddock at Riverside is broken into, and the following morning Bo is missing. Search parties scour the area in vain, and Josie becomes distraught and inconsolable.

Suspicion falls on Scott; particularly when someone claims to have seen a young boy swim the river alongside Eyre's estate the night of the break-in; another maintains he saw Scott leading a pony along the bluffs the following morning. Under pressure from Ellison, who only wants to comfort his daughter and intimidate Scott into returning the pony, the police formally charge the boy with horse thievery.

Ellison visits the Pirie farm and begs Scott to return Bo. He promises not only that the charges will be dropped, but that Scott can have his pick of any other pony and 20 pounds as well. Scott refuses.

When Kit's father, a lawyer, hears that Eyre's wealth and influence have been used to make charges against Scott despite scant evidence, he decides to defend him in court. The rest of the town takes sides, and soon the normally peaceful community is filled with division.

In a tense court battle, Quayle promises to produce the pony when all charges are dropped. Then another court hearing will be held to determine the rightful owner. Both parties agree, and Scott brings in the pony, which he has been hiding.

The hearing ends without a decision, so Quayle suggests a sporting proposition—Josie and Scott will be placed on opposite sides of a roped-in field. The pony will be freed between them, and whichever one he comes to will be considered his owner. The terms are accepted.

On the day of the "natural" trial, excitement and tempers run high. When the pony is released, both Josie and Scott, who is also seated so as not to take unfair advantage of Josie in her wheelchair, begin shouting "Bo" and "Taff." At first the animal moves toward Josie, but after much hesitation, he walks over to Scott and gives him a friendly bite. Then he goes to Josie to nuzzle her. It is now clear that Taff and Bo are the same, but his first choice is Scott. Josie takes her defeat graciously, and, after she apologizes to Scott for trying to take Taff from him, the boy promises to bring the pony to Riverside on weekends to visit her.

Thematic Material

This story of two young people divided by love for the same pony shows what powerful bonds can exist between humans and animals. The folksy, homespun nature of the narrative adds to the good natural humor, excitement, and mounting suspense. The concept that justice is not determined by wealth or station in life is an important subtheme. The reader also learns a great deal about life in the bush country of Australia, and of the disposition and training of ponies.

Book Talk Material

A description of the conflict between Josie and Scott and their differing backgrounds can serve as a good introduction. Some passages that will arouse interest are: the problem introduced (pp. 3-5; pp. 5-6, pap.); Scott's pranks (pp. 25-27; pp. 28-30, pap.); Scott searches for Taff (pp. 30-33; pp. 33-36, pap.); he finds Bo at the fair (pp. 71-74; pp. 75-79, pap.); and Mr. Eyre makes an offer (pp. 100-104; pp. 107-111, pap.).

Additional Selections

Shannon Kelly finds out how difficult it is to keep a horse in a housing development in Bianca Bradbury's *My Pretty Girl* (Houghton, 1974, $5.95). Despite obstacles, Mary rides her horse in jumping competitions in

Anabel Dean's *High Jumper* (Benefic, 1975, $5.95). Laurel Ivy is attached to her pet opossum and her friend Hank, a born naturalist, in *Heart of Snowbird* (Harper, 1975, $5.95) by Carol Lee Lorenzo. Some other horse stories are: Enid Bagnold's *National Velvet* (Morrow, 1935, $7.50; pap., Archway, 75¢; condensed in *Juniorplots*, Bowker, 1967); Mari Sandoz's *The Horsecatcher* (Westminster, 1957, $4.95); Phillip Viereck's *Sue's Secondhand Horse* (Day, 1973, $4.95); and Colin Thiele's adventurous suspense story, *Fire in the Stone* (Harper, 1974, $6.95), set in the opal fields of Australia.

Isaac Asimov, *Fantastic Voyage*
Houghton, 1966, $5.50; pap., Bantam, $1.50

Transforming this story into novel form was almost as torturous as the incredible journey it describes. It was first a short story, then a screenplay and highly successful movie, and lastly a novel, to which has been added the fascinating physiological details by the master of both science fiction and nonfiction books about science, Isaac Asimov. The book is enjoyed by adults as well as young readers in the seventh grade and up.

Plot Summary

Jan Benes, world famous scientist and discoverer of a secret that makes him perhaps the most powerful man in the world, is defecting from the Other Side to America. He has been smuggled into the country by agent Charles Grant, a handsome young bachelor. On the way from the airport to the C.M.D.F. secret underground laboratory, the motorcade is ambushed by foreign agents, and Benes suffers a blow that produces a dangerous blood clot on a part of the brain where a conventional operation is impossible.

At the lab's hospital, the commander of the unit, General Alan Carter, and his chief assistant, Colonel Donald Reid, realize that drastic steps must be taken or Benes will die or suffer severe brain damage. The General calls agent Grant and puts him in charge of surely the most dangerous and bizarre mission he will ever undertake. Carter explains that C.M.D.F. stands for a Combined Miniature Deterrent Forces. Both sides in the Cold War have discovered how to miniaturize objects temporarily, but Benes has uncovered the secret of how to make the change permanent. It is, therefore, vital that his life be saved. Carter's scheme is to miniaturize Grant and a group of scientists inside *Proteus*, a nuclear-powered sub and, by means of a hypodermic needle, inject the vessel, reduced to microscopic size, into an artery in Benes' neck. By traveling through the bloodstream, they should be able to reach the clot and disperse it by a laser beam. Then they will be removed through the jugular vein. They have only one hour to do all this before deminiaturization begins. Grant's companions will be: Dr. Michaels, head of the medical division who will serve as pilot; Captain Owens, a scientist who will be at the controls; the noted but much disliked brain surgeon, Dr. Peter Duval; and his beautiful young assistant, Cora Paterson. Carter also tells Grant that there is a chance that one of his four companions might be an enemy agent.

From the beginning the mission has trouble. Misjudgment by Michaels leads them into the jugular vein and away from the target. Headquarters radios another, more dangerous route through the heart. As they approach it, the beating sounds like a gigantic cannon. The heartbeat is stopped electronically for one minute to allow them to get through. On the other side, they find that their reserve air tanks are damaged. They must go to the lungs to refill the tanks. They don diver suits and cut a tiny passage into the lungs large enough for Grant to pass through a tube that will suck up the air. He is almost killed when Benes suddenly exhales.

Back on the *Proteus*, they discover that a transistor in the laser has been damaged, making it unworkable. Michaels wants to turn back. Grant repairs the laser with part of their radio set, thus losing direct contact with headquarters. However, their movements can still be tracked. They reach the lymphatic system and travel upward to the inner ear. Grant, Michaels and Cora leave the ship to clean the clogged intake valves. Outside, in the operating room, a nurse drops a pair of scissors and the sound enters the inner ear as a massive explosion. Cora is knocked against tissue, which she pierces. Immediately, she is attacked by antibodies and almost suffocates before Grant can drag her back to the ship.

With little time left, they enter the brain. Michaels keeps demanding they give up the expedition. Grant orders them to continue, but there are only three minutes left when they reach the clot. The blood clot is dispersed, but Michaels reveals his true colors to Owens. He tells Owens that Benes must die because his discovery will be used only for destruction. He forces Owens out of the vessel and locks the escape hatch, intending to stay there through deminiaturization. Suddenly a great white corpuscle, the scavengers of the bloodstream, envelopes the *Proteus*, crushing it and killing Michaels. The cell pursues the other invaders as they swim frantically along an optic nerve toward a tear duct. With six seconds to go, the four survivors and the white cell fall from the eye in a droplet of water onto a glass microscope slide. The room is cleared and the slide placed on the floor in time for deminiaturization.

No one can later decide whether the many accidents that befell them were caused by Michaels or even if he was a foreign agent or a scientist trying to uphold his own principles. Cora and Grant will discuss the matter on their first date. Benes lives, although, after regaining consciousness, he complains of a slight headache and a soreness in his right eye.

Thematic Material

Readers are enthralled by this exciting story, and they learn much about the wonders of the human body at the same time. They great amount of accurate scientific detail adds realism and authenticity to a story that is both a cliffhanger and an introduction to human anatomy.

Book Talk Material

The process of miniaturization (pp. 38–40; 30–32, pap.) will introduce the book. Other exciting passages are: the mission is explained (pp. 47–51; pp. 38–41, pap.); final miniaturization (pp. 87–88; pp. 68–69, pap.); in the artery (pp. 103–109; pp. 81–85, pap.); the fistula (pp. 110–113; pp. 86–89, pap.); and into the heart (pp. 118–122; pp. 92–95, pap.).

Additional Selections

Good readers might wish to try some of Asimov's other science fiction, such as the trilogy that begins with *Foundation* (Doubleday, 1970, $6.95; pap., Avon, $1.50), or perhaps the three "Dune" books by Frank Herbert, the first of which is *Dune* (Chilton, 1965, $7.95; pap., Berkley, $1.95). Whites live as insects and blacks are the elite in A. M. Lightner's *The Day of the Drones* (pap., Bantam, 75¢). Other good science fiction books are Jay Williams' *People of the Ax* (Walck, 1974, $6.95; pap., Dell, $1.25); Ludek Pesek's *The Earth Is Now* (Bradbury, 1974, $6.95; pap., Dell, $1.25); Patrick Tilley's *Fade-Out* (Morrow, 1975, $8.95); and Richard Parker's *A Time to Choose* (Harper, 1974, $5.50). For nonfiction readers, try Joan Arehart-Treichel's *Immunity: How Our Bodies Resist Disease* (Holiday, 1976, $6.95) and the story of organ transplants, *The Search for Life* (Rand McNally, 1975, $5.95) by Thomas G. Aylesworth.

About the Author

Commire, Anne. *Something about the Author.* Detroit: Gale Research Co., 1971. Vol. 1, pp. 15–16.

DeMontreville, Doris and Donna Hill, Eds. *Third Book of Junior Authors.* New York: H. W. Wilson Co., 1972, pp. 21–23.

Ethridge, James M. and Barbara Kopala, Eds. *Contemporary Authors.* Detroit: Gale Research Co., 1967. Vol. 1, pp. 34–35.

Ward, Martha E. and Dorothy A. Marquardt. *Author of Books for Young People*. (2nd Edition). Metuchen, N.J.: Scarecrow Press, Inc., 1971, p. 21.

Who's Who in America (39th Edition). Chicago: Marquis Who's Who, Inc., 1976. Vol. 1., p. 109.

Alan W. Eckert, *Incident at Hawk's Hill*

Little, 1971, $6.95; lg. type ed., G. K. Hall, $7.95; pap., Dell, 75¢

The author has written many books and articles on nature, chiefly in the adult field. This novel, a Newbery Honor book for 1972, is based on an actual incident and deals with the amazing story of a boy being nurtured by a badger. It is intended for an audience of sixth through eighth graders.

Plot Summary

In 1850, William and Esther MacDonald began homesteading on sprawling prairie land close to the Red River, about 20 miles north of Winnipeg. They built their first cabin on the side of a knoll they named Hawk's Hill. As their farm grew and prospered, so did their family. Their firstborn was a son, John, followed by two daughters, Beth and Coral, and then another son, Ben. By 1870, John is now 16 and the youngest is six.

His parents are worried about Ben. He is a shy, withdrawn, undersized child who rarely speaks even to those family members who try most to understand and protect him—his mother, John and Coral. Instead, he develops a kinship with the farm animals and the wildlife in the fields. With amazing accuracy, he is able to mimic their sounds and actions to the point where some of his family believe he can communicate with them. His father is afraid that Ben is retarded, but his mother, aware of the boy's great sensitivity and loneliness, believes that he can empathize and relate to these small animals because they too are defenseless and vulnerable.

Their new neighbor, a fierce-looking farmer and fur trapper, George Burton, rides to the MacDonald's one day with his equally fierce-looking dog, Lobo, to ask permission to place some animal traps on the MacDonald property. Burton has a reputation as a dishonest person, but MacDonald grants him permission because two of his horses had to be destroyed recently after breaking legs in badger holes. Ben is terrified by this burly man and his false heartiness and sincerity, but, to everyone's amazement, the boy is able to subdue Lobo's fierceness by falling on his knees and imitating the dog's whines and movements.

Meanwhile, two miles north of Hawk's Hill, a female badger is intent on building a burrow to raise her family. She is a four-year-old who has one battle scar, a notched right ear. With her massive front claws, she first digs an opening 15 feet in length, hollows out a large domed inner chamber, and then creates an escape passage on the other side almost 50 feet long. Lastly, she covers the nesting chamber with grass and moss.

Exploring in the meadows, Ben uncovers the nest of a jumping mouse he has seen being killed by a sparrow hawk. It contains four newly born mice. Suddenly there is a rustling in the grass—the female badger. On all fours, Ben imitates her chattering and feeds her the orphaned mice. Before leaving, she allows him to touch her cheek and mangled ear.

The badger's three babies are born and she must hunt ferociously to keep up her strength. Her mate is also hunting in the area and detects a scent. It is the sardines that Burton placed on one of the traps. The trap snaps on its two front paws. Two days later Burton finds the animal, crushes its skull with a mallet handle, resets the trap and takes his catch to show McDonald.

Ben is struck with horror at the sight of the dead badger, even though he knows by examining its ears that it is not the one he befriended in the prairie. When his father begins to skin the animal, Ben lashes out at him and is slapped. Ben retreats to the barn. Later his father apologizes, but Ben is too frightened to acknowledge the apology.

The female badger catches part of her front paw in Burton's trap. She can hear the pitiful whining of her unfed pups. She struggles to free herself, and she does so on the third day even though most of her paw has been cut off. It is too late; the pups are dead. She seals the tunnel entrance and finds another den.

Shortly afterward, Ben is once again wandering the prairie. He roams farther afield than usual and becomes lost. A thunderstorm strikes and the boy panics. He runs wildly, deeper into the prairie. By nightfall he has lost both shoes and is exhausted; he creeps into a badger hole for safety. That night the badger tries to enter its hole, but Ben drives it off with snarls and shouts. The next day the badger returns, and Ben recognizes his friend by her ear. Imitating her chattering and whining, he gains her confidence. As she would to her lost pups, she brings him food. Later that day, Ben sees Burton surveying the area on horseback, but he retreats into the hole undiscovered.

As the days pass, Ben sights others on horseback, but he continues to elude them. The badger and Ben form a close relationship. He imitates her actions and sounds and crawls on all fours; she hunts for him, bringing back mice, chipmunks, birds, and prairie dogs, which he learns to eat raw. In turn he nurses her festering paw by licking off the scabs and drawing out the pus.

The badger begins to teach him to hunt. One night they kill the marauding Lobo, who has been stalking their den. By the end of two months, Ben is completely acclimated to his new existence.

The MacDonalds venture out every day still hoping to find their son, even though others have given up. One day John happens on Ben's shoe and sees a shadowy figure crawling into a badger hole. He waits until Ben reemerges, hoists the boy on his horse, and heads for home with the badger in hot pursuit.

The boy's adjustment is speeded by allowing the badger to enter the house as a pet. Shortly afterward, Burton again visits the farm and when the badger attacks him, the man draws a gun and shoots her. MacDonald drives Burton off his property, but Ben cannot be consoled. But as he is about to bury the animal, he notices a flicker of life. There seems little chance for the badger to recover, but Ben and his family will try their best.

Thematic Material

The amazing bond between the boy and the badger is both tenderly and convincingly presented. The elements of family love and personal courage are additional points in the story. The author's extensive knowledge of animal life, particularly of badger lore, adds fascinating sidelights to the story, as do the details of pioneer life in the Canadian West.

Book Talk Material

Some of the author's descriptions of badgers, as given in Chapters 2 and 4, will serve as an introduction, along with a brief résumé of the plot. Specific passages of interest are: Ben subdues Lobo (pp. 9–10; pp. 28–29, pap.); Ben is discussed by his parents (pp. 16–19; pp. 35–39, pap.); the badger digs her nest (pp. 28–32; pp. 48–52, pap.); and Ben finds the badger (pp. 47–51; pp. 69–73, pap.). With a small group, John Schoenberr's excellent illustrations also could be used, although they are murkily produced in the paper edition.

Additional Selections

Two black kids in the rural South help a stray dog and her litter in Charlotte Baker's *Cockleburr Quarters* (Prentice-Hall, 1972, $4.95; pap., Avon, 95¢) for a younger audience. Fifteen-year-old Link develops an interest in the wilderness in Keith Robertson's *In Search of a Sandhill Crane* (Viking, 1973, $5.95). In Barbara Corcoran's *All the Summer Voices* (Atheneum, 1973, $6.25), David tries to save his horse from being sold. Also use Jean George's many titles, including *My Side of the Mountain* (Dutton, 1967, $6.95; pap., $1.95; condensed in *Introducing Books*, Bowker, 1970) and

Julie of the Wolves (condensed in this volume). Two fine nonfiction works are Constance Colby's *A Skunk in the House* (Lippincott, 1973, $6.95) and Michael Fox's *Sundance Coyote* (Coward, 1974, $5.95).

About the Author

Kinsman, Clare D., Ed. *Contemporary Authors*. Detroit: Gale Research Co., 1975. Vol. 13, p. 242.
Who's Who in America (39th Edition). Chicago: Marquis Who's Who, Inc., 1976. Vol. 1, p. 888.

Jean Craighead George, *Julie of the Wolves*

Harper, 1972, $4.95; lib. bdg., $4.79; pap., Harper Trophy, $1.25 (same pagination); lge. type ed., G. K. Hall, $6.95

It seemed natural for Jean George to turn to nature writing. Her father was an entomologist and her twin brothers became wildlife ecologists. As a child, the Craighead home was filled with an assortment of pets—from dogs to such esoteric wildlife as opossoms, owls, raccoons, and falcons. After a career as a reporter and magazine author-illustrator, she wrote a series of nature stories with her husband, John George. She has continued her writing career alone and with outstanding success. *My Side of the Mountain* (Dutton, 1967, $6.95; pap. $1.95; condensed in *Introducing Books*, Bowker, 1970) was Newbery Honor Book of 1960 and also, like *Julie*, was made into a successful motion picture. Two of her books that have appeared on the ALA Notable Children's Book list are *Gull Number 737* (Crowell, 1964, $3.95) and *Spring Comes to the Ocean* (Crowell, 1966, $3.95). The 1973 Newbery Award was given to *Julie of the Wolves*.

Plot Summary

The story is told in three parts. The first and third tell the story of a young Eskimo girl's amazing journey alone across miles of arctic tundra. The short middle section is a flashback of the girl's life up to her decision to leave the town of Barrow, Alaska, on this trek that she hopes will lead to a new life in San Francisco.

Julie, also called by her Eskimo name of Miyax, lives her first four years in the settlement of Mekoryak on Nunivak Island. When her mother dies, her father, Kapugen, gives up the white man's ways and leaves his home and possessions to live with his daughter in the true Eskimo way in a remote seal camp. Here Miyax absorbs the language and culture of her people. She develops an affinity and respect for nature. Kapugen helps her to understand and love all wildlife, including the wolves whom Kapugen says love each other and "if you learn to speak to them, will love you too."

Shortly after her ninth birthday, Miyax is forced by Aunt Martha to return to Mekoryak to attend school. Before Miyax leaves, Kapugen arranges that she will be married at age 13 to David, son of Kapugen's hunting partner, Naka. After her departure, Kapugen grows more despondent. Within a month, Miyax receives news that her beloved father has not returned from a seal hunt and is presumed dead.

In her gussack, or white man's, environment, Miyax gradually becomes Julie. She makes friends with her schoolmates and becomes pen pals with Amy Pollack, a San Francisco girl of Julie's age. Julie becomes envious of Amy's life of prosperity and ease, and she hopes one day to accept her friend's invitation to visit San Francisco.

Life with her stern, unfeeling Aunt Martha becomes increasingly difficult. But when she reaches 13, Miyax is summoned by Naka to Barrow to marry David. Her life in Barrow is even more intolerable. Naka is frequently drunk and quarrelsome, to the point of physically abusing his wife, Nuson. David proves to be retarded, but their marriage remains one in name only. Julie becomes a household drudge, forced to spend hours each day sewing boots and parkas for the tourists.

One day David tries to attack her sexually. She escapes and with the help of her friend Pearl, gathers together a few essentials in her backpack and leaves Barrow to trek the 300 miles to Point Hope, where she hopes to get work on a ship heading for San Francisco.

Julie is traveling during the arctic summer, the time of the midnight sun. After five days, or "sleeps," away from Barrow, at the point where she is completely lost and almost without food, she happens upon a small pack of wolves. Remembering her father's words, she tries to communicate with them and tell them of her plight. She builds a sod house at the bottom of the frost heave that separates her from the wolves' den and begins to observe them closely. At first she is unsuccessful in her attempt to imitate the sounds and body language of the wolves, but within a few days she learns the basic vocabulary and, to her surprise, becomes an adopted member of the pack. Miyax grows to love and respect her new family, and she even gives them names. The leader, who becomes her wolf-father, is Amaroq (Eskimo for "wolf"). The other adult members are Silver, the mother of the pups, a second male, Nail, and Jello, the last adult, for some reason treated like an outcast. He lives physically and socially outside the pack's close family circle. There are five pups. The liveliest and most friendly Miyax names after her father, Kapu. The others are Sister, Zing, Zat, and Zit.

With her full acceptance by the wolves, Miyax no longer has to worry about her food supply. The wolves take care of her through their frequent kills of caribou. Miyax begins to cure and store a supply of meat because she realizes that when summer ends the wolves will move on and she will be alone once more. She and the wolves share their lives and livelihood for several weeks, but when summer ends, the wolves leave.

When Miyax returns to her sod house, she discovers that Jello, now a complete outcast, has attacked her camp, destroyed her sleeping gear, and eaten most of her food supply. That evening she hears the howling of her wolves and knows that they can't be far ahead, but by morning Jello has attacked again, this time stealing her pack filled with equipment and the remaining food. In the morning, close to her camp, Miyax finds the torn body of Jello. Amaroq had turned on him and killed him.

Miyax rejoins the wolves and constructs a makeshift sled with which she is able to travel fast enough to keep up with them. She also finds a sick golden plover whom she adopts and names Tornait, the bird spirit.

At the first signs of civilization—some empty oil cans—Miyax becomes fearful for the wolves in an area where the white man has placed a bounty on their skins.

One day a small plane carrying hunters spots the wolves in a clearing. From the air, they shoot and kill Amaroq and seriously wound Kapu. To Miyax the plane suddenly represents the white civilization—no longer something to be sought but a hateful monster that has killed her beloved protectors. Miyax slowly nurses Kapu back to health. He now becomes the leader of the pack and, at Miyax's insistence, leaves her while he leads the pack back to the wilderness and safety.

Instead of traveling to San Francisco, Miyax decides to live truly like an Eskimo. She builds herself a snow house and begins to live off the land. One day an Eskimo family on their way to hunt caribou visits Miyax and tell her of the village, Kangik, they have left and of the mighty hunter who lives there, Kapugen. She sets out for the village with dreams of a reunion with her father untainted by the white man's civilization. Her father, kindly and loving as before, is overjoyed to see his daughter. But Miyax soon realizes that Kapugen has adopted many of the gussack ways; he has even married a white woman.

Crushed, Miyax returns to her ice house. Her pet, Tornait, dies and she is once more alone. In her complete solitude, she wonders if it is still possible to live as in the olden days, or if one must make compromises with the changes that time brings. Slowly she realizes that "the hour of the wolf and the Eskimo is over," and, with resignation, leaves her ice house to join her father in Kangik.

Thematic Material

The facts of wolf lore in this novel have all been authenticated by the author. She had been sent to Alaska to do research for an article on the habits of arctic wolves. From the vast amount of data she collected came the inspiration for this novel. But *Julie* is more than a nature story rich with fascinating details of animal life in the arctic. It contains a wealth of other themes, the most importrant being the conflict within a young girl between modern culture and the primitive life of the Eskimo. Julie's resolution of this conflict reflects her growing maturity. The novel also explores relationships and responsibilities within an animal family and suggests parallels and applications in our own lives. Perhaps, most of all, this is a novel of human survival in spite of extreme adversity, and of the courage and self-will that make this victory possible.

Book Talk Material

Jean George's Newbery Award acceptance speech (reprinted in *Horn Book*, August 1973) contains most interesting background material. Young people can be introduced to the "first" Julie (pp. 342–343) or to the typical home life of the wolf as seen by the author (p. 344). Some interesting passages are: Miyax's first sucessful attempt at talking to the wolves (pp. 21–22); she becomes one of the pack (pp. 24–26); and the wolves save her from a grizzley attack (pp. 131–133). John Schoenherr's excellent illustrations—the author said he "made Julie and her wolves walk off the pages into life"—could be used, as well as part of the Newbery Award record (3040, $6.95, also available on cassette) based on this novel.

Additional Suggestions

Jean George's other book about wolves is the *Moon of the Gray Wolves* (Crowell, 1969, o.p.). Scott O'Dell's *Island of the Blue Dolphins* (Houghton, 1960, $3.95; pap., Dell, 1971, 95¢; condensed in *Juniorplots* Bowker, 1967) is an excellent companion piece to Jean George's books. Two other books dealing with accounts of wolves are: Russell Rutter and Douglas Pimlott's *The World of the Wolf* (Lippincott, 1968, $5.95; lib. bdg., $5.82), which follows the life cycle of the wolf from pup to full maturity, and *Black Lobo* by Billy Warren (Golden Gate, 1967, $3.95), a novel dealing with the frustrations and fun of trying to raise a wolf. Two teen-agers, brother and sister, leave their pampered existence with its false values to live with their uncle in the wilderness in Barbara Corcoran's *A Star to the North* (Nelson, 1970, $3.95). An Indian girl, like Julie, discovers kinship between humans and other living things in Katy Peake's *The Indian Heart of Carrie Hodges* (Viking, 1972, $4.95). Walt Morey's *Canyon Winter* (Dutton, 1972, $4.95) is an outdoor story with conservation as an important theme.

About the Author

Commire, Anne. *Something about the Author.* Detroit: Gale Research Co., 1973. Vol. 2, p. 112.

Ethridge, James M., Ed. *Contemporary Authors.* Detroit: Gale Research Co., 1963. Vols. 7-8, p. 188.

Melvin, Helen. "Jean Craighead George." *Horn Book*, Vol. 49 (August 1973), pp. 348-351.

Ward, Martha E. and Dorothy A. Marquardt. *Authors of Books for Young People.* New York: Scarecrow Press, Inc., 1971, p. 196; 1964, p. 88.

Who's Who of American Women (2nd Edition). Chicago: Marquis Who's Who, Inc., 1958. Vol. 2 (1961-1962), p. 364.

Fred Gipson, *Savage Sam*

Harper, 1962, $6.95; lib. bdg., $6.27; pap., $1.25

At the end of Fred Gipson's earlier novel, *Old Yeller* (Harper, 1956, $6.95; pap., 95¢; condensed in *Juniorplots*, Bowker, 1967), the young hero, Travis Coates, has taken as his new dog, one of the pups Old Yeller sired before his death. In this continuation, a little more than a year has passed. It is 1870, and Travis, now 16, is still living with his parents and young brother, six-year-old Little Arliss, on their small ranch in Salt Flats, along Birdsong Creek in the Texas hill country. Boys and girls from grades six through eight enjoy this exciting animal story.

Plot Summary

Papa Coates jokingly named the pup Savage Sam because of the way he tears into the bowls of scraps that are his food. However, Travis, who has carefully watched the dog mature, is amazed at his uncanny ability as a trail dog in following scents.

A neighbor, Bud Searcy, and his 13-year-old granddaughter, Lizbeth, ride over to the Coates to warn them of reports of Indians raiding ranches and stealing horses in the area. Although the news may be only a rumor, Mama asks Travis to go find Arliss and bring him home. Travis mounts his horse, Blue, and Lizbeth tags along on the Coates' old plow mule, Jumper. A distance from the ranch they hear Sam's distinctive cry and soon discover the reason—Arliss and Sam have cornered a bobcat in his hole. Travis and Lizbeth get caught up in the excitement of the chase, when suddenly they realize to their horror that they are surrounded by Indians.

All three children are captured. While trying to save them, Sam receives a deep back wound from an Indian tomahawk and can't continue the pursuit. Travis' hands are tied and his feet lashed together around a horse's belly. Lizbeth and Arliss are each double-mounted with an Indian captor. As they are about to leave, rifle shots are heard. One Indian is hit in the leg, but the band escapes with their prisoners and the horses they rustled.

Except for the wounded Indian, all are Apaches. The wounded man is taller than the others and wears different clothing. Travis recognizes him as a Comanche warrior. For a moment, Arliss manages to fight loose from his captor, and in the struggle bites off part of his ear.

The Indians stop for the night and cook a wild longhorn calf. The Comanche gives food to the three youngsters. During the night, Travis gets Lizbeth to cut his bonds with his pocket knife. He is planning escape when an Indian makes a lunge for Lizbeth and Travis stabs him. This wakes the others, who seize Travis, strip him, and torture him with firebrands. For the rest of the night he is hung by his hands and feet face down from a cottonwood tree.

In the morning come the first signs of hope—they hear Sam's trail cry. The Indians hear it too, and, believing they are being followed, they break camp. That day is torture for Travis, his body seared and festering. The Indians come upon two white horse raiders whom they kill and scalp. In spite of constant prodding, the old mule Jumper is unable to keep up with the party. An Indian slits the mule's throat and Jumper becomes the midday meal. In spite of their terrible hunger, the children cannot eat.

In the late afternoon, a small band of cavalry are spotted and give chase. The Comanche, who has been walking alongside Travis to ease his wounds, must now flee quickly with the rest. He knocks Travis off the horse and gallops off, leaving the boy behind. From afar Travis watches the battle and, with dismay, sees all of the cavalry killed by Indians.

Travis is filled with despair until he comes upon a watering hole and an unexpected guest—Sam. Together they go to the site of the battle and Travis begins the grisly business of stripping bodies so he can have clothes, guns, and ammunition. Sam is still able to pick up Arliss' trail, but his pace is so fast that Travis is forced to put him on a leash. When he stops for sleep, he is awakened by someone touching him. It is Herb Haley, a neighbor from Salt Falls. He is soon joined by the rest of the search party, including Mr. Searcy and Travis' father.

All night they follow Sam's baying cry, but in the morning there is quiet. They come across a recently abandoned campfire and a mystified Sam. Signs show that the Indians have split into three groups and taken different trails. Which is the right one? Sam tries all three trails and begins his wild yapping when he sniffs the third.

The group must take shelter when a fierce hailstorm strikes. When the hail turns to a drizzly rain, they start out again. Sam's footpads are so worn and cut that he leaves a trail of blood behind him. The Indians are sighted camping in a low valley. Breaking into groups, the settlers separate the Indians from their horses and ambush them. The Indians are killed and Lizbeth and Little Arliss are rescued unharmed.

As Travis comes down the mountainside he sees the Comanche badly wounded and weaponless, lying in the grass. They stare at each other. Travis can't bring himself to kill him. He leaves, hoping that he will somehow survive.

On the way home, Sam gets special treatment and is allowed to ride with the horsemen. Mr. Coates claims he is being spoiled, but even he knows that Sam deserves it.

Thematic Material

This is a story of courage and perseverance, as well as an exciting adventure tale complete with a breathtaking chase. Through the remarkable devotion of Sam to his master, the author reveals the close bond that can exist between human and animal. There are many scenes of great brutality as well as heroism. It also contains interesting details of pioneer life in late nineteenth-century Texas and of the lore and customs of the Apache.

Book Talk Material

To introduce *Savage Sam*, use pages 1–2. Other incidents are Travis and the rest are captured (pp. 16–21; 12–15, pap.); Arliss gets a taste of ear (pp. 35–39; pp. 24–27, pap.); how the Indians start a fire (pp. 46–47; pp. 32–33, pap.); and Travis is tortured (pp. 57–59; pp. 40–41, pap.).

Additional Selections

The Sam of Barbara Corcoran's *Sam* (Atheneum, 1967, pap., 95¢) is a girl suddenly placed in a new environment, whose main interest is her dog she is preparing for a dog show. Walt Morey's *Kävik the Wolf Dog* (Dutton, 1968, $5.95; pap., 95¢) describes the remarkable trek of a dog from Seattle to return to his former master. *The Incredible Journey* (Little, 1961, $5.95; pap., Bantam, 95¢; condensed in *Juniorplots*, Bowker, 1967) by Sheila Burnford is about a similar trek involving three animals. Other interesting dog stories are Jane and Paul Annixter's *Windigo* (Holiday, 1963, $4.95); Jim Kjelgaard's *Lion Hound* (Holiday, 1955, $4.95); and Joseph Lippincott's *Wilderness Champion* (Lippincott, 1944, $5.95).

About the Author

Commire, Anne. *Something about the Author*. Detroit: Gale Research Co., 1971. Vol. 2, pp. 118–119.

DeMontreville, Doris and Donna Hill, Eds. *Third Book of Junior Authors*. New York: H. W. Wilson Co., 1972, pp. 101–103.

Ethridge, James M. and Barbara Kopala, Eds. *Contemporary Authors*. Detroit: Gale Research Co., 1967. Vols. 1–4, pp. 371–372.

Kinsman, Clare D., Ed. *Contemporary Authors*. Detroit: Gale Research Co., 1975. Vol. 45, p. 189.

Walbridge, Earle F. "Biographical Sketches: Fred Gipson," *Wilson Library Bulletin*, vol. 32, no. 2 (October 1957), p. 96.

Ward, Martha E. and Dorothy A. Marquardt. *Authors of Books for Young People*. Metuchen, N.J.: Scarecrow Press, Inc., 1971, p. 199.

Walt Morey, *Gentle Ben*
Dutton, 1965, $5.95; pap., Avon, $1.25

Gentle Ben was Walt Morey's first book for young readers. It has won the Dutton Junior Animal Book Award and the Sequoyah Children's Book Award, in addition to being turned into a motion picture and forming the basis for a successful television series. Its setting is Alaska in the not-too-distant past, but before it had become a state. Since this novel appeared, the author has written several other stories about animals and outdoor adventures. They are all suited to an audience of upper elementary and junior high school students.

Plot Summary

Thirteen-year-old Mark Anderson is growing up on the outskirts of an Alaskan fishing village called Orca City. He is a frail, sensitive boy who has had difficulty adjusting to the great loneliness he felt at the death of his only brother, Jamie, from tuberculosis. In the past few weeks however, Mark has found a new interest. On his way home from school, he begins stopping at the shed behind Fog Benson's shack to visit the huge, five-year-old bear, Ben, that Benson keeps chained there. Over four years ago, Benson shot Ben's mother and brought her cub back as a trophy. Benson, a mean and quarrelsome man, has ignored and half starved the animal, but each day Mark leads the bear by the chain into the sunshine, feeds him scraps from his school lunch, and, when the bear lies down, playfully strokes him and scratches his ear. The boy feels the same love and gentleness for the bear as he would a pet dog, and Ben responds in kind.

One night Karl Anderson tells his wife, Ellen, and Mark that Benson plans to sell Ben for $100 or, failing that, to raffle him off to hunters for his hide at $5 a try. Mark is horrified, and, after confessing to his after-school activities, he begs his father to buy Ben. Anderson refuses, not only because he is short of cash, but also because he is fearful that the animal one day will turn vicious. Brokenhearted, the boy goes to bed, and into the night he hears his mother trying to persuade her husband to buy Ben. She argues that Dr. Wacker is fearful that Mark might also develop tuberculosis, and an interest like taking care of Ben will give the boy exercise and fresh air. But Mark's father is adamant.

At sunrise, Mark steals out of the house to see Ben once more. He leads him into the meadow and frees him, but the bear will not leave. Hours later, Anderson finds Mark and Ben curled up together asleep. He agrees to buy Ben under specific conditions, one of which is that Mark earn Ben's keep by helping his father and fishing mate, Clearwater, on the *Far North*, Anderson's boat, during the oncoming salmon fishing season.

Not only is Ben saved, but Mark proves his worth aboard ship, and during the month-long season helps bring in a good catch of seven loads and two half-loads. When they stop at small fishing villages, Mark buys stale bread from general stores and gets Mike Kelly, superintendent of the cannery in Orca City, to freeze it so Ben will have food in the future. Before the salmon stop running, fishing pirates rob the traps of their family friend, Six-Fathom Johnson, and, although Mr. Anderson has no clear proof, he is convinced that Fog Benson is behind it.

One wintery night, Benson is bragging in the local tavern how he taught Ben to drink beer from a bottle. His cronies don't believe him, so they sneak up to the shack behind the Anderson's home for a demonstration. Fog cruelly tries to rouse Ben from his winter sleep by kicking him. When this doesn't work, he swings a scythe at the bear's head and cuts off part of an ear. Enraged, the bear strikes out, clawing Fog in the face.

The intruders flee, but the next morning, the news spreads of Ben's assault, a delegation of townspeople arrive at the Anderson's, demanding that Ben be destroyed. Anderson and a reluctant Mark agree to an offer made by Arnie Nichols. His boat is going to Ketchikan, and he volunteers to take Ben and release him on an island in the straights. A cage is constructed for Ben and he is hoisted aboard Nichols' boat, *The Hustler*, well named because Arnie plans to take Ben to Seattle and sell him to a traveling zoo. Shortly after leaving Orca City, the boat runs into a severe storm and Ben's cage is broken open. He is thrown into the water and swims to shore on the same island where Six-Fathom Johnson has his salmon traps.

During the winter, Mr. Anderson contracts to use the *Far North* as a mail carrier, but in another storm the ship sinks and Clearwater is drowned. Mark's father, fortunately, is saved.

Without a boat during the salmon run, Anderson accepts Johnson's offer to be a warden for his traps, and the family moves to the island. It is Karl who first sees Ben on the island, and he is reluctant to tell his son, but one night Ben frightens off Fog Benson and his gang, who are trying to rob the salmon traps.

A hunting guide, Mud-Hole Jones, has learned from Nichols the whereabouts of Ben and begins flying in hunters eager for an easy kill. One is Peter King, a wealthy businessman from the States. While Nichols flies back to Orca City for provisions, King strikes out on his own. He falls in the woods and his leg is trapped under a rock. The giant brown bear he has been stalking suddenly hovers over him, but, at that moment, Mark, who has been out looking for Ben, appears. With Ben's help the rock is removed, and a disbelieving King is able to stroke the gentle bear's chin.

In gratitude, King pays Jones to protect Ben from other hunters and agrees to help finance Anderson's plans to buy Johnson's traps. Both the family and Ben are safe and secure.

Thematic Material

In spite of a somewhat contrived plot and a tendency toward anthropomorphism, this is an exciting adventure story, in which the boy's attachment and devotion to his pet are well presented. Mark's assumption of responsibilities and his developing maturity are important subthemes. There are also interesting details on salmon runs and wildlife in Alaska.

Book Talk Material

Chapter 1 (pp. 11–20; same pagination, pap.) gives a good introduction to Gentle Ben and Mark's problems. John Schoenherr's illustrations also could be used. Some other interesting passages are: Mark begs his father to buy Ben (pp. 23–27; pp. 23–26, pap.); Mark tries to save Ben and is found by his father (pp. 39–45; pp. 37–44, pap.); his father agrees to buy Ben (pp. 47–50; pp. 45–48, pap.); Ben is taught to fish (pp. 74–76; pp. 70–72, pap.); and Benson taunts the bear (pp. 108–110; pp. 99–102, pap.).

Additional Selections

An 11-year-old boy nurses a hawk back to health in Jack M. Bickham's *Baker's Hawk* (Doubleday, 1974, $6.50), and in Anne DeRoo's *Cinnamon and Nutmeg* (Nelson, 1974, $5.95), a New Zealand farm girl secretly takes care of two orphaned animals. Arthur J. Roth's *The Iceberg Hermit* (Four Winds, 1974, $6.95; pap., Scholastic, 95¢) tells how a 17-year-old boy is stranded in the arctic, and in Colin Tiele's *Blue Fin* (Harper, 1974, $4.95), a boy gets into trouble while working on his father's fishing boat. An orphan boy moves to relatives on a sheep ranch in Australia in Patricia Wrightson's *The Nargun and Stars* (Atheneum, 1974, $5.50). Other outdoor stories are Ester Wier's *The Hunting Trail* (Walck, 1974, $6.95); John Reese's *Big Mutt* (pap., Archway, 95¢); and Jim Kjelgaard's *Wildlife Cameraman* (Holiday, 1957, $4.95).

About the Author

Commire, Anne. *Something about the Author.* Detroit: Gale Research Co., 1972. Vol. 3, pp. 139–140.
DeMontreville, Doris and Donna Hill, Eds. *Third Book of Junior Authors.* New York: H. W. Wilson Co., 1972, pp. 201–202.
Kinsman, Clare D. and Mary Ann Tennenhouse, Eds. *Contemporary Authors.* Detroit: Gale Research Co., 1972. Vol. 29, p. 426.
Ward, Martha E. and Dorothy A. Marquardt. *Authors of Books for Young People.* (2nd Edition). Metuchen, N.J.: Scarecrow Press, Inc., 1971, p. 372.
Who's Who in America (39th Edition). Chicago: Marquis Who's Who, Inc., 1976. Vol. 2, p. 2234.

Wilson Rawls, *Where the Red Fern Grows*
Doubleday, 1961, $4.95; pap., Bantam, $1.25

According to an old Indian legend told in the Ozarks, a beautiful red fern once grew on the spot where a young Indian girl and boy had perished during a blizzard. Since that time, the red fern has been considered sacred. At the end of this warm story of a boy and his two hunting dogs, the legend takes on new significance. Parts of the book are autobiographical, drawn from the author's own experiences growing up on a small farm on Cherokee land in northeastern Oklahoma. This novel, also the basis of a fine motion picture, is enjoyed by adults and by youngsters in the fifth grade and up.

Plot Summary

After rescuing a bedraggled, old redbone hound from a dog fight, the narrator, Bill Colman, remembers what an important part two such dogs played in his boyhood over 50 years ago.

Bill catches "dog fever" when he is 10 years old and growing up with his parents and three younger sisters on an isolated farm in the Ozarks. He begs his parents to buy him a pair of hound dogs for coon hunting, but money is scarce and if there is any to spare it is spent on such important items as starting a fund so the family can move to a town where there is a school.

After a year of pestering, the boy realizes he will have to earn the money himself. He begins selling bait, vegetables, and berries to fishermen and pelts of small animals he has trapped to his grandfather, who runs a general store. It takes him two years to accumulate the necessary $50 in his "bank," an old baking powder can. Grandpa orders the pups for the boy from a kennel in Kentucky.

After weeks of waiting, word comes that the dogs have arrived at the railway depot in Tahlequah, the nearest town, 20 miles away. Unable to wait until he can hitch a ride, that night the boy takes a few provisions and sets out into the woods on foot. By midmorning the next day, he has his two pups safely in his gunny sack. Because they cost only $40, Billy buys gifts for his family—a pair of overalls for his dad, dress material for his mother, and candy for his sisters. That night on his way home he takes shelter in a cave, building a fire for warmth. During the night he is awakened by the screams of a mountain lion, but he is able to frighten the cat away by stoking the fire and throwing rocks down the mountainside.

The boy and his dogs become inseparable, and the two pups show as much devotion to each other as they do toward Billy. The larger and more ferocious is a male, Old Dan, and the other, less bold but more intelligent, is a female, Little Ann. With the help of one of his grandfather's hunting tricks, Billy catches a large raccoon and uses its skin to train the dogs carefully and painstakingly to become excellent coon-hound dogs. Within a few months the dogs are ready, and Billy sets out with his ax (his parents won't allow him to use a gun) for his first coon hunt. The dogs behave splendidly and soon tree a raccoon in the largest sycamore in the valley. Unwilling to be disloyal to his pets and admit defeat, he begins the almost impossible task of chopping down the huge tree. It takes him two days, many aching muscles, and blistering, bleeding hands, but the tree is felled and they make their first kill.

The three share many adventures together and their hunting success is phenomenal. Billy is able to give substantial amounts of money to his mother from the sale of skins. As the fame of his dogs spreads, Billy is challenged by two of the meanest boys in the area, Rubin and Rainey Pritchard, to hunt down an elusive raccoon on their property. The animal is known as the "ghost coon." The dogs are successful, but when they begin fighting with the Pritchards' scrappy blue hound, Rubin grabs Billy's ax intending to kill Old Dan and Little Ann. But, while running across the field, Rubin trips, falls on the ax, and is killed.

Grandpa pays the fee to enter Billy and his dogs in a championship coon hunt. Billy, his father, and grandfather travel two days to the site. Although 25 hunters enter the contest, Billy and his dogs win and Little Ann is awarded first prize as the best-looking hound. They come home with two cups and more than $300 in prize money.

Out hunting one night, the dogs tree a mountain lion. Before Billy can drag them away, the cat springs. Although the boy kills the lion with his ax, both dogs, trying to save their master, are badly cut. Billy carries Old Dan back home, with Little Ann limping and whining at his side. Old Dan dies, and Billy buries him on a hillside under a tree. Little Ann refuses to eat, and within a few days she too dies and is buried alongside Old Dan.

The following spring the Colmans leave the valley. By combining their savings with the money Billy won in the competition, they have enough to move to town. With an aching heart, Billy climbs the mountainside for the last time to the red oak, and there he sees, as if by a miracle, that a beautiful red fern has grown between the two graves.

Thematic Material

Through this story, the author shows the remarkable bonds of love and devotion that exist between a boy and his dogs. Billy's transition from childhood to adolescence, and his courage, sacrifice, and engaging innocence make him appealing and believable. The wholesome family relationships and interesting use of local color add to the book's beauty and impact.

Book Talk Material

One could use as an introduction the first chapter (pp. 11–15; pp. 1–6, pap.), in which the narrator is reminded of his childhood. Other passages of importance are: Billy tries out his traps (pp. 19–21; pp 10–13, pap.); he earns $50 (pp. 24–27; pp. 17–21, pap.); he collects the pups (pp. 39–41; pp. 35–38, pap.); the night in the cave (pp. 46–48; pp. 43–46, pap.); and the training period (pp. 64–66; pp. 66–68, pap.).

Additional Selections

In Wilson Rawls' later book, *The Summer of the Monkeys* (Doubleday, 1976, $6.95), a 14-year-old in Oklahoma encounters a tree full of monkeys escaped from a circus. On a remote island in New England, a 12-year-old boy breaks out of the protective cocoon others have built around him in Bianca Bradbury's *Boy on the Run* (Seabury, 1975, $5.95). A boy's longing to participate in an ostrich hunt is a main theme in *The Ostrich Chase* (Holt, 1974, $5.95) by Moses L. Howard. A young Oriental boy tries to save his pet in S. T. Tung's *One Small Dog* (Dodd, 1975, $4.95). Frank Walker's *Jack* (Coward, 1976, $7.95) is a huge Belgian sheepdog growing up in Yorkshire. Other animal stories are: Helen Griffiths' *Just a Dog* (Holiday, 1975, $5.95; pap., Archway, $1.25); Sterling North's *The Wolfling* (Dutton, 1969, $6.50; pap., Bantam, 95¢); and Jack O'Brian's *Silver Chief, Dog of the North* (Holt, 1933, $3.95), plus its many sequels.

Glendon Swarthout, *Bless the Beasts and Children*
Doubleday, 1970, $5.95; pap., Pocket Books, $1.25

Glendon Swarthout's novel about an unlikely group of young heroes and their bizarre plan to save a herd of buffalo has steadily gained in popularity, partially because of the movie version. The story is told by a combination of present action and flashback. Originally intended for adults, it is enjoyed by both junior and senior high school readers.

Plot Summary

Box Canyon Boys Camp, whose motto is "Send us a Boy—We'll Send You a Cowboy!", is located in the Arizona mountains close to Prescott. At a handsome price, for eight weeks each summer the camp accepts 36 scions of wealthy easterners. There are six boys and a counselor in each cabin. No formal room assignments are made, but during the first week, by a method known as the "shake down," each boy is to choose the friends with whom he will share a cabin.

Through the process of natural selection, 15-year-old John Cotton finds himself bunking with five obnoxious, rebellious misfits—the rejects and unwanteds from the other cabins. In taking stock one evening, Cotton realizes that he is stuck with a teethgrinder, a headbanger, two bedwetters, one of whom also sucks his thumb, and a nailbiter who overeats. Their ability at organized sports is matched only by their ineptitude in all other camp activities. Their counselor, nicknamed Wheaties because of his "all-American boy" attitude, knows he is stuck with a bunch of goofballs, whom he calls "dings," and he tries to tyrannize them until Taft, a juvenile delinquent in the true sense, blackmails him into submission by threatening to reveal to the director that Wheaties has liquor, cigarettes, and sex magazines in his locker.

Each week, prizes and Indian tribe names are awarded to the cabins on the basis of points scored in the week's activities. During the first award ceremony, Cotton's cabin is, as expected, lowest, and by camp tradition they are dubbed the Bedwetters; their trophy, a chamber pot. At this point, Cotton decides to take charge and become their leader. He is a tough, self-reliant but compassionate boy who has personal problems of his own, such as his much-married mother, but he rarely speaks of them. Like a drill sergeant, he sets down such rules as no more crybaby attitudes and no complaining letters or phone calls home. Slowly the boys begin acting as a team, gradually gaining a bit of self-respect and independence.

During their last week, the Bedwetters go on an overnight camping trip to the Petrified Forest. On the way back, the boys persuade Wheaties to take a detour to see a herd of buffalo on the state's game preserve. Their visit coincides with the second of a three-day thinning of the herd. Hunters have paid $40 each to shoot down the captive animals. The boys are sickened and appalled by the slaughter. Back at camp, Goodenow, who is severely maladjusted, upchucks, and that night Lally 2, infantile and overprotected, tries to run away. The boys sneak out of camp, and, after finding him, decide that somehow before morning they must get back to the preserve, some two hours away by car, to free the animals that are to be shot the next day.

The boys take six horses from the corral. Taft steals a rifle and box of ammunition, and Goodenow carries along the buffalo head whose custody the Bedwetters had won from the Apaches on a bet. In Prescott they leave the horses and transfer to a pickup truck, again with Taft's stealing abilities. Against Cotton's better judgment, they stop in Flagstaff for hamburgers. They are chased by teen-age ruffians, but Taft shoots out one of their tires.

One mile from the preserve, the boys run out of gas. To test them, Cotton suggests that they go home, but the others refuse. Cotton is delighted because now they have shown the courage and independence for which he had hoped. After much difficulty, the buffalo are released from their pen and wander into a large enclosure from which they must be led in order to escape. With quickness of mind, the boys take one of the preserve's trucks, fill the back with hay, and, with the animals following, drive the truck to the end of the compound, where they find the exit blocked by a gate of heavy chains. Cotton once more takes charge. He orders the boys off the truck and drives headlong at the gate, breaking the chains.

Cotton turns the truck around and drives the animals out of the enclosure to safety. But the truck goes out of control and plunges over a steep gorge. When the rangers arrive, they find the remaining five boys red-eyed at their terrible loss, but triumphant in their accomplishment.

Thematic Material

The convincing transformation of Bedwetters into heroes through the efforts of an idealistic, courageous young boy is told effectively, and, despite its tragic ending, with a great amount of humor. Throughout, the author makes a searing indictment of our treatment of natural resources, including wildlife, and paints a scathing picture of the tawdry communities that have displaced the natural beauty of the West. Anyone who has lived through summer camp will find the details of life at Box Canyon both realistic and full of insight.

Book Talk Material

A description of the Box Canyon Bedwetters will provide a wonderful introduction. The author's outcry at the shame of the buffalo slaughter is given on pages 119-120 (p. 110, pap.). Other important passages are: the "shake down" into various cabins (pp. 19-21; pp. 24-26, pap.); the awarding of prizes (pp. 28-30; pp. 32-33, pap.); Wheaties is tamed (pp. 49-51; pp. 48-49, pap.); Cotton takes over (pp. 64-66; pp. 61-63, pap.); and stealing the trophies (pp. 144-147; pp. 134-136, pap.).

Additional Selections

Many reviewers have compared this novel to John Knowles' *A Separate Peace* (Macmillan, 1960, $5.95; pap., Bantam, $1.25). Two teen-age boys share an interest in freshwater biology and a concern for man's intrusion into the balance of nature in Don Moser's *A Heart to the Hawk* (Atheneum, 1975, $6.95). Jack Denton Scott's *The Survivors* (Harcourt, 1975, $7.50) tells of 12 North American animals that have survived the same civilization that brought extinction to other species (Harcourt, 1975, $7.50). In the translation from the original German, *The Hunters of Siberia* (Walck, 1969, $6.95) by Barbara Bartos-Hoppner makes a plea against hunting. Also use James Herriot's moving and delightful *All Creatures Great and Small* (St. Martin's, 1972, $8.95) and *All Things Bright and Beautiful* (St. Martin's, 1974, $8.95; pap., Bantam, $1.95), and Robert F. Leslie's *The Bears and I* (pap., Ballantine, $1.25).

About the Author

Ethridge, James M. and Barbara Kopala, Eds. *Contemporary Authors*, Detroit: Gale Research Co., 1967. Vol. 1, p. 923

Ward, Martha E. and Dorothy A. Marquardt. *Authors of Books for Young People.* (2nd Edition). Metuchen, N.J.: Scarecrow Press, Inc., 1971, p. 497.

AUTHOR–TITLE INDEX

Titles fully discussed and summarized in *More Juniorplots* as well as those listed as "Additional Suggestions" are cited in this index. An asterisk (*) precedes those titles for which full summaries and discussions appear.

229

SUBJECT INDEX

The subject index is designed to suggest themes for book talks beyond the goals or chapter headings under which the titles in *More Juniorplots* are arranged and discussed. This brief listing includes only those titles fully summarized and discussed in the book. Additional titles relating to these subjects can be found in the "Additional Suggestions" that accompany the discussion of the books listed below.